T0058160

Jean Hugard's Complete Course in Modern Magic

Skills and Sorcery for the Aspiring Magician

JEAN HUGARD

Racehorse Publishing

THIS BOOK IS DEDICATED TO THE MAGI-
CIANS OF THE PAST AND PRESENT WITH
THE HOPE THAT IT WILL LEAD OTHERS
TO FOLLOW IN THE ILLUSTRIOUS FOOT-
STEPS OF MY FRIENDS, HOUDINI, THUR-
STON, KELLAR, HERMANN, HARDEEN,
CARDINI, AND THAT GREAT MASTER OF
LEGERDEMAIN, ROBERT HOUDIN, TO
WHOM ALL OF US OWE OUR START.

JEAN HUGARD

First published 1939 by Harper and B

First Racehorse Publishing Edition 2018

Foreword © 2018 by Steve Cohen

Racehorse Publishing books may be purchased in bulk at special discounts for sales promotion, corporate gifts, fund-raising, or educational purposes. Special editions can also be created to specifications. For details, contact the Special Sales Department, Skyhorse Publishing, 307 West 36th Street, 11th Floor, New York, NY 10018 or info@skyhorsepublishing.com.

Racehorse Publishing™ is a pending trademark of Skyhorse Publishing, Inc.®, a Delaware corporation.

Visit our website at www.skyhorsepublishing.com.

10 9 8 7 6 5 4 3 2

Library of Congress Cataloging-in-Publication Data is available on file.

Cover photos: Shutterstock

ISBN: 9781631582455
eISBN: 9781631582479

Printed in the United States of America

CONTENTS

INTRODUCTION
by
Julien J. Proskauer

In this book is compiled the knowledge obtained during more than forty-five years' experience in magic. In it, Mr. Hugard has assembled magic of the past, present and future. For thirty-five years, Mr. Hugard was one of vaudeville's famous performers of magic. His name has been in lights in the biggest cities in every country. He knows magic as a performer and as an author. He is the world's most prolific writer on magical subjects, but this is the first book he has ever written for other than those in the inner circle of magic. In it, are workable effects that will bring pleasure and entertainment to your audience and much happiness to you.

I have been interested in magic for more than thirty years and have known all the great magicians—and the not so great—over this period. Professionals and amateurs alike find in magic a release for their natural talents as well as a means of livelihood or hobby which brings happiness and pleasure to others. All magicians, famous professionals as well as novices, are bound by a code of "never tell how a trick is done." Let me ask you in the name of all of them to be sure to keep this in mind.

Readers of this book must be interested in entertaining others—there can be no entertainment when the secrets of magic are revealed. This is a textbook by one of magic's great masters. You owe it to Mr. Hugard as well as to yourself and to the myriads of magic enthusiasts everywhere to refuse to explain how you do any trick.

Mr. Hugard has been more than careful in his explanations of how to do magic, but it will be easy to see before you read too far that no one magician can be perfect in all branches of magic. Houdini, and his brother, Hardeen, specialized in escapes, Thurston worked with large illusions, Cardini works with cigarettes using cards to add color to his performance, John Mulholland in the style of a lecturer, uses his magic, Nate Leipzig does a full vaudeville act with cards only, Jack Gwynne became famous because of his "fishbowl" illusion, Fred Keating is the "vanishing bird cage" magician in the eyes of many—and so on down the line we find magicians specializing in those branches of magic which experience has taught them is their forte. You must do the same.

Find the branch of magic you like—then devote all your time to developing it. Read this book carefully with that idea in mind. Select effects you think you can do, then, after you have finished the entire book, go back and reread those effects you first liked. Experiment with them in front of a mirror, rehearse patter and then try out the finished effects before a few known friends. That will tell you which ones should be developed further, and which should be dropped from your act.

Be very careful that the effects selected lend themselves to your particular personality. One person does well with cigarettes, another can't use them. Another specializes in card magic, whereas another may believe that billiard ball manipulation is more fitted to his physique and speech.

But the "tricks" are not the all-important item in being a good magician, a likable entertainer. This is shown by the fact that all of us realize that "magic" is based on the principle of giving the appearance that miracles are visibly taking place, when actually nothing beyond explicable procedure has deceived the eyes, and, therefore, the minds of the on-lookers. To achieve such results successfully, it is essential that one study and obtain some knowledge of applied psychology, on a minor scale, of course.

According to the dictionary, psychology is a science of mind, its nature and functions. When a magician keeps this definition in mind, he will always remember that the brain recognizes as fact that which the eye is ready to believe.

For example, in a card trick where a pack of cards is placed against a subject's head, and the magician immediately thereafter announces the name of a previously selected card, reason if permitted to function, would convince anyone that the deck has nothing to do with the magician's ability to tell the name of the card. Suggestion that such a procedure was under way, leads the subject to believe "mind reading" is taking place.

All magicians worthy of the name count on the "patter" or description of what is being done to suggest to the eyes and ears of the audience just what he wishes their minds to believe. It is obvious, therefore, that the application of psychology to magic resolves itself into the use of suggestion on the part of the magician.

There are scores and scores of wonderful magical effects explained in this book, but the ability to perform them successfully rests entirely upon the magician's skill to deceive the audience with words and "misdirection."—as well as a well grounded knowledge of the effect.

Misdirection is fixing the attention of the audience on one thought, while something entirely different is taking place somewhere else. Misdirection is, therefore, essential to the performance of a "miracle." The successful professional magician operates along lines of verbal and visual deception with his patter and moves designed to draw the attention of the audience away from some essential act on his part.

One thing for magicians always to keep in mind, particularly amateurs, is that any magical effect can go "wrong." By covering up the failure of the trick with an impromptu phrase or two gives time to check and correct the error so that the mistake is covered up and to the minds of the audience the effect has been successfully performed. It is, therefore, essential that a magician never tell in advance what is to happen.

A rule of all good magicians is to refrain from repeating the same trick before the same audience the same night. If anyone pleads: "O.K., do that again," the wise magician pretends not to hear the request, but immediately starts performing another and totally different effect based on another principle. This diverts the mind of the inquirer from delving too deeply into what last transpired.

It is extremely essential that a magician size up every person in his audience. Experience has taught magicians that the man or woman whose eyes are too close together will not make a good assistant. The character of this type of person might be such that he or she would think it funny to be "wise," and thus spoil the trick. If you need an assistant in an effect, pick some jovial looking person. If you want someone to do exactly as told, pick a man or woman with a fairly well-rounded chin. Avoid at all costs, the person who is too eager to help, unless you know that it is someone who will not try to "steal" the center of the stage.

Another good point to remember is that hands are "tell-tales." Never select as a helper an individual with chubby fingers. With all the best intentions in the world he may be clumsy and spoil your act by dropping something. Select someone with graceful fingers, a pretty girl or woman if possible. Femininity adds a touch of interest to your performance.

Be confident in your power to deceive the audience, but never be so arrogant and aggressive that your attitude will annoy those whom you are endeavoring to entertain.

In every audience, there is someone who "knows how it is done." Select such an individual as your assistant when you are about to do some effect that you know particularly well, one that can't go wrong, one with a surprise finish. If you handle this person carefully, you will turn a prospective enemy into a friend and you will find his cooperation later will be of great help for the balance of the entertainment.

Outstanding performers use a "sales" angle to their patter. The simplest trick well "sold" makes you a miracle man. "Selling" a trick consists primarily of using a persuasive attitude for certain effects, a fast line of patter of almost meaningless words for others, and other effects require that every word be calculated to hold interest. The magician must believe that he is a salesman talking to a buyer. With that thought in mind, he cannot go wrong.

For those who do magic with apparatus, I must also give a word of advice. Never do an effect as soon as you get it. Practice it before mirrors, rehearse the patter (many effects on sale at the magic stores come with patter) and be letter-perfect in speech and action before showing any effect.

Max Holden, a magician of many years' vaudeville and stage experience, tells every novice to study the necessary moves first, to learn the patter next, and then to time the words with the moves.

Educational nights which the Assemblies of the Society of American Magicians hold at various meetings stress this point also. There are Assemblies, or branches of the Society, in almost every large city. Serious magicians owe it to themselves to affiliate with magical societies. Besides the Society of American Magicians, there are others such as the Pacific Coast Magicians Alliance and the International Brotherhood of Magicians.

Magicians should read publications devoted exclusively to magic. Among the best known are *The Sphinx*, published in New York, *The Genii*, Pasadena, California, and *The Linking Ring*, Kenton, Ohio. Published in England are *The Magic Wand*, *The Magician Monthly*, and Goldston's *Magic Quarterly*. Some dealers publish house organs which have a trade journal slant. Of these, *The Tops* is an example.

Of course, the majority of these remarks are addressed to beginners in magic because those with years of experience realize their importance.

The magical fraternity of this generation and of the generations for years to come owe a debt of gratitude to Jean Hugard for *Modern Magic Manual*.

FOREWORD
by
Steve Cohen, The Millionaires' Magician

The broad range of knowledge required to become a master magician cannot possibly be contained in a single textbook. If there were a university course for new conjurers—let's call it Magic 101—the professor would likely assign a reading list containing a variety of specialized books. Upon examination, students would notice the name "Jean Hugard" pop up multiple times next to the assigned titles. Hugard is highly regarded as one of the most prolific and articulate teachers in the history of magic. He authored nearly thirty books during his lifetime, each focusing on a narrow area of study: cards, coins, thimbles, mental magic, and so on. His *Royal Road to Card Magic* (co-written with Frederick Braue), in particular, is considered a standard primer for beginners interested in sleight of hand card tricks.

In most cases, magic neophytes are eager to learn a few tricks they can perform in social settings. During Hugard's lifetime, this genre was known as "pocket tricks," but it has more recently been rebranded as "street magic." In this style, the magician removes a prop from his pocket, performs the trick, and puts it away. If the audience reaction is encouraging, the magician performs a second trick, and then repeats until either he exhausts his repertoire, or the audience becomes exhausted with him . . . whichever comes first.

For the professional magician, however, magic is more than simply a succession of tricks. There is a degree of artistry involved in knowing what dictates a good opener, a strong second trick, and a stronger closer. Learning how to structure an act, even a short one lasting only a few minutes, is challenging. There is a well-known expression, "If the only tool you have is a hammer, every problem looks like a nail." Similarly, if you've only studied sleight of hand in relation to card tricks, your range of knowledge is limited to the manipulation of fifty-two pieces of paper. It would behoove you, as a student of magic, to expand your toolkit in order to attain a macro view of what is even possible.

The volume you now hold, *Hugard's Complete Course in Modern Magic*, zooms out the telescope lens to provide expert instruction in a wide variety of magic genres. In addition to card and coin sleights, there are tricks with handkerchiefs, rope, flowers, and golf balls. There are close-up tricks with thimbles, rings, and thread, as well as stage tricks that can be performed in front of larger audiences, including the classic Chinese Linking Rings.

Although it is common for new magicians to want to focus exclusively on smaller-scale sleight of hand tricks, I recommend learning two or three routines that "play big." Once your reputation as a magician starts to grow, you will often be called upon to entertain larger groups of people. If you have only mastered tricks that require an audience to look down at your hands, the people further back will only have a view of the top of your head! This book contains dozens of tricks that allow you to present to people situated both near and far, and to provide larger groups with a robust magical experience.

Modern Magic Manual was first published in 1939, and in the ensuing decades, tricks with cigarettes and cigars have become less popular due to the changing tide of public opinion about the effects of tobacco on health. My advice, however, is to not skip the chapter that teaches cigarette manipulation, as the sleights can be applied to similar-shaped objects, such as crayons or lollipops. The same advice applies to the chapter describing pocket watch tricks. Modern audiences do not carry pocket watches – many people no longer even wear a wristwatch. Yet the premises introduced in the chapter on pocket watch magic are applicable to other objects. In fact, I performed a variant of one routine ("Watch and Loaf") on a national television talk show in England to a rousing response.

Also, do not overlook Chapter I—"The Wizard's Wand." Even if you never perform the tricks described, consider using a wand, or similar object, to assist in concealing an item in your hand. Holding a wand gives you a logical reason to keep your hand closed when an object is hidden inside. Psychologically, people cannot conceive that you can hold two items in the same hand.

The wand is an indispensable tool that is built into the very infrastructure of the "Cups and Balls" (described in Chapter V). There are multiple moments in this trick when the wand covers a multitude of concealments and secret loads. If you do not own a wand, feel free to substitute a spoon, a pencil, or even the cross rod of a wooden hanger. In a pinch, any of these objects can serve the same purpose as a wand. Personally, I am a fan of the "Coffee Cups and Balls" described in Chapter V, as this follows the impromptu nature of Max Malini's famous performances. Malini borrowed three coffee cups, acquired some cherries from the bar (in lieu of balls), and used a celery stalk as his wand. The apparently extemporaneous use of natural objects is extremely disarming, and makes the final appearance of large fruits that completely fill each cup even more surprising.

Chapter VIII offers valuable lessons in "Silks and Sorcery," a genre of magic that no longer enjoys the same popularity as it did in decades past. Within the trade, magicians call handkerchiefs "silks," and tricks with silks take advantage of their flowing, visual nature, as well as the ease with which they can be compressed into small spaces. Ade Duval, a famous magician at the time this book was released, played in the world's most celebrated theaters (including Radio City Music Hall and the London Palladium) with an all-silk act titled "Rhapsody in Silk." He produced thousands of colorful silks both from empty tubes and from his bare hands, ultimately filling the stage with swirling, jubilant silk banners. While other magicians were plagued with imitators, Ade Duval's silk act was never duplicated. The reason? Probably because it took him one and a half hours to prepare the silks before every twelve-minute performance! If you want to try your hand at silks, Chapter VIII teaches the special folds and pleats that enable you to unfurl one, or a dozen, in an eye-pleasing production.

You will also learn some great knot tricks, including "Upsetting a Square Knot." This is the basis of Slydini's famous silk routine, which he performed brilliantly on the Dick Cavett Show in 1977. We are fortunate to have a recording of that broadcast preserved on the New York Times website. An internet search for "Slydini" and "Dick

Cavett" will guide you to this masterful performance. Slydini expanded upon the simple sleight described by Hugard, transforming a po-
tentially trivial trick into a full-fledged and genuinely baffling routine
that is worthy of your study.

If you are inclined to learn card magic, Chapter XVII offers a solid
roundup of effective sleights and tricks. The first nine pages of this
chapter are devoted to shuffles—the overhand shuffle, riffle shuffle,
and the Hindu shuffle. I recommend that you study Hugard's description of the false overhand shuffle subtitled "To retain the whole deck
in a set order." I use a version of this false shuffle in my performances,
and the method described in this chapter is both easy to learn and
utterly deceptive. Your audience will believe that you have shuffled the
deck, while in fact not a single card has changed position.

Hugard reveals an intriguing bit of trivia: he himself coined the
term "Hindu shuffle" after seeing an Indian magician in Australia
execute this style of shuffle, common to the people of India and East
Asia. Hugard's coinage of the "Hindu shuffle" has been adopted by
professional magicians worldwide ever since. In most western coun-
tries, however, the more prevalent method of mixing cards in casual
gaming is the overhand shuffle.

One of the first bits of advice I received as a beginner is that you
only need to know three sleights: a pass, a palm, and a force. By combining these three maneuvers, you will have the ability to perform a
wide variety of entertaining card tricks. Chapter XVII offers solid,
workable methods in each of these categories, as well as fully formu-
lated routines that build upon the sleights you have just learned. For
further study, I recommend Hugard and Braue's *Royal Road to Card
Magic* and Hugard's *Encyclopedia of Card Tricks*.

As a veteran magician, I want to remind new students that you do
not need to learn every version of every sleight. Young magicians often
pride themselves on the sheer number of moves they can do, the more
difficult the better. Their skill serves as a badge of honor, and fellow
magicians reinforce this notion by praising flawless execution of challenging sleights. If, however, you know twenty-five methods to control a selected card, yet only one method to reveal it, audiences will
believe you know only one trick. On the flip side, if you know one

method to control a selected card, and twenty-five methods to reveal it, your audience will believe you know twenty-five different tricks. Pay attention to the various discoveries taught in Chapter XVII, including a pleasing sequence contributed by legendary magician and mentalist, Theodore Annemann.

When I began learning magic forty years ago, I loved multi-subject books like this. Between two covers lay a gold mine of tricks using cards, coins, rope, linking rings—all items I dreamed about performing on stage one day. Two more favorites, similar in scope, are Henry Hay's *The Amateur Magician's Handbook* and John Northern Hilliard's *Greater Magic*. Each of these volumes felt like a Sears catalog of magic, heavy books describing hundreds of attractive and peculiar sleights, and I felt compelled to learn them all. If you are a new magician, I envy you. You are about to embark on a journey of exploration that can inspire a lifelong love of magic.

Steve Cohen
The Millionaires' Magician
Lotte New York Palace hotel
June 1, 2017

I

THE WIZARD'S WAND

*"Come, bring thy wand, whose magic power can wake the
troubled spirits of the deep."*

Hemans—Address to Fancy.

FROM time immemorial the magic wand has been associated
with some supernatural power. Perhaps the earliest his-
torical suggestion of its miraculous virtues is the Biblical story
of Moses' wand which he cast on the ground, turning it into a
serpent. Again we have the dividing of the Red Sea at a wave
of his wand and the gushing of water from a rock on its being
struck with the wand. Down through the ages the belief has
persisted in the popular mind that the magician accomplishes
his miracles by the aid of his wand. Was there ever a magician
depicted in books, on canvas, or in the mind's eye without a
wand? Yet the modern performer too often passes up this invaluable aid toward building up the character he is supposed to
portray. He may use it for an opening trick by causing it to
vanish but, after reproducing it, he lays it aside. A most illogical
procedure.

Apart from its suggestion of magical powers, the wand is of
great practical use to the magician. It gives him something to
do with his hands at awkward moments, it gives a logical reason
for keeping the hand closed when some object has to be held
secretly in it, and it is a powerful aid in misdirection. A mere tap
with it on a table will draw all eyes to that spot, giving the
operator an opportunity of making some necessary motion with
his other hand imperceptibly. The habitual use of the wand cannot be too strongly recommended to the student.

1. THE MAGICAL PRODUCTION OF THE WAND

Take a small rubber band and tie a knot in the middle,
making two small loops. To one of these fasten a small black

1

safety pin and insert the end of the wand in the other. Fasten the pin under the coat on the right-hand side near the armpit in such a way that the lower end of the wand is just above the edge of the coat. To produce it, you pretend that you have forgotten to bring it but that, as you are powerless without it, you will make it come to you. "You will see it appear," you say, "either on this side"—and you fling out your left arm to full length, looking at it yourself—"or on this"—and you rapidly extend the right arm to the right, showing the wand. At the moment the left arm is stretched out you seize the end of the wand with the right hand, draw it out, and swing it into view as the arm reaches its fullest extension and as you turn to the right. By the time the spectators are looking in that direction the trick is done. It is a good plan to toss the wand into the air at once, making it revolve lengthwise several times and catching it again in the right hand.

2. The Magnetic Suspension of the Wand at the Fingertips

(1) With a few words about the magnetic qualities of the wand place it against the palm of the left hand, supporting it,

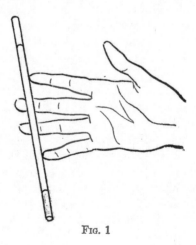

Fig. 1

upright, with the left thumb, and rub it vigorously with the tips of the right fingers. Then place the right fingers on the side of the wand as shown in Fig. 1, the tips of the two middle fingers slightly bent and pressing the wand against the tips of the first and fourth fingers, which are on the side of it. Only the flesh under the nails of these last two fingers should touch the side of the wand.

By using a light unvarnished wand you can turn the hand in any direction and even let the wand slide downwards, stopping it again at will, the wand continuing to adhere to the fingers. Naturally some little practice is necessary.

(2) In this case a loop of fine black thread is placed round the top joints of the middle fingers of the left hand. When the wand is to be suspended, place one end against the tips of these two fingers, withdraw the tip of the third finger from the loop, and insert the end of the wand. Push the wand through until the loop is at the middle and let it lie across the top joints of the fingers. By pressing the middle finger back a little the loop will hold the wand quite firmly; you can turn the hand in any direction and even allow the wand to slide downwards by relaxing the pressure slightly and applying it when you wish to stop it. With practice it will be found that the wand can be suspended in a number of different positions, and at any time desired the thread can be broken and dropped to the floor imperceptibly.

3. Vanishing the Wand and Recovering It

The latest and most simple method is of recent introduction. The wand used is black with white ivorine tips, and another

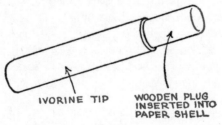

IVORINE TIP   WOODEN PLUG INSERTED INTO PAPER SHELL

Fig. 2

wand, duplicating this in appearance, has detachable tips (Fig. 2) which fit into a tube of black paper. The real wand is placed beforehand in the inside breast pocket of the coat and the faked wand is carried on openly. Because of the wooden tips this can be rapped on the table, giving the impression of solidity. To vanish it, you take a sheet of newspaper, roll the wand in it, screw up the paper at the ends, and again rap the end of the packet on the table, apparently proving that the wand is still there. Then, holding the packet between the hands, one hand on each end, clap the hands together, crumpling the paper, and roll it into a ball. The wand has vanished; toss the paper aside and bring the solid wand from the breast pocket.

This is the usual procedure; but there are two effects that can be added to make it still more effective: one is the spontaneous appearance of the wand from the vest pocket, and the other is the tossing of the crumpled paper to the spectators to be examined.

To provide for the appearance of the wand, cut a hole in the bottom of the upper left vest pocket, and have a bag of rather stiff cloth, which will take the wand and allow it to slide easily, sewed to the slit in the vest. The length of the bag is such that when the wand is placed in it the upper end is just out of sight in the vest pocket. Attach a small weight to a length of black silk, drop it into the bag, bring the thread down, and tie it to the lowest vest button; then place the wand in the bag. A pull on the thread will naturally cause the wand to rise out of the pocket. See Fig. 3.

To enable you to throw the ball of paper out, an exchange must be made for a piece of paper crumpled similarly. This you have under your vest on the right-hand side. With these preparations made, you proceed thus: When the paper supposed to hold the wand is crushed, your hands are brought just in front of the body; in rolling and squeezing the ball of paper, slip the right thumb under the thread and bend the thumb to hold it. Hold the ball of paper in the right hand and with the left grasp the left side of the coat and pull it open. Look down at the vest pocket and at the same moment let the right hand move downwards and to the right, thus making the wand rise from the vest pocket. At the same time turn toward the right so that the right hand comes over the outside pocket of the coat at that side, let the paper ball drop into it, and then close the fingers again. Take the lower end of the wand in the left hand, let the thread slip from the right thumb, toss the wand in the air to show it is not attached in any way, and at the same moment take the duplicate paper ball from under the vest. Finally toss the empty paper out to the spectators. The weight will pull the thread taut against the vest, where it will be safely out of your way.

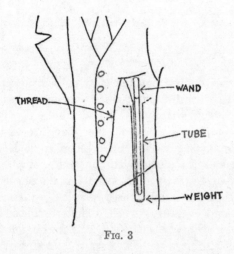

FIG. 3

Someone is sure to open up the paper, and if you have the word STUNG printed in very large letters on it his expression on reading it will cause considerable amusement to the rest of the onlookers.

The paper tubes and the ivorine tips with solid wand to match can be obtained very reasonably at any magic shop. There are also many kinds of mechanical wands for the production, vanish and exchange of silk handkerchiefs and the like —but these are outside the scope of this work.

II

CONJURING WITH COINS

"Everyone will have noticed with what skill a coin let fall upon the ground runs to hide itself, and what art it has in making itself invisible."

Victor Hugo—Les Miserables.

THERE is no doubt that tricks with coins long antedated tricks with cards. Coins were in common use ages before cards were made available to all and sundry by the printing press. Probably the operators of the "anciente and honorable plaie of the balles"—cups and balls—soon applied to coins the peculiar processes they employed in their manipulations with balls. It is strange, however, that there is no printed record of the different passes and palms with coins earlier than the middle of the nineteenth century, when Ponsin published his book *Nouvelle Magie Blanche Devoilée* (1853). Fifteen years later Robert-Houdin, in his work *Les Secrets de la Prestidigitation et de la Magie*, gave the first complete explanation of magic with coins. In spite of this there was but little progress in the way of new principles or sleights until 1895, when T. Nelson Downs invented the back and front palm with coins, and a number of other new principles and sleights, which practically revolutionized the art of coin manipulation.

Tricks with coins are always effective and they have this great advantage—coins are always available and anyone who has acquired some skill in their manipulation can stage a little magical performance anywhere at a moment's notice. I shall treat the basic principles first, then the new sleights and manipulations, and finally tricks in which these are put to practical use.

I. THE SECRET HOLDS

1. THE REGULAR PALM

This is the foundation upon which all sleight-of-hand magic has been built; it is the acquired faculty of holding any small object in the palm of the hand without the aid of the fingers. The first step is to learn how this unconventional hold is made. If you place a half dollar in the middle of the palm of your hand and contract the hand slightly, you will find that the coin will be gripped by its sides between the two fleshy pads, one at the base of the thumb, the other opposite this one and in line with the third and fourth fingers. At first, in order to exert enough pressure on the coin, the hand will assume a very cramped position; however, in a short time the muscles will become educated and it will be found that a coin can be held in the palm with a contraction so slight that the hand retains a perfectly natural appearance.

Palming is the backbone of sleight of hand and it is useless to try to proceed further until it is acquired. This is easily done if you make a practice of always having a coin—a half dollar, for example—in your pocket and form the habit of holding it in your palm at odd times. A half dollar is the best coin to start with and once you are able to hold it easily in the palm of the hand you will find very little difficulty in applying the same grip to coins of any size. It must always be borne in mind that the ideal to be aimed at when palming a coin, or any other small object, is to hold the hand in a perfectly natural way. The first impulse of the beginner is to stretch out the fingers and the thumb to the utmost; guard against this by studying the appearance of your hand when it is at rest, and copy that.

From the very first acquire the habit of always keeping the palm of the hand toward the body when you palm a coin, so that the action will become automatic. The most perfect palm is wasted if the hand is unconsciously turned toward the spectators. The fingers must also be trained to act freely and independently when a coin is in the palm of the hand. An excellent practice is to hold a coin in the palm when writing or playing cards.

Several coins can be palmed at once; they should not be laid on the palm in a pile but slightly overlapping one another toward the roots of the fingers. The greater the number of coins, the greater the necessary contraction of the hand will be; but it is seldom that more than three or four will have to be palmed at the same time.

The second step is to learn how to place the coin in the correct position in the palm secretly. Take the coin between the first finger and the thumb, flat; turn the hand over and slide the

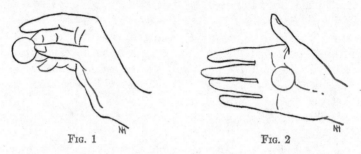

Fig. 1   Fig. 2

coin onto the tips of the second and third fingers with the help of the thumb (Fig. 1). Remove the thumb and place its tip against the tip of the forefinger to prevent its automatic extension outwards, a fault that many performers never realize; at the same time bend the two middle fingers and press the coin into the palm, which retains it (Fig. 2). At once extend the two middle fingers and again place the tip of the thumb against them, bringing both into exactly the same position as before but without the coin. Practice the movement until you can place the coin in the palm in an instant.

2. THE OBLIQUE PALM

This method marks the first great stride forward in modern coin manipulation. Invented by T. Nelson Downs and first used by him publicly in 1895, it has become indispensable in coin conjuring. The new grip is easily acquired once the regular flat palm has been mastered.

In the oblique palm the coin is held at an angle of about 45 degrees, the free end directed toward the tips of the fingers (Fig. 3).

The best and quickest way to learn this palm is to put the coin in the oblique position in the palm with the other hand and learn to hold it there by the contraction of the muscles of the palm only. As soon as you are able to hold it securely in this position, the next step is to learn how to produce the coin thus held, at the tips of the fingers. To do this bend the fingers, place the nail of the second finger against the thumb side of the coin and the top joint of the third finger on the other side, thus gripping the coin between the top joints of these two fingers (Fig. 4); then stretch them out and carry the coin away. Place

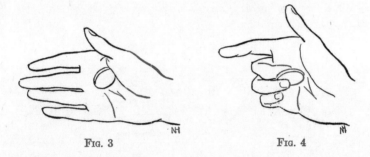

Fig. 3   Fig. 4

the tip of the thumb below the coin and slide it to the tip of the first finger.

When this movement of lifting the coin from the oblique palm to the tips of the forefinger and thumb can be done easily and surely, the reverse action—that is to say, the placing of the coin in the oblique palm—must be learned. To do this, hold the coin between the tips of the thumb and first finger, bend the top joint of the second finger, and place its nail against the coin on the thumb side and touching the thumb; then place the third finger behind the coin, gripping it against the nail of the second finger, and release the thumb. Bend these fingers and place the coin in the oblique palm. Note particularly that the tip of the third finger must be behind the tip of the second finger and not parallel with it. Contract the muscles of the palm to grip the coin and immediately extend the fingers.

Do not attempt to make the moves rapidly at first; execute them slowly and correctly until the fingers become accustomed to them. The necessary speed will come with practice.

These two methods of palming are the only difficult moves to be learned. Once they are mastered the other sleights will be found comparatively easy.

3. The Finger Palm

In this position the coin is held at the roots of the two middle fingers, which are bent in and grip it between the folds of the first and second joints (Fig. 5). The first and fourth fingers take no part in the action and are slightly extended.

The coin can be slid into this position from the regular palm by lowering the hand and letting it glide into the bend of the middle fingers. Several coins can be held in this easy and natural position at the same time.

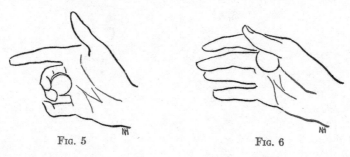

FIG. 5   FIG. 6

4. The Thumb Palm

This is a very easy hold, the coin being perpendicular to the palm and gripped in the fold at the base of the thumb by the pressure of the latter against the first finger. The coin must not pass behind the hand, and the tip of the thumb must be separated from the first finger.

To place the coin in the thumb palm, hold it between the tips of the thumb and first finger, the tip of the first finger resting on its upper edge; push the coin downwards with the first finger, making it slide along the thumb and supporting it with the second finger underneath until it reaches the fork of the thumb. Grip it there by pressing the base of the thumb inwards and at once extend the fingers (Fig. 6).

With very little practice this palm can be made with extreme rapidity. The coin can be transferred to the regular palm or the finger palm by simply releasing the thumb pressure and letting the coin fall into the hollow of the hand or the bend of the middle fingers.

5. THE FORK OF THE THUMB PALM

In this position the coin is held horizontally between the side of the thumb and the base of the first finger, well down in the fork. To place it there, hold it between the tips of the thumb and first finger, put the top joint of the second finger on the thumb side of the coin, release the thumb and separate it widely,

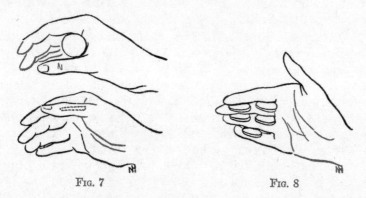

Fig. 7   Fig. 8

at the same time gripping the coin between the top joints of the first two fingers. Bend these fingers and carry the coin well into the fork and hold it there in a horizontal position by closing the thumb on it (Fig. 7).

To produce the coin from this palm, the movements are simply reversed; that is to say, you bend the fingers, grip the coin between the top joints of the first two fingers and extend them, place the tip of the thumb under the coin, release the second finger, and show the coin at the tips of the thumb and forefinger. Some very brilliant effects can be obtained with this sleight, since it permits the secret hold of a number of coins which can be produced one by one after both sides of the hand have been shown.

6. THE PINCHES BETWEEN THE FINGERS

A coin can be held perpendicularly by its edge between two fingers, either at their tips or bases. It is not necessary to go into details of the various positions; the front pinches are shown in Fig. 8, and from any one of these the coin can be transferred to a back pinch by pushing it through the interval between the fingers with the thumb. The pinch that is most useful is that between the first and second fingers, at either the front or the back of the hand.

II. THE VANISHES

1. THE COIN, LYING ON THE PALM OF ONE HAND, IS TAKEN BY THE OTHER HAND

Show the coin lying on the palm of the left hand in the exact position for palming it in that hand. Bring the right hand over; pick up the coin with the fingers in front of it, the thumb at the back, and move the hand away, closing the fingers on the coin as you turn to the right. This is the feint. Replace the coin in the same position in the left hand as before, under pretense of showing the right hand empty. Now make a pretense of picking up the coin, making exactly the same movements; but this time contract the left hand, palming the coin, and turn it slightly, bringing its back toward the spectators. Close the fingers of the right hand on the supposed coin, move the hand away toward the right in a diagonally upward direction, and fix your whole attention on that hand. Point the forefinger of the left hand toward the right hand as it moves away, thus giving a reason for turning its back to the onlookers. Immediately begin rubbing the tips of the fingers of the right hand against the palm, as if you were crumbling the coin to nothing. Finally, after a few moments' delay to let the spectators become used to the idea that the coin really is in the right hand, open the fingers one by one, beginning with the little finger, and show that the coin has vanished.

The whole action must be natural, without haste, and the best way to convince the spectators that you have taken the coin is to appear to be convinced yourself. Never show the hand empty immediately after having pretended to take it. The supposed crumbling of the coin is designed to give the onlookers time to forget the previous action of taking the coin from the left hand. The principles of the feint, the fixing of attention on the hand supposed to hold the coin, and the pretended pulverization apply equally to all the vanishes and will be taken for granted in their description.

2. The Tourniquet

This vanish, which has been used by generations of magicians, is still one of the best when skillfully done.

Show the coin in the left hand, for example, held flat between the tips of the thumb and the second and third fingers. Bring the right hand over, palm downwards, pass the thumb well under the coin (Fig. 9) and close the fingers from above. At the

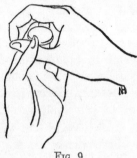

Fig. 9

moment that the coin is hidden by the right fingers, relax the grip of the thumb and let the coin fall. It strikes against the right thumb, turns vertically, and lands in the finger-palm position in the left hand, where a very slight contraction of the two middle fingers holds it securely. At the same moment close the fingers of the right hand completely, apparently seizing the coin, and move that hand upwards to the right in a diagonal direction. Turn the left hand over a little and point to the right hand with the forefinger, at the same time making a turn of the body toward the right. Complete the vanish as described above.

I cannot emphasize too strongly the fact that sleights must not be regarded as tricks; they are simply devices to be used secretly in the execution of tricks, of which the spectators should not have the slightest suspicion. In this case, after having shown the coin in the left hand, turn your attention to the spectators and, in the course of your patter, execute the sleight casually, without looking at your hands, and turn your eyes on the hand supposed to hold the coin only after you have raised it to about shoulder height. You may then open the hand a little, keeping its back to the front so that the spectators cannot see into it, and say something about a peculiar mark on it and even pretend to turn it over with the other hand. The whole idea is to convince the audience that the coin is actually in the hand which is supposed to hold it. If you succeed in doing this, then the resulting vanish becomes a real feat of magic; anything short of this is failure. This is the reason that so many performers who execute the mechanical part of these sleights fail in the presentation of the tricks in which the sleights are used. They emphasize the sleights instead of the trick and completely overlook the fact that it takes misdirection and presentation in addition to the sleights to make any trick really illusive.

Naturally the movements required in making the sleights must be carefully studied and practiced until they can be done perfectly, but in the final analysis it is the presentation and misdirection which are the principal parts of the trick itself. It would be impossible to treat these points fully in connection with each sleight. Every performer must work them out for himself. Time spent in this way will bring a much greater reward than hours wasted on learning complicated maneuvers.

3. THE REGULAR PALM

The vanish by the regular palm is the one most often used and is the method implied when palming is spoken of without any details being given.

Show the coin between the thumb and forefinger of the right hand and move the right hand toward the left as if to place the coin in it. The right hand naturally turns over; as soon as the back of the hand conceals the coin, slide it onto the tips of the second and third fingers, put the tip of the thumb against that of the forefinger, bend the middle fingers and press the coin into the palm, immediately afterward extending the two middle fingers to their first position. Rest the tips of the right thumb and fingers on the half-closed left hand for a moment as if depositing the coin, then move the right hand away and close the left hand completely. At first it will be found that the distance between the two hands is not sufficient to allow time for the execution of the palm; so you make a turn of the whole body toward the left, thus prolonging the journey of the right hand.

To acquire a perfect palm, practice before a mirror. First put the coin really into the left hand; then repeat the action, but palm the coin, and continue the practice until you cannot detect the least difference between the two actions. Finish the vanish as prescribed.

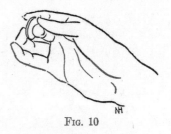

The vanish can also be made by using the thumb palm instead of the regular palm, and with this advantage—that you can vanish the coin completely. To do this, after you have apparently placed the coin in the left hand, move the right hand towards the left shoulder to pull up the sleeve and, as it passes over the left outside coat pocket, let the coin drop in.

FIG. 10

4. THE OBLIQUE PALM

Show the coin held between the tips of the right thumb and forefinger near the edge with as much of the coin showing as possible, the other three fingers being closed on the palm. Bring the right hand

FIG. 11

over to the left hand, place the outer edge of the coin against the left palm, and begin to close the left fingers. At the moment that the coin is hidden by them, place the first joint of the right second finger in front of the coin and that of the third finger behind it (Fig. 10), grip the coin with them, bend the two fingers, and carry the coin to the oblique palm in the right hand (Fig. 11). Immediately close the left fingers on the right thumb and forefinger and then slowly withdraw them. To all appearance the coin has been placed in the left hand.

Raise the left hand diagonally to the left and turn slightly toward the left; point to the left hand with the right forefinger and make the usual movements to complete the vanish.

5. Actual Deposit of the Coin and Its Withdrawal Under Cover of the Fingers

Show the coin in exactly the same way as in the preceding vanish and place it flat against the palm of the left hand (Fig. 12). Retain the grip of the thumb and forefinger and begin to

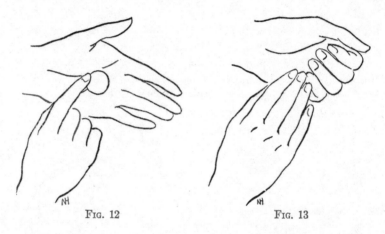

Fig. 12   Fig. 13

close the left fingers. As soon as they hide the coin from the eyes of the spectators, extend the last three fingers of the right hand over the coin (Fig. 13), and, a moment before the left fingers close completely, withdraw the right hand, retaining the coin between the thumb and forefinger and hidden by the other three fingers. Raise the closed left hand diagonally to the left, your eyes fixed on it, and drop the right hand quietly as you press the coin into the regular palm with the middle fingers.

With both these last vanishes several coins can be made to disappear in succession, but care must be taken in palming the second and the succeeding coins that they do not "talk." To avoid any sound they must be slid one onto the other.

III. THE CHANGES

It is necessary very often to substitute a coin of your own for one that has been marked by a spectator. Many methods have been devised for accomplishing this, but the following are the best.

1. BY THE REGULAR PALM

Hold the substitute coin in the regular palm in the left hand and keep the hand with its back to the front. Take the marked coin with the right hand and go through the motions of placing it in the left hand, really palming it in the regular palm. Raise the left hand vertically; at the moment the right hand reaches it, turn it horizontally, palm upwards, and rest the tips of the right fingers on the substitute coin for a moment, then move it away. So far as the spectators are concerned, you have simply transferred the coin from one hand to the other.

2. BY THE THUMB PALM

In this case you hold the substitute coin in the regular palm in the right hand and you receive the marked coin in the same hand. In the action of apparently placing this coin in the left hand, thumb palm it and let the substitute coin fall from the palm of the right hand into the left. The change can be made by using the regular palm, but the action is more difficult and there is no compensating advantage to be gained by using it.

3. THE SINGLE-HANDED CHANGE

Secrete the substitute coin in the finger palm in the right hand and take the marked coin between the first finger and thumb of the same hand; then make the following moves:

(1) Slide the marked coin down the face of the thumb with the forefinger, bend the top joint of the thumb, and grip the coin against the fold at the base of the thumb.

(2) Place the tip of the thumb on the finger-palmed coin and push it upwards, over the middle finger to the tips of the forefinger, into view.

(3) This action will have pushed the upper edge of the

marked coin against the base of the two middle fingers. Bend these fingers inward, grip the opposite edge of the coin and pull it back into the finger palm in exactly the same position from which the substitute coin has just been removed.

In spite of the necessary length of this explanation, the movements blend into one another so perfectly that the change can be done in a flash. The change must be made with the hand in motion; for example, in putting the coin on the table or in simply raising the hand to note the private mark on the coin, it will then be imperceptible. Note particularly that at both the start and the finish of this change you can allow the palm of the hand to be seen.

Whenever you have to exhibit a coin to the audience, either at the start of a trick or at the final production, be careful to hold it by the extreme edge between the tips of the thumb and forefinger and close the other three fingers into the palm (Fig. 14). The habit of holding the coin in this manner should be cultivated from the very beginning. A coin is only a small object, and if the spectators cannot see it plainly the effect of the trick is ruined.

Fig. 14

IV. THE BACK AND FRONT PALM

It will probably never be settled satisfactorily to whom should go the credit for the invention of the back and front palm with cards, but it is generally accepted that the same principles with regard to coins were invented by T. Nelson Downs. Briefly the back and front palm consists in making a coin pass from the front to the back of the hand, and vice versa, in such a way as to be able to show both sides of the hand empty in succession.

The writer of Mr. Downs' book *Modern Coin Manipulation* gave a detailed description which purported to be an explanation of the method used by Mr. Downs. Briefly stated, the reader is told to hold the coin on the fingers at the first joints; grip its sides with the first and fourth fingers; make it revolve to the back, the hand being held palm outwards; pinch it between the first and second fingers, with the other two fingers spread wide apart; grip it between the second and third fingers, spreading the first and fourth fingers; pinch it between the third and fourth fingers, spreading the first and second; then repeat all these movements in the reverse order before finally placing the coin in the oblique palm.

As a matter of fact,. these gymnastic finger exercises were never used by Mr. Downs in his public performances, not even the revolution from the front finger hold to the rear finger hold. The fact, of course, is that even if the moves could be done so perfectly that the spectators could get no glimpse of the coin at any time their very execution would simply telegraph to the most stupid onlooker exactly where the coin was at any given moment. Mr. Downs was too great an artist to do that. He used the back and front palm only incidentally and in a natural way to prove, apparently, that the hand was empty on both sides, the coin having vanished into thin air.

Unfortunately, because of the large sale of the book and the great reputation achieved by Mr. Downs, this so-called explanation of the sleight has done great harm, not only by putting a stumbling block in the path of beginners, but by the attempted performance of the moves in public by performers who ought to know better. The two methods which follow are entirely practical and are not difficult. No others are necessary.

1st Method. Stand with your left side to the audience, the right arm stretched out to the right, palm outwards, the thumb pointing upwards, the fingers extended and joined, the coin in full view against the top joints of the two middle fingers, and the sides of the first and fourth fingers pressing lightly on the edge of the coin (Fig. 15).

Under cover of a pretended throw upwards bend the tips of the middle fingers under the coin, making it revolve to the rear, and pinch its upper edge between the top joints of the first and second fingers. Do not separate the third and fourth fingers; merely bend them a trifle inwards. The front of the hand is thus shown empty (Fig. 16).

To show the back of the hand, begin to close the fingers at the first joints only—that is, keeping them extended—and turn the hand and the wrist without moving the arm. When the back of the hand is toward the spectators, in an almost vertical position, place the tip of the thumb on the edge of the coin and pull it into the front pinch. Stretch the fingers out again and

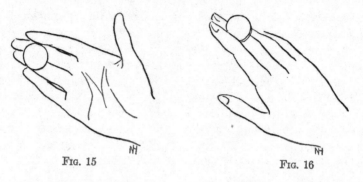

FIG. 15   FIG. 16

show the back of the hand. Both sides of the hand have thus been shown empty.

2d Method. Proceed exactly as in the first method up to the point where the hand is held palm outwards with the coin at the back, pinched between the first and second fingers. Bend the

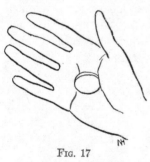

FIG. 17

fingers and turn the hand and wrist as explained; pass the third finger, stretched out, above the coin, pinching it between the second and third fingers; bend these two fingers into the palm and press the coin into the oblique palm; then stretch out the four fingers and the thumb, separating them widely (Fig. 17). The whole movement can be executed so rapidly that the spectators do not realize that the fingers have left their sight for a moment.

To show the palm empty again, bend the fingers as before and pinch the coin between the second and third fingers; stretch them out; place the tip of the first finger on the edge of the coin and hold it pinched between the first and second fingers at the back. The transfer is made with the back of the hand toward the audience, the hand itself being motionless. At this moment turn the hand to the front with the fingers stretched out and joined, thus showing the front of the hand empty with the coin back at the starting point. The whole action can be done in a flash and is quite illusory.

These transfers, in common with all the other sleights, must be executed under cover of natural gestures, purely as a means to an end and not as exhibitions of digital dexterity.

V. FLOURISHES

There are very few of these exercises in pure dexterity with coins, and the few there are produce much less effect than the flourishes with playing cards. I shall explain two only, the steeplechase, which, although useless for stage work, is very effective under more intimate conditions, and the multiplication flourish, a brilliant effect.

1. THE STEEPLECHASE

The effect is that a coin revolves from joint to joint on the back of the hand. To begin, hold the right hand closed, the

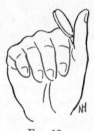

FIG. 18

FIG. 19

palm toward the audience, the first joints of the fingers horizontal, and the back of the hand vertical. Place the coin, a half dollar or dollar, in an upright position between the tip of the thumb and the side of the first joint of the forefinger (Fig. 18). Release the pressure of the thumb and let the coin fall flat on top of the first joint of the forefinger (Fig. 19).

Move the joint of the second finger a little toward the right and raise it; then bring it down to pinch the edge of the coin that overlaps the first joint, making the coin rise to a vertical position and then fall flat on the joint of this finger, turning over in the process. Separate and raise the joint of the third finger in its turn; then lower it to pinch the side of the coin just as you did with the second finger, with the result that the coin turns over and falls flat on the joint of this third finger. Repeat the same movements with the fourth finger, then hold the coin in a perpendicular position between the joints of these last two fingers.

At this point there are three different methods of procedure:

First. Let the coin slide down between the joints of the two fingers onto the tip of the thumb, held underneath the hand, and carry it, thus balanced, back to the starting point between the thumb and forefinger joint.

Second. Let the coin fall flat on the joint of the third finger again; slope the hand a little and make it slide over the joints to the starting point, where the thumb tip nips the edge and raises it to a perpendicular position ready for a repetition of the roll.

Third. Let the coin fall flat on the joint of the third finger; raise the joint of the middle finger, moving it a little to the left, then bring it down, nipping the edge that overlaps and making the coin fall flat onto its joint. Repeat the same movements with the first finger, and turn the coin over onto its joint; then nip its edge with the thumb tip, bringing it back to the starting position.

The flourish must be learned with each hand. Practice the separate movements very slowly at first and make no attempt at speed until the finger movements are thoroughly coordinated. As soon as the roll has been mastered with both hands, proceed to the following routine:

(1) Place a coin between the tips of the right thumb and forefinger joint, roll it to the little finger, let it slide down onto the thumb, and carry it back under the hand to the starting point. Again roll it to the little finger, then roll it back over the hand to the thumb.

(2) Bring the left hand over to the right hand and let the coin turn over and fall into the starting position between the left thumb and first joint of the left forefinger. Roll it over the

left joints and back again, and then again into the starting point in the right hand.

(3) Take a second coin with the left hand and make the coins in each hand roll back and forth simultaneously.

The flourish is a very graceful one and gives the onlookers a high opinion of the operator's dexterity. As an incentive to the reader, though it may seem almost incredible, the author vouches for the fact that Mr. Ross, the Philadelphia magician, performs the feat with four coins in each hand, the coins rolling separately and simultaneously.

Vanishing a Coin by Means of the Steeplechase Flourish

After the roll with two coins, put the coin in the left hand on the table and repeat the roll with the right hand, bringing

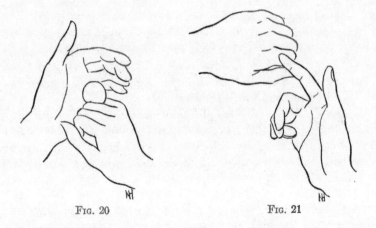

FIG. 20   FIG. 21

the coin to the little-finger position. Bring the left hand over, pretend to take the coin (Fig. 20), and move the left hand away closed. In reality, let it slide down between the third and fourth fingers and pinch it there. Close the second, third, and fourth fingers into the palm and point to the left hand with the right forefinger (Fig. 21).

The coin is now pinched on the inside of the right hand between the third and fourth fingers. Open this hand, keeping its back to the front, the fingers pointing to the right; place the tips of the left fingers against those of the right hand, pinch the coin between the left second and third fingers, and stroke the right hand from the fingertips to the wrist, making a turn to the right at the same time. Close the last three fingers of the left hand into the palm and point to the empty right hand with the left forefinger. Drop the left hand behind the right knee and produce the coin between the tips of the left thumb and forefinger.

2. THE MULTIPLICATION FLOURISH

Hold five coins (dollars or half dollars), by the edges and facing the spectators vertically, between the first joints of the thumb and forefinger of either hand, the palm of the hand to the front (Fig. 22). Place the second finger against the thumb and press it against the lower edge of the rear coin; raise the finger and lift the coin with it to the space between the first and second fingers (Fig. 23).

At once bring the third finger down against the lower edge of the coin (Fig. 24) and raise it to the space between the second and third fingers (Fig. 25). Repeat the same moves with the little finger, with the result that the coin finally fills the space between the third and fourth fingers.

Next, by means of the same movements of the second and third fingers, roll the rear coin from between the thumb and first finger to the space between the second and third fingers; then with the second finger raise the next coin and hold it between the first and second fingers, with a final result as shown in Fig. 26.

Hold the four coins thus for a few moments for the effect to register, then drop the coin between the first and second fingers onto a plate and instantly roll the rear coin of the two between the thumb and forefinger into the space thus made vacant. The clash of the coin on the plate impresses the spectators with the fact that the coins are real and enhances this brilliant effect. This little stratagem should be used occasionally in any manipulative effect with coins.

Some difficulty will be found at first in keeping the coins in a vertical position as they roll from finger to finger, but the effect is well worth the practice required. The production of coins in this manner is one of the finest effects in coin magic.

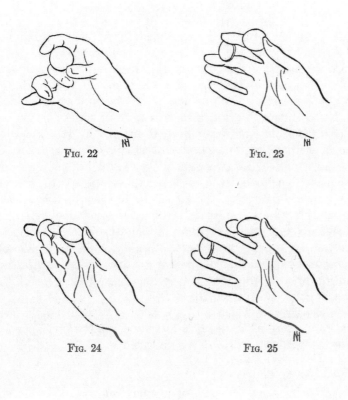

FIG. 22   FIG. 23

FIG. 24   FIG. 25

FIG. 26

VI. TRICKS WITH COINS

There are numerous pieces of apparatus for the performance of coin tricks which are automatic in their working, but these do not come within the scope of this book. As Robert-Houdin says, "Cleverness at this sort of work is of the same order as that of the musician who produces a tune by turning the handle of a barrel organ. Such performers will never merit the title of skilled artists and can never hope to attain any real success." Even in the handling of such apparatus it is only the performer who has acquired skill in sleight of hand who can produce any real effect. The whole trend of modern magic is away from the use of apparatus specially designed to produce certain effects. The magical entertainer of today must depend upon his skill with familiar articles of everyday use and his mental acuteness. There are, of course, secret accessories which are of invaluable assistance, but of these the spectators know nothing. These accessories, or gimmicks, will be explained in the course of the tricks in which they are used.

The experiments which follow depend entirely upon the performer's mastery of the sleights already explained and upon his ability to present them in a convincing way.

1. THE FLYING COIN

Effect. The invisible flight of a coin from one hand to the other.

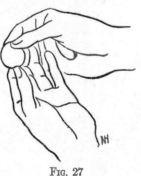

FIG. 27

1st Method (Robert-Houdin). Have a coin secretly in the right hand, holding it in the regular palm. With the same hand show another coin of the same value and put it between the tips of the thumb and fingers of the left hand. Show this coin and all parts of the left hand, turning slightly toward the left as you do so. Bring the right hand over, the back of the hand to the front, and take the coin in such a way that a great part of it is always visible to the spectators;

but at the moment when the two hands come together (Fig. 27), take advantage of the fact that the palms are hidden to drop the palmed coin from the right hand into the palm of the left hand.

Fix your attention on the coin in the right hand, showing the coin and all parts of the hand; close the left hand, turning its back to the spectators and extending it to the left. Under cover of a pretended throw toward the left hand, palm the coin in the regular palm in the right hand. Finally open the left hand and show that the coin has arrived. The trick bears repetition.

2d Method (*M. Trewey*). Stand facing the audience, both hands with the palms upwards and about a foot apart, the fin-

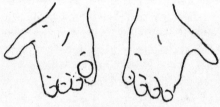

Fig. 28

gers joined and stretched out to the front, the elbows touching the sides. Show a coin lying on the first and second joints of the right third and fourth fingers (Fig. 28). Announce that the coin will pass invisibly into the left hand.

To do this, rapidly turn the hands over inwards, letting the coin shoot over into the left hand; instantly close both hands, moving them upwards in a circular direction—first outwards and then backwards and downwards to their original position (Fig. 29). If you make the movement of the hands and the

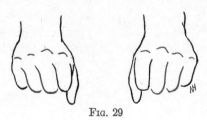

Fig. 29

secret throw of the coin quickly enough, it will be impossible for
the spectators to see the coin as it passes across the small space
between the hands at this moment.

Having done the trick, you pretend to begin to do it. Raise
your right fist above your head, the back of the hand to the
front, and pretend to drop the coin into the right sleeve. Move
the arm as if aiding it in its descent; wiggle the shoulders;
finally shake the left arm, held down at the side of the body, and
make a motion of catching the coin as it drops from the sleeve.
Then show the coin at the tips of the left thumb and fingers.

The trick can be repeated with a second coin. To do this,
retain the coin in the left hand on the lower joints of the third
and fourth fingers and place the second coin in the same position in the right hand. When the second throw is made, as before, close the left third and fourth fingers on the coin in that
hand and receive the flying coin in the folds of the first and
second fingers in such a way that the two coins do not come
into contact. Repeat the same pretended journey via the sleeves;
but, this time, in the final movement make the two coins clink.

3d Method (*L'Homme Masqué*). Stand facing the spectators;
show the left hand empty, close it, and hold the knuckles upwards—the arm bent and the fist opposite the middle of the
body, directed toward the right. Show a coin in the right hand
and announce that you are about to pass it invisibly through
the back of the hand into the palm.

Hold the coin in the position of the finger hold, the thumb
pressing it against the top joints of the two middle fingers and
the fingers joined. Strike the back of the left hand with the tips
of the right fingers, backs outwards, counting "One." Lift the
hand to repeat the blow and quickly palm the coin in the regular
palm, realigning the fingers and thumb instantly; then strike
down again, counting "Two." Repeat the blow and count
"Three." Begin to turn the left hand over, the right fingers still
masking it; open the fist slightly, let the coin fall from the right
palm into it, and close it again instantly. Immediately afterward turn the right hand over toward the front, keeping the tips
of the fingers on the back of the left hand; at the same time
complete the turn of the left fist, bringing it palm upwards. On
the completion of the turn the right hand is below the left fist

and is palm upwards; you point the right forefinger at the left fist, showing the right hand empty, and then slowly open the left hand to prove that the coin has arrived.

The illusion depends on the coordination of the turning of the hands, which should appear to be simultaneous and merely to show the palms of the hands in order to prove that the coin has passed through the back of the left hand.

4th Method (*M. Trewey*). Make a pretense of slyly taking a coin with your left hand from a pocket on the left side. Close this hand and hold it, back upwards, about waist high. Show a

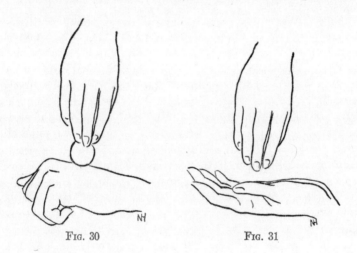

Fig. 30   Fig. 31

coin in the right hand and hold it between the tips of the thumb and fingers with about half the coin visible. Announce that you will pass it through the back of the left hand. Place the coin perpendicularly on the back of the left hand (Fig. 30), and push downwards so that the coin passes out of sight behind the fingers. At this point pretend to overhear someone say that you already have a coin in the left hand. Turn that hand over and open it, showing it empty (Fig. 31).

Turn the left hand the reverse way, closing it, and at the precise moment when the tips of the right fingers are hidden by the left hand drop the coin, close the left hand immediately, and again apply the tips of the fingers of the right hand to the back of the left fist. Pretend to press the coin flat, and then rub the fingers on the back of the fist. Finally lift the right hand, turn the left hand over, open it, and show the coin.

Here again the least hurry or the least delay will spoil the illusion. The hands must act in perfect unison.

These four solutions of the same problem by these celebrated magicians are worthy of the closest study.

2. THE ACE OF CLUBS, THE SIGN OF MONEY

Effect. A half dollar is extracted from an unprepared Ace of Clubs.

Method. We will suppose that you are seated at the bridge table and that you have a coin—a half dollar, for example— palmed in your right hand. Take a pack of cards and shuffle it. You may even spring the cards from hand to hand; the palmed coin will not interfere with the action. Run through the pack— being careful, of course, to keep the back of the right hand toward the spectators—and take out the Ace of Clubs, at the same time explaining that in cartomancy this card represents money. Take the card in the left hand by one end at the tips of the fingers and put the pack down with the right hand.

Let the coin drop to the finger hold in the right hand and take the card from the left hand by the free end, at the same time sliding the coin onto its back with the right thumb. Show the left hand empty on all sides and take the card and the coin with that hand, sliding the latter onto the back of the card with the thumb and holding it there. Now show all parts of the right hand and at the same time secure the coin in the left finger palm and hold the card by the extreme end at the tips of the fingers. Flick the back of the card with the right hand; turn it and flick the face, to show there is nothing concealed in it. Turn it again, face outward, at the tips of the left fingers and again slide the coin on the back.

Remove the card and coin with the right hand, sliding the coin under the right thumb as before. Turn the card upright and grip the top left corner with the left thumb and forefinger, hold- ing the coin at the back. Slide the right hand down the card, fingers in front and the thumb at the back, several times, each time showing the hand empty. At the third movement nip the coin with the thumb and carry it downwards, producing it from the lower end as if it had been squeezed out of the body of the card. At once hand both for examination.

3. The Passage of Three Coins One by One from One Hand to the Other

Effect. Three coins are taken in each hand; three are then made to pass invisibly, in succession, to the other hand, the coins in each hand being counted at each stage—until finally all six are in one hand and none in the other.

1st Method. Borrow six coins of the same denomination and secretly hold a seventh palmed in your right hand. Or you may have six coins in your right trousers pocket; in bringing them out, palm one and count the remaining five onto the table, then, saying you need six coins, borrow one from a spectator. Any idea that you might have a supplementary coin is thus subtly negatived. Make two piles of three coins and place them a few inches apart.

Pick up one pile with the right hand and drop the coins into the left hand, secretly letting the palmed coin drop at the same time. Close the left hand. Pick up the other three coins with the right hand, close it, jingle the coins, get the bottom coin into the position for palming, and grip it there by the regular palm. Make a motion of throwing a coin across to the left hand; turn the right hand back upwards; and drop two coins, one by one, opening the fingers widely for a moment as the last coin drops. Without pausing, open the left hand and drop its four coins onto the table, counting them.

Without haste, but without delay, pick up the four coins with the right hand and drop them into the left hand, again releasing the palmed coin. Show the right hand on all sides and pick up the other two coins. Again get one into the palm, making the throwing motion, and then drop one coin from the right hand. Count out five from the left hand.

For the last coin, sweep the five coins off the table into the left hand, releasing the palmed coin at the same moment. Give the lot into a spectator's hand, making him close it on the coins and hold them above his head. Show the last coin and pretend to put it in the left hand, really palming it by the thumb grip. Extend the left arm and move the right hand over to the left shoulder to pull up the left sleeve and, as the hand passes over the left outside coat pocket, let the coin fall inside. Pull up the sleeve, make a throwing gesture with the left hand, and show both hands empty. The spectator counts the coins and finds that he has six.

2d Method. In this version the supplementary coin is suppressed, the effect remaining the same. A new move is necessary, which is not difficult but requires careful timing.

In order to save time you may very well provide all the coins yourself. It is never worth while to delay matters by borrowing articles unless the nature of the effect makes this absolutely necessary. Arrange the coins in two piles of three on the table. Take one coin with the right hand and apparently put it in the left hand, really palming it by the regular palm; count "One." Take a second coin with the right hand; show it at the tips of the thumb and second and third fingers, with the back of the hand to the front; turn the hand palm downwards over the left hand, and apparently drop this second coin into the left hand, which opens just enough to receive it and then closes.

In reality, at the moment the backs of the right fingers touch the tips of the partly open left fingers, drop the coin from the palm of the right hand so that it strikes against the coin on the top joints of the right fingers in its passage into the left hand; immediately palm this second coin in the right hand by closing the two middle fingers, thus carrying it to the regular palm. Close the left hand and point to it with the right forefinger, counting "Two."

Properly timed, the illusion is perfect—the jingle of the two coins being conclusive evidence to the spectators that the two coins are really in the left hand. Take a third coin with the right hand and really let it fall into the left hand, imitating the previous action exactly so that it produces the same sound by falling on the single coin already there. Take the other three coins with the right hand, counting them, close the hand, and hold both hands with the backs downwards and well apart. Make a throwing motion with the left hand toward the right. Open the left hand and drop the two coins it holds, one by one, onto the table. Then count out four coins from the right hand and again show both hands empty.

Pick up one coin with the right hand and apparently place it in the left hand, palming it as before; then take a second coin and repeat the move explained above, to produce the jingle in palming this coin, counting "One, two." Pick up the remaining four coins with the right hand, counting "Three, four, five, six." Make the throwing motion with the left hand toward the right; open the left hand, showing one coin only; drop the coin on the table. Drop the five coins from the right hand, counting them, and show both hands empty.

For the last coin the action is varied a little. Take one coin with the right hand and really place it in the left hand, using exactly the same gestures as when you palmed the coin. Pick up a second coin with the right hand; then stop and say, "I don't want you to think that I use my sleeves"; put the two coins down and pull the sleeves back a little. Once more apparently place a coin in the left hand, palming it this time; close the left hand and stretch it out to the left. Take the five coins with the right hand, close it, and hold it extended to the right. Repeat the throwing motion; open the left hand, showing it empty, and drop the six coins, one by one, onto the table.

4. THE PASSAGE OF FOUR COINS FROM A HAT INTO A GLASS

Effect. Similar to that of the preceding experiment but more striking. There are two methods: one by pure skill; the other by means of a simple accessory.

1st Method. A hat, a glass, and four coins—half dollars preferably—are required and all of them may be borrowed, the only preparation being the palming beforehand of a fifth coin in the right hand.

Place the hat, glass, and coins on the table; pick up the coins with the right hand and drop them into the hat, counting them one by one. Grasp the glass by the rim with the tips of the right thumb and fingers so that the palm overarches its mouth. Dip the left hand into the hat, pick up the four coins, show them and jingle them in the hand; then place the hand in the hat, drop three coins only, and retain one coin in the finger palm. At once grasp the hat by the brim, the fingers inside pressing the stolen coin against the side of the hat.

Face the spectators, holding the hat in the left hand and the glass in the right, the arms outstretched. Announce that one coin is to pass from the hat to the glass. Give the mystic command; shake the hat, making the coins jingle; follow the supposed passage of one coin with your eyes; and let the palmed coin fall into the glass.

Place the glass with the coin in it on the table and with the left hand turn the three coins out of the hat into the right hand. Count them and jingle them in the hand, getting one coin into position in the regular palm; thrust the hand into the hat, let two coins fall, and retain one in the palm. Seize the glass with this hand as before, stretch the hands wide apart, and order a second coin to pass. Jingle the two coins in the hat, follow the supposed flight of a coin to the glass with your eyes, and let the palmed coin fall into the glass.

There are now two coins in the hat and two in the glass; you have one secretly in the left hand, held against the side of the hat. Place the glass down and take the two coins out of the hat with the right hand. Show them and drop one coin into the hat, letting the hand go just out of sight in the hat in the action. Show the second coin and repeat exactly the same action of dropping it into the hat, but really palm it and at the same moment drop the coin from the left hand. Take the glass in the right hand and follow the same procedure as before for the passage of the third coin, letting the palmed coin drop into the glass.

Place the glass with the three coins on the table; thrust the right hand into the hat; take one of the two coins, quickly slipping it under the fingers of the left hand, and bring the other out openly at the tips of the fingers. Show the inside of the hat empty by raising it and turning it over with the left hand. Pretend to drop the coin from the right hand as before, palming it and with a finger of the left hand giving the side of the hat a fillip to imitate the sound of a coin falling into the hat.

Order the fourth coin to pass, and let the palmed coin fall into the glass from the palm of the hand. Turn the hat over and show it empty. Pour the coins from the glass onto the table; at the same moment slide the coin hidden by the left fingers under the sweatband of the hat, and lay it mouth downwards on the table. Count the coins and incidentally show both hands empty. The coin can be secretly removed when returning the hat to its owner.

2d Method. In this case the extra coin is attached to a thread which runs from the armhole down the left sleeve; the length of the thread is such that when the arm is stretched to its full length the coin rests in the palm of the hand, but that when the arm is bent and held near to the body the coin will fall about six inches below the hand. It will be understood, therefore, that this attached coin can be let drop freely into a hat held in the left hand close to the body and that the mere action of extending the arm will cause the coin to be drawn up into the hand holding the hat, thus causing its disappearance. This is the principle on which the trick depends.

As in the first method, you borrow a hat, a glass, and four coins. Place the hat and the glass on the table. Pick up the first coin and apparently place it in the left hand, counting "One"; really palm the coin in the right hand and show the attached coin in the left hand. Actually place the remaining three coins, one by one, into the left hand, counting "Two, three, four" and keeping the back of the right hand to the front throughout to conceal the palmed coin. Hold the hat under the left hand, the left arm bent and close to the body, and drop the four coins into it. Then take the hat with the left hand by the brim, the fingers inside, the thumb outside.

Pick up the glass with the right hand by the rim, as already explained. Jingle the coins in the hat and stretch the left arm out, thereby causing the attached coin to mount to the fingers of the left hand, which press it to the side of the hat and conceal it. Order the first coin to pass from the hat to the glass, use the same pantomimic action, and let the coin fall from the right hand into the glass. Turn the hat over and let three coins fall on the table.

Repeat exactly the same procedure for the remaining coins, the right hand palming one coin and the left hand showing the attached coin in its place. When the extra coin has been drawn up into the fingers for the last time, break the thread; then slip the coin under the sweatband and finish as in the first method.

5. THE COIN AND ORANGES

Effect. A borrowed and marked coin is passed into the middle of two oranges in succession.

Articles required. Two oranges, two half dollars, a plate, a table knife, a napkin, and a penknife.

Preparation. Make a bold mark, a cross for example, on one of the coins with the penknife and make an exact duplication of this mark on the other coin. Cut a slit, large enough for the insertion of a half dollar, in each of the two oranges and push one of the marked coins into the slit in one of the oranges. Put the fruit and the table knife on a plate and set the plate on your table—the slits in the oranges to the rear, of course. Place the napkin alongside and put the second marked coin and the penknife in your right trousers pocket.

Routine. Begin by borrowing a half dollar; take it in your right hand and, while showing it to everyone, let it be seen that your hands are otherwise empty. Hand the coin back to the owner, asking him to mark it so that he can identify it easily. Thrust your right hand into your trousers pocket and bring out the penknife. Open a blade and hand the knife also to the owner, remarking casually, "Just scratch a mark on the coin, a square, a cross . . . anything you like so that you will know it again." Take both coin and penknife with the right hand; put the coin in your left hand, at the same time noting the mark; then place the knife in your trousers pocket and at the same time finger palm the duplicate coin.

Take the borrowed coin at the tips of the right thumb and fingers and move the hand upwards toward your eyes as if to examine the mark closely, at the same time executing the one-hand change. If the spectator has reacted to your suggestion and has scratched a cross on the coin, remark, "I see you have marked it with a cross. An easy way of signing your name." If, however, a mark of another kind has been made, content yourself with saying that the coin has been plainly marked.

Hold the substitute coin at the tips of the thumb and fingers, the palm of the hand to the front and visible, the bent fingers concealing the borrowed coin, and give this substitute coin to a spectator at a little distance; ask him to note the mark carefully so that he, too, will be able to identify the coin. Return to your table and under cover of your body, keeping the elbows pressed to the sides, push the borrowed coin into the slit in the second orange. At once pick up the table knife and, with this in your right hand, turn to the spectators. Point to the oranges with the knife and have the owner of the coin choose one, the right or the left. Using the old equivoque, you make the choice settle on the orange which has the borrowed coin in it. Push the point of the table knife into the slit and carry the orange, thus impaled, to the owner of the coin and ask him to hold it in full view.

Go to the second spectator; take your substitute coin from him; lay it on the palm of the left hand, asking him to take a final look at the mark. Then apparently pick it up with your right hand, really palming it in the left hand; rub it with the fingers for a moment or two; and pretend to throw it toward the orange. Take the plate off the table with the right hand, putting the second orange aside for the moment; pick up the napkin with your left hand, and go to the owner of the coin. Have him cut the orange in half and take out his coin himself. When he has identified his mark, take the coin from him and, in wiping it with the napkin, change it for the palmed coin in your left hand as you go to the second spectator. Ask him to identify the mark also, which, of course, he does in good faith. In the meantime you have slipped the borrowed coin into your right trousers pocket with the napkin.

Pretend to overhear a request to do the trick again and acquiesce readily. Thrust the knife into the second orange, give it to the second spectator to hold, and take the coin from him. Show it and apparently put it in your left hand, really palming it in the right hand. Move the right hand toward the left shoulder and take advantage of this action to drop the palmed coin in the outside left coat pocket; then pull the left sleeve up a little. Pretend to throw the coin at the orange, and show both hands empty on all sides. Let the spectator cut the orange, take out and identify the coin; this he does readily enough, since it has the same mark as the coin he saw before.

In the meantime you have taken the napkin from your pocket and have palmed the borrowed coin. Take the substitute coin; exchange it for the borrowed coin in the act of wiping it with the napkin; and finally return it to the owner, who once more identifies it as his property.

6. The Coin and Silver Boxes

Effect. A marked coin is borrowed and the owner is given a purse to hold as security. The coin vanishes, and the spectator finds a small packet in the purse. Unwrapping this, he finds: first, several silks; then some yards of ribbon wound round in all directions; and finally a small silver box, closed by rubber bands, and inside it another little box, which is locked. When this second box is unlocked, he finds, inside it, his marked coin.

Articles required. The two small boxes—the innermost one of which is self-locking when the lid is closed—and a coin slide; these can be obtained at a magic store. Three or four yards of inch-and-a-half ribbon, several silk handkerchiefs, a duplicate coin, a penknife, a sheet of paper about five inches by four, a glass, a box of matches, and a purse with a drawstring.

Preparation. Put the small box inside the other, place the end of the coin slide inside the inner box, and close the lids as far as they will go. Stretch several small rubber bands round the boxes both sideways and lengthways, so that on the withdrawal of the slide they will force the lids down. Now wrap the ribbon round the boxes until they are completely concealed, but let the outer end of the coin slide protrude. Do the same with the silks, and finally stretch several small rubber bands round to keep the parcel intact. Place it in the purse with the end of the slide protruding; pull the drawstring tight to keep the slide in position; and put the purse in your inside breast pocket, the mouth of the slide upwards. Finally scratch a mark—a cross, for example—on the duplicate coin; put it with the knife in your right trousers pocket, the matches in the left trousers pocket, the glass and the paper on your table.

Routine. Borrow a coin of the same denomination as yours; take it, letting it be seen that your hands are empty; then, as an afterthought, hand it back to the owner to be marked with your knife, which you take from your pocket and hand to the spectator. This done, take the knife back, return it to your pocket, and seize the opportunity to palm the duplicate marked coin in the finger palm. Work the single-hand change in the manner described in the preceding trick, and drop the substitute coin in the glass on your table.

Turn to the owner of the coin and, pretending to think he looks worried about his property, offer to give him security for it. Grasp the left side of your coat with your left hand; thrust your right hand into the breast pocket; slip the coin into the slide; withdraw this, letting it fall into the pocket; and bring out the purse, holding it by the drawstring and pulling it tight. The left arm aids in the withdrawal of the slide by pressing the purse against the body. Hand the purse to the owner of the coin to put in his pocket.

Take the piece of paper and the coin from the glass. Place the coin against the middle of the paper and fold the lower third upwards over it, then the upper third down, and finally the ends

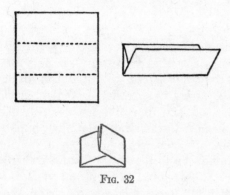

Fig. 32

inwards—wrapping up the coin securely (Fig. 32). Pretending to overhear an objection, open the paper, take out the coin, thrust it close to a spectator's eyes as you say, "You see the mark?" Then place it again on the paper, turn the lower fold upwards, the coin and the fold being toward your body and in the left hand. Lift the coin out of the fold and show it once more; replace apparently in the fold but really on the outside; fold the top down over it, then the ends. It would seem that the coin has been wrapped up fairly; really it is on the outside but covered by the end folds. Squeeze the paper round the coin, so that an impression is made in the paper; let the coin be felt and knock it against the glass. Finally let it slip secretly into your left hand, take the packet with the right hand, and thrust the left hand into your trousers pocket. Leave the coin there and bring out the matches. Set fire to the paper and let it burn away completely.

It only remains to make the most of the situation. You may apologize to the owner for the loss of the coin, try to borrow another, and so on. Finally you recall that he holds a security. Let him take out the purse and open it; unwrap the silks and the ribbon, revealing the outer box; then from this remove the inner, locked box. Hand him the key and for the climax have him identify his coin.

The trick is a modern version of the old ball-of-wool trick, the unwinding of which was too tedious an operation for modern audiences. In its present form it is one of the most mystifying tricks possible.

7. THE FIVE COINS

A routine of manipulations suitable for performance with the coins collected in the Miser's Dream (see page 42).

Stand with your left side to the front and display five coins in the left hand at the tips of the left thumb and fingers. Show the right hand back and front, the fingers apart. Take one coin from the left hand with the right thumb and forefinger; make a pretended throw into the air; and, under cover of that action, instantly pass the coin to the rear finger hold, then to the upper pinch between the first joints of the first and second fingers.

Under cover of a downward circular motion of the hand transfer the coin to the oblique palm with the back of the hand to the front, the fingers stretched wide apart. By reversing the movement bring the coin back to the same rear pinch as before, the fingers outstretched and joined, the palm of the hand to the front.

Bring the left hand up to the right hand, take one of the four remaining coins with the right thumb and forefinger, and at the same time, under cover of the back of the left hand, pass the last three fingers of that hand behind the right hand and pinch the first coin between the tips of the second and third fingers. Lower the left hand, leaving the second coin at the tips of the right thumb and forefinger, and transfer the first coin to the oblique palm in that hand.

Proceed in exactly the same way with the vanish of the second

and third coins. The position then will be this: In the left hand
you have one coin visible at the tips of the left thumb and forefinger and three coins in the oblique palm; in the right hand
you show one coin at the tips of the thumb and forefinger. Hold
up the left hand, showing the last coin and looking at it yourself;
then transfer your gaze to the coin in the right hand and at the
same time let the left hand drop, transferring its coin to the
oblique palm and at once realigning the thumb and fingers as if
they still held the coin. Vanish the coin from the right hand;
bring the left hand over and pretend to place the last coin between the right thumb and forefinger, at the same time stealing
the fourth coin and in due course transferring it to the oblique
palm.

Hold the right thumb and forefinger together as if they really
held a coin; keep the hand in motion and then suddenly throw
the imaginary coin in the air, opening the fingers widely and
showing both sides of the hand. Pause a moment, then make a
catch in the air with the left hand. Jingle the coins in that hand
and then drop them into the right hand, counting them to show
that all five have been recovered.

8. THE VANISH OF FIVE COINS SIMULTANEOUSLY FROM THE
   FINGERTIPS

Hold the left hand stretched out horizontally, palm upwards,
the fingers and thumb wide apart.
Place a coin on the tip of each
finger and the thumb (Fig. 33);
hold them balanced there while you
place the right hand palm downwards, fingers and thumb extended
so that their tips are on the coins
but the palms of the hands remain separated. The coins are thus
gripped between the corresponding
fingers and thumbs of each hand.
Turn the hands vertically and turn
to the right.

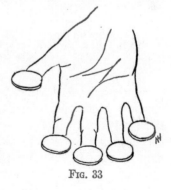

FIG. 33

Under cover of several up-and-down movements of the hands
in the vertical plane, bring the fingers and thumbs of each hand

together so that the coins slide behind one another—that between the third fingers going to the left of the coin between the little fingers, and the other coins going in the same way.

The moment they are in a pile, grip them between the right first and second fingers and carry them to the thumb-fork palm; this move must be made at the bottom of the vertical movement of the hands. At once bring the hands upwards, separate them, and open the fingers. Follow the supposed flight of the coins in the air.

To reproduce the coins, first point to the empty left palm, which faces the spectators, with the right forefinger; bring the tips of the right forefinger and thumb lightly together and turn to the right; point to the empty right palm with the left forefinger.

Turn again to the right, bending the right forefinger as before to hide the coins; bend the tip of the middle finger under the pile and draw out the bottom coin a little, pinch it with the tip of the forefinger, and extend the two fingers; place the tip of the thumb under the coin and press it upwards; release the second finger and display the coin above the tips of the thumb and first finger, keeping as much of it in view as possible (Fig. 34).

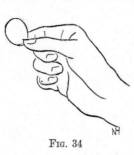

FIG. 34

Take the coin with the left hand, and produce the second in the same way. Continue the production until all the coins are in the left hand. After the production of each coin and before it is transferred to the left hand, you can turn the palm of the right hand toward the spectators and show that it is empty.

Some performers prefer to reproduce the coins by placing the hands together and sliding the coins back to their original positions between the tips of the respective fingers and thumbs. The necessary action is the exact reverse of that for the vanish. It requires considerable practice.

THE MISER'S DREAM

The Miser's Dream, the coin trick par excellence. It is showy, amusing, and astounding and, above all, it is not difficult. The necessary manipulations are well covered by movement from place to place; but, while no special dexterity is required, the feat does call for good showmanship and a ready tongue. It is for this reason that every aspirant for magical honors should include the trick in his studies. Almost without exception every famous magician has featured it at one time or another. Under various titles—such as the Shower of Gold, the Rain of Silver, the Fortune Hunt, the Coin Chase, the Aerial Treasury, Money in the Air, the Aerial Mint, the Miser's Dream, etc.—it has figured in the programs of the great magicians—the two Herrmanns, Kellar, Devant, et al., while Nelson Downs acquired fame and fortune by his masterly handling of this one feat.

The trick itself is an old one. It was first explained in print by Robert-Houdin and, since he does not claim it as his invention, it was probably an old trick even in his time. Since then the procedure has been expanded in many ways by the application of new sleights and new ideas; however, a brief description of the original method will facilitate a clearer understanding of the later developments.

ROBERT-HOUDIN'S METHOD

When you come forward you have a coin (a half dollar is commonly used nowadays) in the right hand, in the thumb palm, and seven other coins in the left trousers pocket. Borrow a hat and, in turning to receive it with the right hand, take the seven coins from the pocket with the left hand. Then take the hat in the same hand, so that the coins, covered by the fingers, lie flat against the inner lining of the hat. Pretend to catch a coin from the air with the right hand and produce the palmed coin at the fingertips. Show this coin and pretend to place it in the hat; in reality, at the moment that the hand enters the hat palm the coin in the thumb palm and drop one of the coins from the left fingers. If these two movements are simultaneous, the illusion is perfect and the spectators believe that the coin just shown in the right hand has really dropped into the hat.

Go amongst the spectators and pretend to find coins in various places—in a lady's handkerchief, under the collar of a gentleman's coat, in a child's hair, and so on—each time making the pretense of dropping the coin into the hat, but really dropping one from the reserve in the left hand. When the left hand has released the last coin, affect to find one more and drop this one into the hat openly.

Finally take the eight coins from the hat, count them into the left hand, and then pretend to take them in the right hand by means of the tourniquet. Affect to give them to a spectator and, as you lean to place them in his hand, with your right side turned to him, put them in your left pocket. Tell him to rub them briskly, and bring your two hands together and rub them one on the other. When the spectator opens his hands he finds them empty, and you congratulate him on being able to do the trick as well as you do it yourself.

Such was the original method, undoubtedly a very pretty effect.

MODERN METHODS

In order to give a full explanation of the modern methods, it will be necessary to take each part of the feat in detail.

The coins. For parlor or club work real half dollars should be used, for a great part of the glamour of the feat is the fact that the magician materializes real money from the air. If imitation coins are used at close quarters, the spectators soon discover that they are not real half dollars and their interest quickly evaporates. For stage work, however, the palming coins sold by the magic stores possess several advantages. They are thinner and lighter than half dollars and, therefore, a greater number can be used in a load; the edges are deeply milled, making them easier to handle. Even in this case a special load of real half dollars should be used if the magician goes amongst the audience in the course of the trick. The spectators being allowed to handle some of these will conclude that all the coins are the same.

The receptacle. The passing of the silk hat (deeply regretted by magicians) has compelled the use of other articles to receive the coins. In spite of this, Nelson Downs clung to the use of the "topper" to the end of his career and for good reason. The hat he used was his own and was always handed to him by one of the musicians. It was so constructed that in passing it from hand to hand he could secrete his load of coins under the curve of the brim and was thus enabled to place the hat, with the load, crown downwards on his table, while he turned his sleeves back and showed his hands empty. It would be ridiculous to imagine that this could be done with any borrowed hat, but this fact was carefully omitted in his book explaining his methods.

In the place of a silk hat many performers use a champagne bucket, a small china or glass bucket, or a child's sand bucket. This last serves the purpose very well, particularly if it is suitably painted and used to hold a bouquet until it is required for the trick. All these articles have the great advantage of making the sound caused by the dropping of a coin audible to everyone. If, on occasion, an ordinary hat has to be used, a small plate or saucer should be placed inside it for the same purpose.

The reserve load. This is the first difficulty to be surmounted. As we have seen, the original method was to secure the load from a pocket, technically known as a pochette, but the use of special pockets has gone out of fashion. The load can be placed in the left trousers pocket and obtained by casually thrusting the hand into the pocket, but a pile of twenty coins makes a rather too obvious bulge. A better plan is to place the coins on the table behind a crumpled silk handkerchief and on top of a small round disk of blackened cardboard to raise them a little and so provide for a clean lift when you seize them. To obtain possession of the pile secretly, first show the bucket, then put it on the table in front of the silk in such a way that it will hide the coins when the handkerchief is removed. Take the silk and use it to wipe your hands; then pull back the sleeves, showing your hands empty. Pick up the bucket with the right hand at the same moment that you replace the silk and steal the coins with the left hand. This operation is rendered easier by tying the coins crosswise with a weak thread that can be broken easily.

A very novel idea is to have the pile underneath a small bell, one with a clapper. In this case the bucket is put on the table just in front of the bell, the sleeves are pulled back and the hands shown, then the bell is taken and rung with some appropriate remark to arouse the spectators to special attention. The bell is then replaced with the left hand, which secrets the coins while the right hand takes the bucket.

Again, the load may be on a small wire support or shelf at the back of the top rail of a chair, the bucket being placed on the chair seat. Then in moving the chair back, or to one side, the left hand gets possession of the coins.

Having successfully—that is, secretly—obtained the reserve coins in the left hand, the next step is to get them into the bucket in the proper position and without arousing any suspicion on the part of the spectators. To do this, turn your right side to the spectators; show the inside of the bucket with the right hand, holding it by the rim, the left hand being naturally at the side of the body. Turn the mouth of the bucket toward your body and bring it over to the left about waist high; at the same time raise the left hand, back outwards, to meet it and seize it with that hand, the fingers and the load inside and the thumb on the outside of the rim. At once tap the bottom of the bucket with the

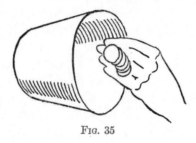

FIG. 35

knuckles of the right hand to prove that it is not prepared in any way and to cover any accidental sound caused by the contact of the coins with the metal, though this can be avoided by careful handling. As you tap the bucket, press the coins against the inside so that they lie in echelon under the left fingers (Fig. 35). Thus the top coin can be pushed forward by the middle finger until it is held at the extreme edge by the tip of the finger, the other coins being held in position by the first and third fingers. At the moment when the right hand apparently places a coin in the bucket, this particular coin can be allowed to fall by merely lifting the second finger. Immediately afterward the next coin is pushed forwards and held in the same way in readiness for the supposed deposit of another coin.

The first coin. As we have seen, Robert-Houdin held one coin palmed in the right hand on entering. Other performers have begun with two coins palmed in the right hand, producing one and openly dropping it into the receptacle, then catching the second and placing the hand inside as if to deposit it but really palming it and dropping a coin from the reserve in the left hand. The objection to both these methods is that the hands cannot be shown perfectly empty before the trick is begun. To overcome this difficulty some performers begin with the right hand empty and merely pretend to catch a coin and place it in the holder, the left hand dropping a coin simultaneously. Again the hand is shown empty and the move is repeated. Then, pretending to overhear an objection that the coins are not real, the operator takes the two coins out and shows them. He then drops one openly and makes a pretense of dropping the second, really palming it and dropping one from the left hand.

Nelson Downs began his act, in the same way, with the imaginary catching of two coins, then taking them out to show them. He dropped the first openly; but in placing his hand into the hat to deposit the second, he swiftly seized and palmed two coins from the reserve in the left hand. One of these he produced from the air and then dropped it into the hat; the other served for the repeated catches. This method is very difficult, great skill being required to take the two coins from the left hand and palm them rapidly.

The best solution is that of M. Gaultier. As before, two coins are supposed to be caught and dropped, the left hand letting a coin fall each time; immediately afterward this hand pushes forwards two coins and holds them in readiness with the tip of the middle finger. In order to show that the coins are real, the right hand is thrust into the hat, the two coins in it are palmed instantly, and the two under the tip of the middle fingers are seized and brought out at the tips of the thumb and fingers of the right hand. These are shown, and also the interior of the receptacle; then one is dropped in from a height of about six inches, and the second also but with the hand a little nearer to the mouth of the receiver. One of the palmed coins is then produced from the air, and this also is dropped openly from the hand held immediately above the receptacle. The second palmed coin, having been produced, is shown and apparently deposited; but this time the right hand goes inside, just out of sight, and palms the coin while the left hand drops one from the reserve.

As they have seen three coins actually dropped into the receptacle, the repetition of the same gesture and the sound of the falling coin will convince the spectators that the rest of the coins really are deposited in the same way.

Various maneuvers. The coins are caught—sometimes in the air; sometimes behind the arm, the elbow, the knee, the shoulder; sometimes from the leg of the artist's trousers, the flame of a candle; etc., etc.—but from whatever point they are produced, the operator must first pretend to see a coin at that very spot and then catch it. It has a good effect to pretend that you are about to catch a coin, then stop and say, "Not worth while. It's only a penny."

Standing with your right side to the front, you may vanish a coin by pretending to throw it in the air and palming it; follow its imaginary flight with your eyes, step a pace or two to the left, hold out the bucket, and let a coin drop from the left hand at the precise moment when your gaze rests on the bucket. A little later you may repeat the maneuver; but this time pretend to have missed the catch and turn away with the remark, "I missed it that time." A moment later let a coin drop from the left hand. With a surprised start you say, "No, there it is after all."

Pretend to place the coin in your mouth, blow it in the direction of the hat, and let a coin fall in the usual way. Again, make a pretense of rubbing a hole in the side of the bucket with the edge of the coin and then throw it through the hole from a distance. Or hold a coin against the side of the receptacle between the tips of the right thumb and fingers and apparently push it right through, really sliding the fingers over it. Or you may appear to make it pass through the bottom by showing the coin at the finger hold, the palm of the hand to the front and the fingers vertical, and passing it to the rear finger hold; in each case the left hand drops a coin simultaneously.

In the older version of the trick the coins were always produced with the back of the hand toward the spectators; by using the new sleights, they can be caught just as easily with the palm of the hand to the front. For example, in turning to the right, pass the coin to the rear finger palm or the rear pinch, reach into the air with the palm of the hand to the front, and produce the coin at the fingertips. By bringing the bucket over to the right side of the body, the coin can be deposited in it, apparently, with the palm of the hand to the front, by back palming it under cover of the bucket and bringing the hand out the same way; then, with the palm still toward the spectators, the coin is again produced at the fingertips. This method should be used several times in the course of the trick, for it goes far to convince the most skeptical that the coins really are caught in the air.

The left hand reserve. When the reserve in the left hand has been exhausted and you do not wish to replenish it immediately, the necessary jingle when a coin is supposed to be dropped can be produced by striking the rim of the bucket rather sharply with the wrist when the pretended deposit is made.

To actually replenish the reserve, you can secure a second load by the same means as the first; or you may take the bucket in the right hand, dip the left hand in and seize a handful of coins and let them drop back into it from above. Repeat this several times and, the last time, retain a certain number of coins in the bend of the second and third fingers, keeping the back of the hand to the front and let the rest of the coins fall as before. Retake the bucket with the left hand and press them into the required position.

It is advisable to load the right hand in this way at least once during the trick, and then produce the coins thus stolen one after the other rapidly and throw them into the receptacle visibly.

Amongst the audience. Nothing arouses an audience to greater enthusiasm than to see a skilled operator producing real coins from the sleeves, collars, beards, hair, pockets, and even the noses of the spectators. This part of the procedure is not only the easiest but also the most effective. The procedure varies according to the needs of the moment; but in general you begin by extracting single coins from different parts of the spectator's clothing, hair, and so on, then dip the right hand into the bucket, take out a handful of coins and pour them back in a stream. Repeat the action, and the third time retain a number of the coins in the finger palm; produce these rapidly, one by one, really throwing them into the bucket until only two coins remain in the right hand. Thrust this hand into the right coat pocket of one of the spectators, let one coin fall into the pocket, and bring out the other at the tips of the fingers. Thank him and proceed to other catches.

Then return to this person and tell him you will show him how easy it is to catch coins from the air; say that he has only to reach with his hand, close it quickly, and he will get a coin. Make him do this, then hold the bucket just under his fist and tell him to drop the coin into it. He opens his hand and, to the amusement and astonishment of everyone, a coin is heard to drop. Have him repeat the same procedure; the third time tell him he can have the coin and to put it in his pocket. Entering into the joke, he thrusts his hand with the supposed coin in his pocket. Pretending to notice that some of the spectators are skeptical, tell him to take the coin out and show it to everyone. He puts his hand into his pocket and finds there the coin you loaded into it. This interlude never fails to bring down the house. As you are now operating with real half dollars, you take the coin from the spectator, to show it, and then drop it into the bucket.

In the meantime you have had ample opportunity to load both hands with all the coins you require to continue the productions amongst the spectators, and the more boldly and vivaciously you work the better the trick goes. In the same way you can load a person's pocket with several coins by seizing his handkerchief and pretending to shake a coin out of it. In replacing the handkerchief in his pocket, drop another coin in. A little later you pretend to throw a coin to this same spectator and let him take the coin from his pocket himself.

Finish this part of the routine by producing a stream of coins from a spectator's nose. Choose a person who is well in sight of the rest of the spectators and be sure to do it in an inoffensive way, with a smile and an "Excuse me, sir, you didn't know you had all this money."

The finale. Some performers finish by making all the coins vanish, a difficult operation if done by sleight of hand but easy enough if a table with a special coin trap is used. A more effective finish and one that requires no special apparatus or difficult sleights is this: On your table, behind some small object or on a little wire support, you have a load of twenty-five coins; a similar load is in your left vest pocket. When you have concluded the work amongst the spectators, in returning to the platform, hold the bucket in the left hand and jingle the coins noisily. Profit by your back being turned for the moment to take the load of coins from the vest pocket with the right hand and then transfer the bucket to that hand.

Take your stand behind your table and place the bucket on it. Raise your right hand, closed; push out one coin with the thumb and throw it into the bucket; at the same moment steal the table load of coins in the left hand, raise that hand, thumb off a coin, and bring the hand down—throwing the coin into the bucket as the right hand is raised to produce another coin. Continue in the same way, each hand producing a coin and dropping it, alternately, and gradually increasing the pace until you produce a regular rain of coins. Finally pour the coins from the bucket into a glass dish, regulating the flow until the supply appears to be almost inexhaustible, thus bringing the trick to a compelling climax.

There is no better feat of magic for acquiring ease of manner and showmanship than the study *and practice* of the Miser's Dream. As an instance of the possibilities of showmanship, it is recorded that M. Trewey, the famous French magician, was accustomed to perform the trick perfectly without the use of a single coin. So compelling were his gestures and facial expressions that the spectators actually believed they saw him catch real coins; the illusion, of course, was completed by the dropping of coins into a hat by an assistant behind the wing who worked in perfect unison with the magician. The final vanish of the coins was, therefore, a very simple matter. I myself have seen the trick executed faultlessly with the use of three coins only.

III

WIZARDRY WITH WATCHES

"A poor life this if, full of care,
We have no time to stand and stare."
William Henry Davis—Leisure.

WATCHES have probably been used by magicians for their nefarious purposes ever since they were invented; but the old-time magicians satisfied themselves with one plot, that of the apparent destruction of a watch and its subsequent restoration. On this theme they played innumerable variations and, thanks to the incurable perversity of mankind, the theme is still popular. Of recent years a new idea has been introduced—that of building routines with watches, consisting of manipulations only, vanishes, reproductions, and multiplications. Speaking broadly, there are at the present time two distinct classes of tricks with watches, tricks properly so called and manipulative routines. Each of these classes will be treated separately.

I. PROCESSES FOR TRICKS WITH WATCHES

The various passes accomplished by pure sleight of hand will be dealt with in the second section; there are, however, certain processes which require the use of accessories and, as these are useful in set tricks, they will be explained here.

1. THE VANISH OF A WATCH WITH AN UNPREPARED HANDKERCHIEF

Lay a silk handkerchief over the palm of the left hand and place the watch on its center. Lift the front half of the silk and fold it over the watch toward your body, letting it fall. Fold the right-hand side over the left and then the left-hand side over to the right. Do not make these folds too close to the watch; leave at least an inch of space on each side, so that the watch can slide away easily. The middle of the silk now forms a kind of tube, with the opening at the rear. Seize the watch and apparently turn it over toward yourself; in reality, let it slide in the tube, turning the silk only. Repeat this process until the watch slides out onto the palm of your left hand and the folded handkerchief rests on top of it.

So far as the audience is concerned, the watch has been wrapped up fairly. You can palm it and dispose of it as required for the trick, while the parcel supposed to contain it remains in full view—on top of a glass, for instance. Later, a corner of the silk is taken and it is shaken out empty; it is at that moment that the watch apparently vanishes.

2. SWITCHING A WATCH WITH A HANDKERCHIEF

In this case you have a watch palmed in the left hand, face up. Spread a handkerchief so that its middle covers the watch. Then show the watch you wish to change and place it on the handkerchief over the palmed watch. Under cover of a half turn to the right transfer the handkerchief and the watches from one hand to the other, making the switch in the process in this manner: Place the right hand on the borrowed watch, palm downwards, in the act of turning to the right so that the handkerchief is transferred to the right hand, the duplicate watch is brought above the handkerchief, and the borrowed watch is concealed below it in position to be palmed and carried away by the right hand.

3. PAPER FOLD TO VANISH A WATCH

A piece of paper about ten inches square is required. Fold this twice, reducing it to a five-inch square. Place the borrowed watch on the center of the paper (Fig. 1A); fold one-third of the paper from the front back over the watch (Fig. 1B); fold the right-hand side to the front (Fig. 1C); then the left-hand side in the same way (Fig. 1D); finally turn the packet round sideways and fold the last end down to the front (Fig. 1E). The side folds must not be made too close to the watch. The result is that the watch, to all appearances fairly inclosed in the paper, is really in an open fold and will slip out into the hand at will. Press the paper (which should be rather stiff) firmly round the watch, so that its shape will show after it has been allowed to slip out into your palm. A startling vanish results if flash paper is used for this trick fold.

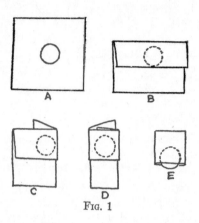

FIG. 1

4. BAG TO VANISH A WATCH

Various kinds of bags have been devised for the vanish or the switching of a watch. One is made by sewing the hems of two handkerchiefs together with the exception of about three inches at one corner, where a pocket is made between the two. A shoe button is sewn on this corner to enable the fingers to find it easily. To use the handkerchief, palm the duplicate watch in the left hand and throw the handkerchief over it, letting the corners hang down below the hand. Seize these corners with the right hand and bring them upwards, at the same time withdrawing the left hand and leaving the duplicate watch inside the bag thus made. Invite the owner of the watch you are borrowing to drop it in, while you open the mouth of the pocket to receive it. Twist the fabric round the duplicate watch, and in so doing squeeze the borrowed watch out of the pocket into your right hand and palm it.

The disposal of the duplicate then depends upon the requirements of the trick in hand. If the watch is to be smashed (apparently) then, in handing the handkerchief to a volunteer assistant you let all the corners go, except the one with the button sewn to it, just as he is about to take the bag. The duplicate watch drops, and as this is merely an old case filled with loose parts you have a very satisfactory accidental smash.

Another useful accessory for getting possession of a borrowed watch, while apparently smashing it effectively, is a prepared stocking. It has a small pocket at the opening. To use it, place the duplicate watch at the top—inside the stocking but not in the pocket. Roll it into a compact parcel. Produce this from a spectator's pocket, keeping the duplicate watch at the top. Borrow a watch and openly drop it into the pocket, at the same moment releasing the dummy watch; the passage of this can be seen as it slides down to the toe, and this will naturally be taken for the borrowed article. It is then a simple matter to squeeze the borrowed watch into the palm of the hand. A favorite method of procedure, then, is to remark that the watch is a little slow and swing the stocking round rapidly, sling fashion, to make it go faster. Unfortunately you have unwittingly come near your table, and the watch strikes it with the usual untoward result.

One more method of using a handkerchief should be mentioned. In one corner sew a little pocket and secure in it a filbert nut. Fold the borrowed watch in the handkerchief as explained in the first method, palm the watch, and place the folded handkerchief on the floor. A moment or two later you step on it by accident, bringing your heel on it with a "scrunch" which simulates very satisfactorily the crushing of the watch. However, when you shake out the handkerchief the watch has vanished.

II. TRICKS WITH WATCHES

1. THE FLYING WATCH

Effect. The magician borrows a watch; wraps it in a piece of colored tissue paper, and puts the packet in the outside breast pocket of his coat, leaving the ends of the paper visible. He borrows a hat and gives it to a spectator to hold above his head amongst the audience. Returning to his place, he takes the package from his pocket and orders the watch to fly to the hat. He tears the tissue to pieces, the watch has vanished, and the spectator finds it in the hat.

Method. One watch only is used, a borrowed one. The trick

lies in the performer's coat; the pocket into which the watch packet is placed is slit at the bottom and a long cloth tube is sewn to it. The tube is then stitched to the lining of the coat and carried back and down to the tail on the same side, ending inside a pocket there. When the magician places the tissue packet in his coat he squeezes it, breaking the paper just below the watch so that it slides down into the pocket, then into the tube, finally into the tail pocket, while the ends of the tissue paper remain in full view above the opening of the outer breast pocket.

In going for the hat, the magician has ample opportunity for getting the watch into his hand. He takes the hat in the same hand, his fingers covering the watch as he shows the inside, and makes some remark about the maker of the hat. He hands it to another spectator to hold high above his head with both hands —crown downwards, of course. The rest follows.

This is an excellent opening trick and never fails to score. The same tube arrangement can be adapted to ordinary suits by using an upper vest pocket to receive the packet and carrying the tube down to the trousers pocket.

2. The Watch in the Loaf of Bread

Effect. This denouement, the production of a borrowed watch in a loaf of bread, is still one of the best and most popular.

Preparation. To prepare for the trick, take an oblong loaf of bread, remove the waxed paper carefully, and cut a slit in the bottom large enough for a watch to be pushed into it. Fold the waxed paper in such a way that when you again inclose the loaf the edges of the paper will come together at the slit underneath, without overlapping. Cut several sheets of wrapping paper just large enough to inclose the loaf, without overlapping. Wrap the loaf in the first sheet and tie it with string or tape as shown in Fig. 2, so that the string does not cross the slit. Do the same with three or four other sheets, tying each one in the same manner. Free access to the slit in the bread is thus left, and at the finish of the trick each sheet can be shown intact as it is taken off. Place the parcel in a brown paper bag and make a slit in this exactly opposite the opening in the papers and the slit in the loaf. Set the parcel on the seat of a chair on the right-hand side of the stage, laying it on its side with the slit to the back.

You will also require a tray and a breadknife; place these in readiness on your table.

Method. For the first part of the trick you can choose any of the methods already explained. We will suppose that the watch has been switched, the duplicate smashed up, and the pieces vanished. You have the watch palmed in the right hand and your right side is to the front. Your right arm is at your side as you point with the left hand to the parcel on the seat of the chair. Go over to it and pick it up, the left hand in front and the right hand at the rear. Thrust the watch straight into the slit and

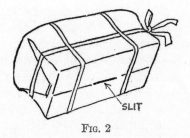

FIG. 2

push it well in with the tips of the right fingers, the right thumb resting on the top of the parcel.

Remove the wrapped loaf from the bag and crumple the bag, being careful not to allow the slit to be seen. Place the loaf on the tray on your table and pick up the bread knife. Cut the string on the outside wrapper and remove the paper, showing it intact. Do the same with the other sheets. When you come to the waxed wrapper, pick up the loaf with both hands, one hand covering the slit, and show all parts apparently intact. Remove this wrapper and cut off a slice of bread from each end of the loaf, about an inch in thickness; then stand the loaf on end on the tray, with the slit to the rear still. Cut the loaf about half-way down, in line with the slit, until the knife meets the watch; then complete the cut through the crust on each side, thus obliterating the slit. Break the loaf in half and show the watch embedded in the bread. Carry this down to the owner of the watch and allow him to remove it himself.

Presented in this way, the trick will be remarkably effective.

3. The Watch in the Dinner Roll

Effect. The effect of this trick is similar to that of the preceding one; but it is much simpler, both in the working and the preparation.

Preparation. You will require a ten-inch square of flash paper and three dinner rolls, two unprepared and one with a hole in one end large enough to take a small watch.

Method. To present the trick you begin by borrowing a watch, preferably a lady's. Receive it on the middle of the flash paper —which you have folded twice, making a square of five inches. Fold the paper round the watch, using the trick fold already explained; hold the resulting package at the tips of the left thumb and fingers, with the opening downwards. Call attention to the rolls—which you have on a plate, the prepared one being in the middle of the other two. Have one chosen; if the middle one is selected, toss the other two out to the spectators. If an outside roll is chosen, toss it out and have a choice made between the other two, the one on the right or the one on the left. By resorting to the equivoque "My right" or "Your left," you force the answer to apply to the prepared roll.

Pick up the prepared roll, and place it in the left hand for a moment as you thrust your right hand into your pocket for matches. Place the roll in such a position that the hole in the end is directly under the open fold of the watch packet, and let the watch slip into the hole. Show the matches in your right hand; then take the roll again in that hand and put it on the plate, the opening to the rear. Move away from the table; show the packet at the tips of the left fingers, the impression showing the shape of the watch being visible to all; call attention to the impression. Take out a match; strike it and light the flash paper, at once tossing it toward the roll on the plate. The paper vanishes in a flash and the watch, so far as the audience is concerned, vanishes at the same moment.

It only remains to pick up the roll, one hand at each end, between the thumb and fingers, and squeeze the "holed" end flat.

Show all parts of the roll as held, then break it in half and reveal the watch embedded in it. Carry it down to the owner to be removed and identified.

4. The Watch and Nest of Boxes

This trick, as generally presented, requires an assistant, but the following method can be worked singlehanded under almost any conditions. It will be found very effective.

Preparation. Three cardboard boxes, with removable lids and graded in size to fit one into the other, are required. The smallest box must be large enough to take a fair-sized bouquet of flowers. To prepare for the trick, attach a length of ribbon to the bouquet and put this in the smallest box. Let the ribbon fall over the side to the rear and place the lid on the box. Tie this round with broad tape, making a bowknot on top so that you can untie it quickly.

Place this box inside the next in size, again letting the ribbon fall to the back. Follow exactly the same procedure with the third box; the end of the ribbon will then hang at the rear of the largest box. Cut this off about an inch below the edge of the lid and attach a small hook of soft wire to it. Thus prepared, place the nest of boxes on a table to one side of the stage or platform.

Method. To begin the experiment, borrow a watch and wrap it in a silk handkerchief, using the trick fold, already described, which leaves the watch in the palm of your left hand. Place the folded handkerchief on top of an inverted glass on your table and at the same time leave the watch behind some small object there. Show both hands empty as you announce the voyage you are about to cause the watch to make. Give the command with a tap of the wand, pick up the handkerchief and shake it out; the watch has departed.

Bring the nest of boxes forwards to this same table, again letting it be seen that your hands are empty. Finger palm the watch, slip it onto the hook at the back of the box, and proceed to untie the ribbon round the outside box. Remove the lid and lift out the second box. Put the first box on the floor and re-place its lid. The watch has been lifted away with the second box and now hangs at its rear. Open this one in the same way and lift out the innermost box. Set the second box on top of the first and replace its lid.

Finally untie and open the third box. Bring out the bouquet and show the watch dangling from it at the end of the ribbon. Put the lid on this box and place it on top of the others. This procedure enhances the marvel of the three boxes having been nested, and all parts of the boxes should be shown as you put them down. It only remains to take the bouquet down to the owner of the watch and have it identified. If natural flowers are used, and you have borrowed the watch from a lady, you should present the bouquet to her after detaching the watch and the ribbon.

5. THE AUCTION

Method. An amusing *mise en scène* for the smashing of a borrowed watch is this: Having switched the watch and wrapped the dummy in a handkerchief, place the package on your table and announce that you have been authorized to sell it to the highest bidder. Take a hammer and start the bidding yourself at ten cents; as the bids come in keep tapping the watch with the hammer, now and then striking a sharp blow on the table as you call, "Going. Going." If you are a good actor, the spectators will enter into the fun and bid fast and furiously as you hit the watch harder and harder in the excitement. Finally call, "Gone"; and bring the hammer down hard on the watch, smashing it to pieces. Profuse apologies follow, then the vanish of the fragments, and the final reproduction of the watch restored to its original beauty.

III. SLEIGHTS FOR MANIPULATIONS WITH WATCHES

There are certain sleights which are peculiar to watches, because of the stems and rings. These must be learned before any routine of manipulations can be presented. They will offer no difficulty to anyone conversant with coin and ball sleights.

1. THE VANISH FROM THE FINGERTIPS

Stand with your right side to the spectators and show the watch in your right hand, a little to the left of the body, holding it by the ring between the tips of the thumb and forefinger so that the body of the watch extends above the thumb and finger (Fig. 3).

Bring the left hand up, palm to the front, behind the watch and enfold it with the fingers. The moment they form a screen in front of the watch, let it drop into the right hand. Close the left hand completely and carry it away upwards in a diagonal direction, agitating the fingers on the palm as if crumbling the watch. Let the right hand drop to the side almost simultaneously with the withdrawal of the left hand—which is turned on its wrist, presenting its back to the front as it apparently grasps the watch and then turns over, palm outwards, as you raise it toward the left. Finally open the left fingers one by one, beginning with the little finger, and show the hand empty.

FIG. 3

2. THE FINGER PALM VANISH

For this sleight you face the spectators, holding the watch by the keeper in the left hand between the thumb and the first two

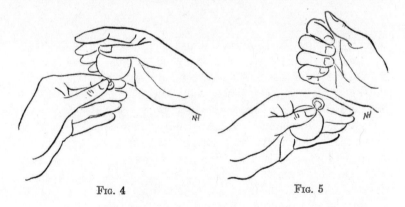

FIG. 4

FIG. 5

fingers, the body of the watch extending above the forefinger, broadside to the front, all the fingers being pressed firmly together and vertical (Fig. 4). Bring the right hand up and enfold the watch, with the fingers curling round it and apparently carrying it away, the left hand remaining stationary.

What you really do is to swing the watch to the left and downwards behind the left fingers and retain it there until you wish to reproduce it (Fig. 5), or you may transfer the watch to the thumb grip by closing the fingers as the left hand drops to the side.

3. The Thumb Grip

The most useful method of holding a watch hidden in the hand is that of gripping the keeper in the thumb crotch by

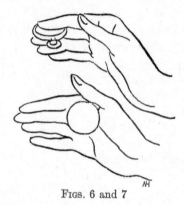

FIGS. 6 and 7

pressing the first joint of the thumb against the side of the hand. In order to place the watch in this position, hold it flat between the top joints of the first and second fingers of the right hand, the keeper being toward the body and the third and fourth fingers doubled back into the hand (Fig. 6).

Bring the left hand over the right two fingers, with its back to the front and the fingers pointing downwards. As soon as they screen the watch, bend the first two fingers of the right hand back, carry the watch to the right thumb crotch, and grip the ring with the thumb (Fig. 7), immediately afterward stretching the right fingers out again and encircling them with the left fingers. Move the left fist away and point to it with the right forefinger. Agitate the left fingers as if crumbling the watch to nothing and finish the vanish as usual.

4. The Illusive Pass

In this very deceptive pass you hold the watch between the right first and second fingers by the ring, which is at a right angle to the body of the watch; the watch is in full view, extend-

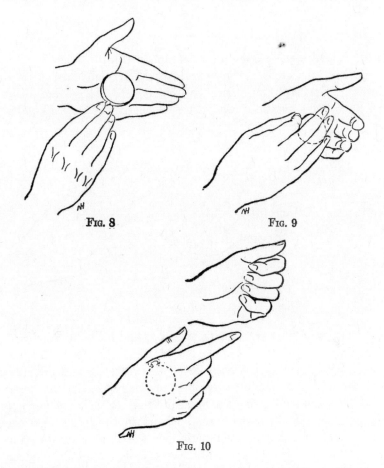

Fig. 8   Fig. 9

Fig. 10

ing outwards from the fingers. Place the watch flat on the palm of the left hand, which is held palm upwards to the left of the body, your right side being to the front (Fig. 8). Close the left fingers; as soon as they screen the watch, extend the right second, third, and fourth fingers in front of it (Fig. 9); taking advantage of this cover, draw the watch back with the first finger and thumb into the regular palm or the thumb grip. Move the left hand away, upwards in a diagonal direction, and point to it with the right forefinger (Fig. 10). Finally make the apparent vanish from the left hand, agitating the fingers and opening them as usual.

5. A BACK HAND PASS

Several of the passes already explained with coins are applicable to watches. The tourniquet is specially useful with watches, as with any other small objects. The pass I am about to describe is an application of the tourniquet to the back palm.

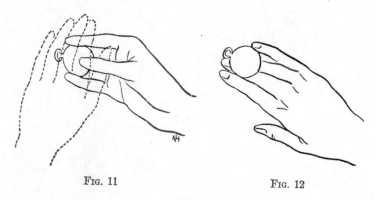

FIG. 11   FIG. 12

Stand with your left side to the front and hold the watch flat on the first joints of the fingers of the right hand, the ring pointing outwards and the sides of the watch against the sides of the first and fourth fingers, the thumb resting on the upper side of the watch. Bring the left hand over to the right hand to grasp the watch, the back of the hand to the front. Pass the left thumb under the right thumb and apparently close the hand on the watch (Fig. 11). In reality, as soon as the watch is hidden by the left fingers make it pivot to the back of the right fingers in exactly the same way as with a coin (Fig. 12). Move the left hand away, closed and the fingers rubbing against the palm as usual, and drop the right hand to the side. Let it pass momentarily out of sight behind the hip, at once reversing the watch to the front of the fingers and transferring it to the regular palm. Then bring the hand up, as you turn to the left and point to the left fist with the extended forefinger.

6. Swallowing a Watch

Hold the watch by the ring only, so that the watch protrudes above the fingers. Lift the watch to the mouth, the back of the hand to the front, and insert the watch in the mouth. Continue the upward motion of the right hand while you retain the grip on the ring, thus withdrawing the watch; then let it fall into the right palm. Push out one cheek with the tongue to simulate the presence of the watch, and make a pretense of swallowing it. In the meantime you have dropped the right hand to the level of the waist, and with the tips of the fingers of both hands you press on the stomach at the bottom of the vest. Slip the watch under the vest with the right-hand fingers and press the thumb against it through the cloth, then raise the bottom of the vest and slowly remove the watch with the left hand.

If you execute this manipulation before you have had any occasion to turn away from the audience, you can have a duplicate watch hooked between your shoulders and, after the swallowing operation, thump your chest with your fist, turn round and display the duplicate watch on your back, at the same time pocketing the palmed watch.

7. The Thumb Crotch Steal

Face the audience and close the left hand into a fist, thumb upwards. Push the watch into the fist just far enough to enable you to hold it as in Fig. 13. With the right hand force it down into the fist by tapping it. At the moment that the ring enters the fist and is brought to a vertical position,

FIG. 13

grip it with the right thumb in the thumb crotch and lift it clear. Tap the fist once or twice more with the right hand; then raise the left hand, agitating the fingers, and finish in the usual way.

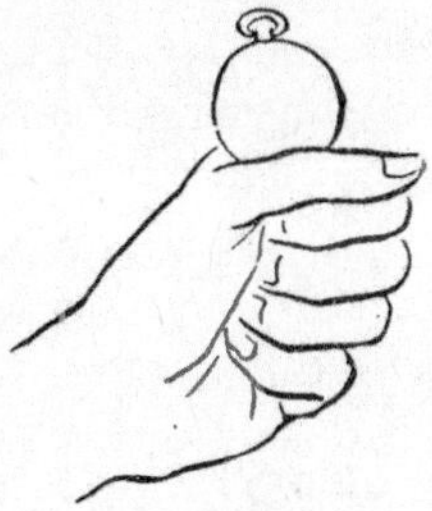

8. The Change Over Pass

Having a watch palmed in one hand, it is necessary sometimes that you show both hands apparently empty. To do this stand with your right side to the front, the watch being held in the right thumb crotch. Show the left hand empty, holding it vertically, palm outwards, and stroke it with the right hand from the fingertips to the wrist; turn the left hand, back outwards, and begin to stroke the back, at the same time turning slowly to the right. As the right hand passes over the back of the left, both hands being now backs outwards, grip the watch with the left thumb, transferring it to the left thumb crotch as the turn to the right is completed. Turn the right hand palm outwards and stroke it from the fingertips to the wrist with the left hand. Both hands have thus been shown empty back and front.

IV. MANIPULATIONS WITH WATCHES

1. CATCHING WATCHES FROM THE AIR

The watches used for manipulative purposes are merely imitation watches, which, being lighter than the real ones, are very much easier to handle. A quite satisfactory article can be purchased at the dime stores or at any novelty shop.

Effect. Five or more watches are caught from the air, one by one, and placed in a hat. Finally the hat is shown empty, the watches having vanished.

1st Method. A catgut loop is attached to the keeper of a watch, and your right thumb is inserted in the loop. The watch can then be allowed to hang out of sight at either the front or the back of the hand.

To prepare for the trick you place the looped watch at the top of your vest with the loop protruding. Begin by borrowing a hat and place it, crown downwards, on your table. To get possession of the watch secretly, stretch out your right arm to the right and pull up the sleeve with the left hand. Turn to the left, stretch out the left arm, and at the same time bring the right hand over across the chest; engage the thumb in the loop and carry the watch away, immediately pulling up the left sleeve.

Produce the watch at the fingertips as if caught from the air; approach the table so that the hat is on your left, and dip your hand into it—apparently depositing the watch in it. Bring the hand up, showing the palm empty by resting the thumb on the brim of the hat (Fig. 14). Turn the hand, bringing its back to

the front, and thus lift the watch into the palm again (Fig. 15).
Proceed in the same manner for as many catches as you wish
to make, each time placing the watch in the hat and secretly withdrawing it. Finally vanish the watch by one of the passes already
explained and drop it into a pocket. Take up the hat and make
a motion of throwing its contents out to the audience. They ex-
pect to receive a shower of watches but the hat is empty.

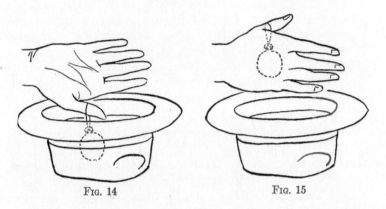

Fig. 14   Fig. 15

If preferred, you can load a number of watches into the hat
when you place it on the table and produce these as being the
ones caught from the air.

2d Method. In this method the watch to be caught from the
air is prepared by having its back covered with a piece of black
cloth, glued onto it, and a small sharp hook soldered to the stem.
Thus the watch can be hooked to the clothing, back outwards
and will be unnoticeable.

With one of these prepared watches hooked to the inside of
your left sleeve, begin by pulling up the right sleeve with the left
hand, then the left sleeve with the right hand, at the same time
stealing the watch in that hand which produces the watch as if
caught from the air. To vanish it you make a pretense of tossing
it to a spectator. As the hand reaches the lowest point preparatory to the throw, hook the watch to the trousers, back of the
hip; bring the hand forward as if it still held the watch; and
make the throw, following its supposed flight with your eyes. The
watch will seem to vanish in mid-air.

Such watches are generally used in connection with a stand, on which they are apparently placed as they are caught. The stand is prepared in this manner: It is covered with black velvet and has a number of recesses cut in it, which are also covered with the same material. Each of these is large enough to take a watch easily. In each of them there is a watch, also backed with black velvet so that when they have the backs to the front they are invisible. The working is obvious. When you catch a watch and go to place it on the stand, you simply palm it and, under cover of the hand, turn over the watch in one of the recesses. The same watch, therefore, is caught over and over again and is placed on the stand only after the last catch.

To vanish the watches you simply turn them in the recesses, bringing the velvet-covered backs to the front as you pretend to take them off the stand. It is the easiest thing in the world to vanish them, either by pretending to pulverize them in the hand or by tossing them in the air. The last watch should be really removed and several passes made with it. Finally pretend to put it in the left hand, really palming it in the right. Reach across to the left shoulder to pull up the sleeve and as the hand passes over the outside breast pocket drop the watch into it in passing. Pull the sleeve back a little, vanish the watch from the left hand, and show both hands empty. It is advisable to have a handkerchief in this pocket to keep its mouth slightly open.

There are a number of different kinds of stands for the production and vanishing of watches, and these should be purchased from the regular magical dealers. Magical apparatus must work with precision, and this is a virtue rarely obtained with home-made articles.

3d Method. This is an interlude with a black-backed watch. Attach a prepared watch to your watch chain and place it in your vest pocket. In the course of your manipulations take it out of the pocket with your right hand and let it hang at the full length of the chain in front of your right thigh. Pretend to take it in your left hand as you pretend to detach it with the right hand but, in reality, turn the watch back outwards and carry the left hand away as if it held the watch. With the right hand grasp the end of the chain and the watch, and put both back into the vest pocket. A moment later vanish the watch from the left hand and bring it out of the pocket with the right hand, showing it is still attached to the chain. You must, of course, turn the watch over in the pocket to bring it face outwards.

V. WRIST WATCHES

There are only a few tricks in which wrist watches play the leading role, and there is a field here for the ingenuity of magicians. The following trick will serve to show the possibilities.

1. THE REAPPEARING WRIST WATCH

Effect. A wrist watch, taken off the wrist and repeatedly vanished, always returns to the performer's wrist.

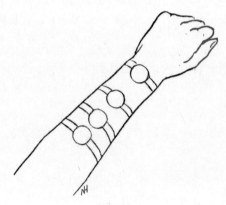

FIG. 16

Method. Four toy wrist watches, such as those procurable at the dime stores, are required. Remove the leather straps and replace them with elastic braid and snap fasteners. Make up three small paper cones of brown paper with secret pockets (see page 74). Place one in your breast pocket; crumple the other two into loose balls and put them in the front corner of your outside coat pocket on the right-hand side. Fasten all four watches on your left arm, one above the other (Fig. 16).

Begin by taking off the first watch; in doing so, engage the fingers in the band of the next one and pull it down as you adjust the sleeve, being careful that it remains out of sight. Take the paper cone from your pocket, open it, and drop the watch into it. After announcing what is to take place—the watch to vanish and return to your arm—open the paper and show it empty. Crush it up tightly; carry it in the right hand to your right coat pocket as you extend the left arm to full length, and look intently at it. At the moment the second watch thus comes into view, drop the crumpled cone into the pocket and pick up one of the empty papers. Bring the right hand over and pull the left sleeve back a little further.

Pretending that you think "that gentleman over there" did not quite follow the trick, offer to repeat it. Open up the crumpled paper cone, detach the second watch, and follow the same procedure as before.

Finally do the trick a third time, and reveal the fourth watch. This time simply drop the cone into the coat pocket and leave it there. The spectators have seen the same paper, as they think, used three times, and any suspicions they might have had of the paper being prepared will have been wiped out.

VI. ALARM CLOCKS

The space allotted to this chapter will allow for the explanation of one trick only:

THE VANISHING ALARM CLOCK

Effect. An alarm clock is shown and the alarm is set off to prove that it is a genuine one. The clock is then covered with a handkerchief and hung on a stand. A hat is borrowed and placed on a table, crown downwards. The magician sets off the alarm again and, while it is ringing, he jerks the handkerchief away and the clock has vanished. Finally it is found in the borrowed hat.

Method. Many different methods have been devised for bringing about this startling effect, most of them requiring a special tray and an assistant. By using the following plan the trick can be worked singlehanded.

Three clocks are required, and care must be taken that all three have the same tone. One is placed openly on your table; the second is hung on a headless nail behind a chair, ready for loading into a hat; the third is fixed under your table, with a lever whereby a touch of the hand will set off or stop the alarm. The handkerchief is double and has a length of flexible cardboard stitched in the middle between the two thicknesses. A small metal ring is attached to the middle of the cardboard and a small slit is made in the material so that the ring can protrude. The last accessory required is the stand. This is simply a metal rod, set in a foot, with a hook at the top.

To present the trick, begin by showing the clock and set off the alarm to prove that it is a genuine one. Put it on the table and throw the handkerchief over it; seize the ring of the cardboard shape and lift the handkerchief, at the same moment dropping the clock into a well in the table or onto the *servante*. Place the ring on the hook of the stand, and the card, bending with the weight of the handkerchief, will simulate the presence of the clock. Put your hand under the handkerchief and pretend to set off the alarm; at the same time touch the lever connected with the third alarm clock and set it ringing—then stop it.

Go into the audience and borrow a hat; place this, mouth upwards, on the chair and turn to your table; then decide to place the chair a little further away. Pick up the hat by the brim with the right hand; with the same hand grasp the back of the chair, bringing the hat over the clock that hangs there. Grip the seat of the chair with the left hand, lift the chair, and set it down a little more toward the side. At the same time scoop the clock off the nail, letting it fall into the hat, and replace this on the chair seat, crown downwards.

Return to the table; pretend to set the alarm ringing (really the one under the table, as before); seize one corner of the handkerchief with the right hand and jerk it free, at the same time stopping the alarm by moving the lever with the left hand. Shake out the handkerchief, crumple it, and drop it on the table. Finally produce the alarm clock from the hat and set the alarm ringing as you take it out.

IV

MAGIC WITH RINGS

"The ring, so worn as you behold,
So thin, so pale, is yet of gold."

George Crabbe

TRICKS with rings always have a fine effect, for the reason that they are done with a borrowed article and therefore appear to be of an impromptu nature. The various sleights already learned in connection with coins are nearly all applicable to rings. The regular palm, the tourniquet, the thumb grip, and the finger holds can all be applied to rings. It is not necessary, therefore, for me to repeat the details; but there is one special sleight, applicable to rings only, which must be mentioned. We will suppose that you wish to exchange a borrowed ring for a duplicate of your own. Secretly place the duplicate on the end of your right second finger and bend the finger into the palm. Hold the right index finger extended and receive the borrowed ring on its top joint. In turning toward your table, bend the forefinger inwards, extend the middle finger, and let the duplicate fall from it onto a plate or into a glass. The exchange is made and you have possession of the borrowed ring.

Note here that, whenever possible, you should borrow a wedding ring. Thus you not only avoid accidents, such as a stone dropping out and being lost, but you are always sure that your duplicate can be shown openly and will be taken for the original. Such rings can be obtained at any of the five and ten stores.

I. ACCESSORIES

The following articles are of general utility in tricks with rings.

1. PREPARED HANDKERCHIEF

To make this you have simply to sew a little pocket in one

corner of a handkerchief, inclosing a ring in it (Fig. 1). If the handkerchief has a fairly wide hem, a simpler method is to open the hem, insert the ring, and sew the fabric so that the ring is secured at one corner. The best way to use this prepared handkerchief in order to get possession of a borrowed ring, leaving the original apparently in full view or even held by a spectator, is this: Take the borrowed ring between the tips of the right thumb and forefinger; show the handkerchief stretched out, one corner held by the tips of the left thumb and forefinger and the opposite corner held between the right first and second fingers. Cross the hands to show the other side of the fabric; then thrust the right hand, carrying both the ring and the prepared corner, against the middle of the handkerchief at the back. With the left hand seize the prepared corner from above, through the middle of the fabric, and at the same time slide the borrowed ring into the right thumb grip. Bring the right hand from underneath, its back to the spec-

FIG. 1

tators, and either twist the handkerchief tightly round the duplicate ring or, better, tie a knot so that the middle of the handkerchief forms a little bag with the duplicate ring inside. In this condition it can be left with a spectator to hold without any danger of untimely revelation.

To vanish the ring apparently, untie the knot, allowing the spectator to retain hold of the duplicate ring through the fabric, seize one corner, and flick the handkerchief in the air. Open it out at once and get the prepared corner between the thumb and fingers; again show all parts of the handkerchief, turning it back and front. It should then be pocketed casually, as if it were an ordinary everyday article.

2. SPECIAL HOOK

This is made of a length of fine black wire, bent as shown

in Fig. 2, the ends AA being sharp. By means of these it can be attached to the clothing at any desired spot, the most useful position being just behind the right-hand trousers pocket, a little to the rear, so that when the right hand is dropped naturally to the side the fingers are brought against the hook and a ring either can be put on it or stolen imperceptibly from it.

3. PAPER CONE

This article is useful only for vanishing a ring. Fold a piece of newspaper in half to the shape shown in Fig. 3a. Paste the two thicknesses together along the lines AB, BC, and

FIG. 2

CA; when dry, fold the paper into a cone (Fig. 3b) with its point at C, and pull the inner fold F over to G. When a ring or any other small article is dropped into the cone, it falls into the

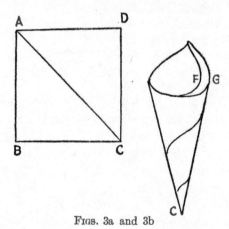

FIGS. 3a and 3b

pocket; and when the paper is opened, it is concealed and thus appears to have vanished. We shall see later that such a cone, made somewhat larger, is very useful in connection with tricks with silk handkerchiefs.

II. TRICKS WITH RINGS

1. The Flying Ring

Under varying forms this trick has long been a favorite with both magicians and audiences. I shall explain the simplest method first; but this must not be despised on that account—quite the reverse, for the effect is very good.

Effect. A borrowed ring is dropped into a glass by a spectator. It vanishes and instantly reappears on the performer's wand, although the ends of this are held by two spectators.

Preparation. Prepare for the trick by attaching a ring to the middle of a handkerchief by a thread about three inches long, and have this in a pocket in such a way that on removing it and holding it up by two opposite corners the ring will be suspended on your side and therefore concealed from the spectators.

1st Method. When you are ready to show the trick, you request the loan of a wedding ring. Then you take out the prepared handkerchief and spread it out, holding the ring corner in the right hand between the tips of the second and third fingers and the opposite corner between the tips of the left thumb and forefinger. Place the corner thus held in the right hand with the corner in the left hand, which then retains hold of both corners. Receive the borrowed ring with the right hand; place it behind the handkerchief; and apparently seize it from the other side at the middle of the fabric with the left hand, which drops the two corners previously held. In reality you slide the borrowed ring to the thumb grip in the right hand, take hold of the suspended ring and push this upward underneath the handkerchief— the left hand taking it from above. Take the ring and handkerchief from the left hand in your right hand; invite a spectator to hold both in his left hand; and give him a glass to hold in his right hand, under the handkerchief and immediately below the ring.

Take the wand in your left hand and, in sliding the other end into the right hand, make it pass through the ring; then move the right hand along the wand to the middle, with the ring hidden under it. Invite a spectator on your right to grip both ends of the wand. Tell the spectator who holds the ring and handkerchief to drop it into the glass at the word "Three"; count "One, two, three"—he drops the ring and everyone hears it fall into the glass.

Once more you count as before. But at the word "Two," seize the middle of the handkerchief just over the glass; at "Three," jerk it rapidly away—straight upwards, so that the suspended ring cannot strike against the side of the glass. "See," you exclaim, "the ring has vanished! I call 'Three,' and here it is threaded on the wand held by this gentleman." Remove the right hand quickly, pressing it against the ring and making it revolve rapidly on the wand. Finally let the spectator holding the wand remove the ring and hand it to the owner for identification. Put the prepared handkerchief in your pocket while all attention is on the sudden reappearance of the ring.

2d Method. In this version the prepared handkerchief is dispensed with. It is necessary, however, to switch the ring, and a good way to do this is to have a duplicate ring palmed in the left hand. After borrowing a wedding ring, show it in the right hand in readiness for the tourniquet (see page 13); then take it apparently with the left hand, really letting it fall into the right and showing the duplicate in the left hand which you drop forthwith into a glass or onto a plate. As in the first method, slide the end of the wand through the ring secretly; move the right hand, and the ring under it, to the middle and have the ends held by a spectator. Take out your handkerchief with the left hand and throw it over the middle of the wand, thus concealing the ring when you remove your right hand.

Pick up the duplicate ring from the glass or plate; show it and pretend to put it in your left hand, really palming it in the right. Keep the left hand clenched, its back to the front, and move it away to the left. With the right hand seize a corner of the handkerchief on the wand on the side nearest to you. Count "One, two, three"; at the word "Three," make a throwing motion with the left hand toward the wand and pull the handkerchief away rapidly and directly toward you, causing the ring to spin rapidly on the wand—a very effective finish. Place the handkerchief in your pocket and take the opportunity of dropping the ring at the same time.

A cane or a ruler can be used instead of the wand, but you

must make sure first that the diameter of the ring is large enough for the article to pass through the ring easily.

3d Method. This method is refined still further, the duplicate ring being also suppressed so that the trick becomes an entirely impromptu one. The working, however, is somewhat more difficult than those of the preceding methods.

Receive the borrowed ring on the palm of the right hand; while showing it thus, shake it into the position shown in Fig. 4, so that a very slight contraction of the hand will hold it securely. Bring the right hand over to the left and, turning it over onto the left palm, pretend to place the ring in the left hand. Close the left fingers immediately and keep the hand clenched.

Take a long pencil from your upper left vest pocket and hold it by the middle with tips of your right fingers so that one end comes against the palm of the hand, the back of the hand being, of course, toward the spectators. Now comes a movement which will require some practice and which must be made by the right hand alone. As you gesticulate while talking and tapping the back of the left hand with the pencil, make the pencil slide through the ring until you get it to the middle, keeping the back of the hand to the spectators all the time.

Fig. 4

With this accomplished, invite a spectator to take hold of both ends of the pencil. Bring the left hand underneath the right, open both hands so that the palms come together with the pencil between them, rub them together, and then suddenly remove both hands. The ring is then seen to be on the pencil, although the ends are still held.

It should be noted in connection with this trick of the ring and the wand that a fine effect can be obtained by using a piece of flash paper and the trick fold described on page 54 in connection with coins. This method dispenses with the duplicate ring; the borrowed ring is obtained directly from the paper, although the impression on it makes it appear that the ring is still wrapped up. A touch with a lighted cigarette will flash off the paper, and the ring appears instantly on the wand held by a spectator.

2. THE RING AND THE EGG

Effect. The effect is that a ring is borrowed, vanished, and made to reappear in an examined egg.

In the original method, which is a very old favorite, a prepared egg cup is used, in the bottom of which there is a slot into which the ring is secretly inserted. The borrowed ring having been vanished, the egg is put into the cup, the top is cracked, and the ring fished out with a wire hook. The modern method is much simpler, more direct and more effective.

Preparation. The only accessory required is a little metal plate with a hook, which is attached to a plate under the rim with a pellet of wax (Fig. 5). The hook is of such a size that any

FIG. 5

wedding ring, no matter how thick, can be slipped onto it. Prepare by placing on your table the following articles: the plate with the hook under the rim at the rear, a glass of water, and a serviette.

Method. Begin by borrowing a wedding ring. Now you may use either of the two prepared handkerchiefs already described, or simply switch the ring for a duplicate. In any case, after the switch, hold the borrowed ring pinched between the first and second fingers of the right hand, approach your table with your left side to the front, and pick up the plate with the egg on it with both hands—the left hand on the front edge, the right hand on the rear. Let the projecting part of the ring slide onto the hook under the rim and then open the fingers. Because of the angle at which the hook is attached to the plate, the ring will be quite secure. Bring the egg forward and have it examined. Your right fingers cover the borrowed ring and the little hook so that you can show the plate freely. Put the plate and the egg back on your table.

Vanish the duplicate ring by one or the other of the methods described above; then return to the left side of your table, take the plate in your right hand, and show all parts of your left hand (the sleeve well back). Take the plate in the left hand and show all parts of the right hand. Then take the plate again in the right hand, covering the hook; pick up the egg with the left hand and show the plate, first lowering to the front to show the top side, then raising it to show the bottom—the ring nat-

urally falling into the hand. Put the plate on the table and take
the egg in the right hand so that it hides the ring. Proceed to
break the egg in the customary way over the plate—first crack-
ing it, then dividing the shell to let the contents fall—and at
the same moment let the ring fall onto the plate.

Finally wash the ring in the glass of water; wipe it, and your
hands, before returning it. Be careful to do this very openly, so
that the ring is visible at all times. If the plate is to be used for
any further experiment, it is a simple matter to detach the waxed
hook and dispose of it.

3. The Flight of a Ring from One Hand to Another

This is one of the most astonishing tricks for impromptu
work, not only with a ring but in the whole range of sleight of
hand. It is not really difficult but requires smooth working
and close attention to misdirection.

Preparation. Have the little hook (already described) in position on your trousers—a little to the rear of the right trousers
pocket, at the height of the right hand when it is dropped naturally to the side. Have also two handkerchiefs of silk, preferably
of different colors, and two rubber bands.

Method. Begin by borrowing a ring. In this case the more distinctive the ring the better, and a gentleman's ring should be
obtained if possible. Invite the owner of the ring to come forward and stand at your left side.

Hold the ring at the tips of the left thumb and first and second fingers, letting a small part protrude above the fingertips,
and show all parts of the hand with the sleeve pulled back a little.
Throw one of the handkerchiefs over the right hand so that its
middle covers the ring. Invite the spectator to feel the ring
through the fabric, to satisfy everyone that the ring is there;
then lower the middle finger and the thumb to carry the ring as
far down into the hand as you can, keeping the forefinger
stretched upwards. The tip of this finger simulates exactly the
shape of the ring, which will appear to the spectators to be still
in the same position under the middle of the handkerchief.

Bring the right hand up from behind and take hold of the
handkerchief near the base of the left thumb; grip the ring with
the thumb and forefinger, so that their tips come together, by

pressing the fabric through the ring. At the same time release the ring from the left thumb and middle finger, and grip a small fold of the handkerchief to hold it fast. Lower the right hand, still holding the ring with the tips of the thumb and forefinger; slide the ring to the edge of the handkerchief and let it drop into the right hand. As far as the audience is concerned, you have simply adjusted the handkerchief.

Invite the spectator to pick up one of the rubber bands from the table; close the left forefinger as if to grip the ring in the left fist, pull the sleeve back a little more, and drop the right hand to the side. Instruct the spectator to gather the handkerchief folds round your left wrist and then to pass the band over the fist, so that it encircles the wrist and holds the fabric securely to it. In the meantime you have placed the ring on the little hook, leaving the right hand free to be shown empty as you instruct the spectator how to fasten the handkerchief round the left wrist.

This done, point to the second handkerchief and, as the spectator gets it, steal the ring from the hook, close the hand, and have the spectator throw the second handkerchief over it and fasten it to the wrist in the same way as the other handkerchief. It only remains to invite the spectator to say on which finger of the right hand the ring shall appear and to slip it onto that finger. Hold your arms at full length on each side, order the ring to pass over, and then have the handkerchief removed from the left hand to prove that it has departed. Finally have the second handkerchief removed; hold your right hand up, back to the front and still closed; then suddenly extend the fingers, displaying the ring in the desired position.

Give this trick the necessary study and you will be more than satisfied with the effect it creates.

4. The Ring, Handkerchief and Glass

This very pretty combination gives the effect of great skill, but it is not at all difficult to perform.

Effect. A borrowed ring is placed in a small glass together with a silk handkerchief, and all three articles are passed, one at a time, into a borrowed hat placed at a distance.

Preparation. You require two small glasses, without feet, and two small silk handkerchiefs, duplicates, about twelve inches square. One glass and one silk you place openly on your table, the other glass with the silk pushed well into it you place under the edge of your vest, lengthwise, with the mouth of the glass toward the right. One other accessory needed is an ordinary handkerchief which has a round piece of celluloid, the same diameter as the mouth of the glass, attached to its middle. Arrange this in your pocket in such a way that when you spread it by two corners the celluloid will be on the side nearest to you.

Method. Begin by borrowing a hat. Take it in your right hand, the fingers on the outside of the brim, the thumb inside. In turning to put the hat on your table, slip the right thumb under the vest and into the glass and twist this out into the hat. This takes but a moment, and if you have kept the right elbow pressed to the side no suspicion will be aroused. Lay the hat on the table, crown downwards, and proceed to borrow a ring. A man's ring is best for the trick, and the larger and more distinctive it is the better. Drop the ring into the glass and push the handkerchief down on top of it in exactly the same way as the silk in the duplicate glass, which is now in the hat.

Announce that you will make the three articles disappear one by one. To do this you must first make an exchange of the glasses, and this becomes a simple matter by resorting to the method of asking the spectators if they wish them to vanish visibly or invisibly. Generally someone will call out at once, "Visibly." "That is very easy," you say; and you place the glass in the hat, standing it alongside the one already there. "However," you continue, "I prefer to do it invisibly." Remove the duplicate glass and stand it on a little table at a distance from the hat. If by chance no one replies, simply say, "If you had asked me to do it visibly, this is what I would have done," and you proceed as already explained.

As matters now stand, the apparent vanish of the ring is mere child's play. Simply pretend to extract the ring and throw it at the hat. Of course, you take nothing; but you act seriously. Remove the silk from the glass and shake it out, then show the glass empty. Lay the silk beside the glass and go to the hat. Lift the silk out of the glass and lay it beside the glass, being careful not to show any part of it above the brim of the hat; then slide the ring up with two fingers, so that it doesn't "talk," and bring it into view between the thumb and fingers. Return the ring to the owner and have it identified.

To vanish the handkerchief you have recourse to a pull (see page 167), which you secure in this manner: Roll the silk between your hands and close the fingers on it, at once putting your right hand, with its fingers almost closed and glancing at it furtively, into your right-hand trousers pocket. There will be knowing smiles and whispers in the audience, if not an open challenge; so you open the left hand and show the silk, remarking that you merely did that to see if the spectators were really following your actions. In the meantime you have secured the pull, previously placed at the top of the pocket; you bring the two hands together and proceed to push the silk into the vanisher as you wave the hands up and down, with your right side to the front. When the silk is safely in the holder—at the moment when the backward motion of the hands brings them near the body—release the pull, which instantly flies under your coat. Continue the up-and-down movement of the hands for a few moments and extend the hands well away from the body. Then close both hands; separate them, working the fingers on the palms; and suddenly open them, spreading the fingers far apart and turning the hands to show all parts of them. Go to the hat and take it by the brim with the fingers inside, pressing the glass against the side of the hat; lift this and turn it over, letting the duplicate silk fall to the floor.

Replace the hat on the table, mouth upwards, as before. The glass only remains to be vanished. Put it on the palm of your left hand, with the right; take out the prepared handkerchief, and throw it over the glass in such a way as to bring the celluloid disk over its mouth. Bring the left hand up until the glass thus covered is on a level with the opening of the outside breast pocket. Grasp the disk from above, through the fabric, between the tips of the right thumb and second finger; with the left hand, under cover of the handkerchief, drop the glass into the outside coat pocket. Stroke the handkerchief several times with the left hand, then, pointing that hand at the hat, call "Go!" and toss the handkerchief into the air. Catch it by one corner, as it falls, and shake it out; then crumple it and put it back in your pocket. Go to the hat and turn it toward the audience, so that the glass can be seen in it. Take it out and return the hat to the owner.

You have fulfilled your contract, and if your work has been well done you will find that this series of magical feats will be received with acclaim by any audience.

V

MAGIC WITH BALLS

". . . they saw Barnaby, head downwards, with his feet in the air, and he was juggling six balls of copper and a dozen knives."
Anatole France—*Our Lady's Juggler.*

IT WOULD perhaps have been logical to treat the manipulation of balls in the first place, for there is little doubt that the whole vast superstructure of sleight of hand has been built upon the discovery, in ages past, that a small round pebble can be held in the palm of the hand without the aid of the fingers. The earliest recorded references to a sleight-of-hand trick are those in Greek and Roman literature relating to the cups and balls trick, small white stones being used by the operators of those days. There are pictures in Egyptian records which suggest that the play of the balls was practiced in the period of the early dynasties; and in ancient tombs these little round stones have been found, together with magic mirrors of metal. Quite recently they have been found in the Celtic burial grounds near Vannes in France. In India and in China the same tricks with balls have been practiced from time immemorial, and with the same basis for the manipulations; namely, the concealment of the ball in the palm of the hand.

Although the trick of the cups and balls has retained its popularity and, indeed, has again become one of the leading items in the repertoire of the close-up worker, the development of billiard-ball manipulation has taken place in quite recent years. There is no satisfactory book on this branch of the art in the English language; the pamphlets that have been written on the subject are merely collections of haphazard sleights, many of them utterly impossible with a ball that would pass for a billiard ball. It is impossible to treat the subject exhaustively in the space allotted to it in this book, but the indispensable sleights will be treated fully in correct order and detail.

In the first place, the balls used should be not less than one and a half inches in diameter; preferably they should be one and three quarters of an inch. If the neophyte finds he cannot handle balls of these sizes, he should content himself with the manipulation of golf balls, which will be treated in the second section of this chapter. The best balls to use are of wood, enameled, polished, and highly varnished and these, together with the half shells to match, can be obtained at any magic store.

I. BILLIARD BALLS

SECRET HOLDS

1. THE REGULAR PALM

In this fundamental position the ball is held in the hollow of the hand by the contraction of the two muscular pads at the opposite sides of the palm, in much the same way as a coin is held. The operation with a ball, however, is more difficult since its rounded surface has a tendency to slip away. This difficulty is increased if the operator has a hard, dry skin; in such case a single drop of glycerine, rubbed in with the tips of the fingers, will be found helpful. With practice it will be found that a ball can be held with a very slight contraction of the hand; when this faculty has been acquired, the next step is to learn to use the fingers freely—to pick up objects and to set them down again without relaxing the pressure on the ball. There is a natural tendency at first to stretch out the thumb and fingers, holding them stiffly and wide apart; this must be carefully avoided. The ideal to be aimed at is the imitation of a hand in repose, in an easy natural position with the fingers partly closed (Fig. 1).

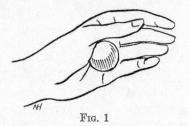

FIG. 1

The next step is to learn how to place the ball in the palm. Hold it between the thumb and forefinger; then roll it onto the tips of the second and third fingers, gripping it by the sides between the first and fourth fingers, and release the thumb. Bend the fingers into the palm and they will carry the ball to the exact spot required. Press the ball home with the tips of the two middle fingers and contract the muscles of the palm to hold it; extend the fingers and hold the hand in an easy natural position. Practice until you can make the whole movement in a flash.

2. The Finger Palm

In this position the ball is held by bending the two middle fingers over it and pressing it against their roots. The first and

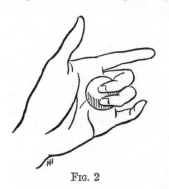

fourth fingers take no part in holding the ball but are kept close to the sides of the other fingers to prevent any glimpse of the ball being held between the fingers, and their top joints are extended slightly (Fig. 2). This is a very easy and useful palm and it enables one to hold two balls hidden in the hand at the same time, one in the regular palm and the other in the finger palm.

Fig. 2

To carry the ball to the finger palm, roll it with the thumb from its position between the thumb and first finger to the roots of the two middle fingers, and bend them over it. To bring it to the same position from the regular palm, simply lower the hand, bend the middle fingers, and let the ball roll into them. Finally, to bring the ball from the finger palm to the ordinary palm, bend the middle fingers in a little more and press the ball into the desired position.

These are the only two positions of practical use for holding a ball concealed in the hand.

3. The Shell

The shell can be palmed in either of these two positions and, further, its convex or concave sides can be against the palm or the fingers. With the convex side against the palm the shell can be palmed more easily than the ball because of its lighter weight, and when the concave side is innermost the edges of the shell afford a good grip.

These are very numerous and are divided into various classes. Only the best and most practical will be explained.

It is necessary, at the outset, that the distinction between the real vanish and the apparent vanish be understood thoroughly. The real vanish takes place when the ball (or any other small object) is secretly palmed in one hand; the apparent vanish is when the other hand is shown to be empty. Of the first the spectators should have no suspicion whatever; their whole attention must be directed to the second. Suppose, for example, you have pretended to take a ball from the left hand with the right. Turn the left hand over, hiding the palmed ball; point to the right hand as it moves away; and follow that hand with your eyes, at the same time turning the body toward the right. As soon as the right hand is closed, puffed out as if it held the ball, begin to work the fingers on the palm as if crumbling the ball away. Then close the fingers tightly and open them one by one, beginning with the little finger, to prove that the ball has vanished. These movements are fundamental, and whenever the vanish is mentioned it must be understood that they are to be made.

Again, it is a good plan to make what is called a feint before the vanish is made; that is to say, you really take the ball in the first place, then return it to the other hand. Take it again, execute the palm and the vanish, copying exactly the moves made in the feint. This process also will be taken for granted in describing the other vanishes.

1. PRETENDED SEIZURES

This class applies to all cases in which the ball is apparently taken from one hand and vanished from the other.

Retaining the Ball in One Hand as the Other Apparently Takes It

Place the ball on the palm of the left hand at the exact spot in which the contraction of the muscles will hold it. Make a pretense of taking it with the right hand by placing that hand over the ball, the tips of the fingers touching the palm in front of it and the thumb behind (Fig. 3). Raise the right hand diagonally toward the right, puffed out as if the ball were really seized, and at the same moment grip the ball in the left palm and turn this hand to hide it. Point toward the right hand with the left fore-

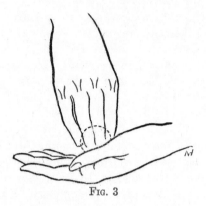

FIG. 3

finger and turn the right hand to bring its back to the front. At once begin the pulverizing movements of the fingers and complete the vanish as described above.

The Ball Falls from the Fist to the Regular Palm

Place the ball on top of the right fist so that it rests on the ring made by the first finger and thumb. Turn your right side to the front and bring the left hand over reversed—the thumb downwards and the fingers stretched out and close together, pointing to the left, to seize the ball (Fig. 4). The moment it is hidden, open the first three fingers of the right hand rapidly in turn, causing the ball to drop until it is stopped by the little finger; then press it into the regular palm with the tip of the two middle fingers. Raise the puffed-out left hand diagonally to the left, the first finger of the right hand pointing to it.

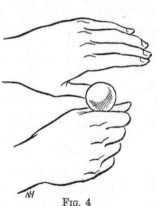

FIG. 4

The whole movement must be made without stopping. When

the hands meet they are kept together for a moment as you make the turn to the left, thus giving time for the ball to drop into the right hand before moving the left hand away.

The Tourniquet or French Drop

Show the ball held between the tips of the thumb and middle finger of the left hand, palm upwards, and the fingers joined. Bring the right hand over (Fig. 5); insert the thumb well under

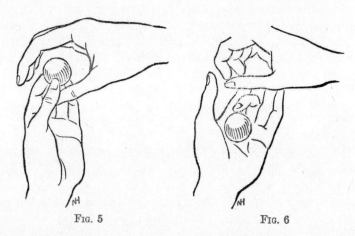

FIG. 5   FIG. 6

the ball and the joined fingers above and in front of it. Turn slightly to the right, moving the joined hands at the same time; release the pressure of the thumb, letting the ball drop into the palm and pressing it there with the tip of the second finger; then close the right hand as if seizing the ball, turn it over, and move it away puffed out as if it held the ball (Fig. 6). Turn the left hand, also to hide the ball, and point the forefinger toward the right hand. Finish the vanish according to the usual routine.

This vanish can be used with balls of any size and with any small objects. It should be done with either hand.

2. PRETENDED DEPOSITS

The Ball, Apparently Placed in the Left Hand, Is Palmed in the Right

Show the ball between the right thumb and forefinger; turn toward the right and place it against the left palm. As you close the left fingers over the ball, quickly roll it to the tips of the right second and third fingers, close them, and carry it to the regular palm. Keep the left fingers puffed out, raise the left hand, and finish in the customary way. The feint, taking the ball really in the first place, should be used and the palm made in exact imitation of it.

The Ball, Rolled Between the Palms, Is Retained in One of Them

Place the ball on the left palm as you turn to the left; put the right hand over it and roll it between the palms of the two hands. Press the ball into the palm of the right hand and, as you remove this hand with its back to the front, close the left fingers, keeping them puffed out as if holding the ball; turn the hand over and move it away toward the left. Complete the vanish in the prescribed manner.

Swallowing the Ball

Hold the ball between the tips of the thumb and the first two fingers of the right hand. Open the mouth and pretend to place the ball in it; in reality, let it fall into the palm under cover of the fingers. Push out the cheek with the tongue; move the hand away with the palmed ball, pointing to the lump in the cheek with the forefinger. Make motions of swallowing, put both hands at the bottom of the vest, thrust the ball under the vest with the right little finger, turn up the edge of the vest, and let the ball drop into the other hand.

3. REAL DEPOSITS FOLLOWED BY RESEIZURE

The Ball, Apparently Pushed into the Left Hand, Is Palmed in the Right

Stand with your right side to the front and show the ball, encircled by the thumb and first finger of the left hand, held vertically, its back to the spectators, the other three fingers bent in. Push the ball into the left hand by giving it little taps with the first two fingers of the right hand, keeping the other fingers bent (Fig. 7). Turn the left hand and show the ball emerging from the left side of the hand. Repeat the operation; but, this time, when the ball is out of sight place it in the right palm with the left thumb and forefinger, move the left hand away, and point to it with the right forefinger. Conclude the vanish as usual.

The Drop Palm

1st Method. With your right side to the front show the ball on the palm of the left hand, held flat. Close the fingers on it

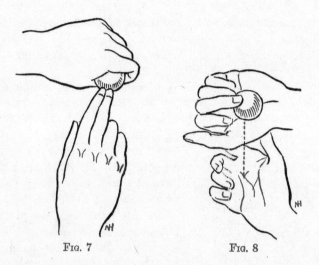

Fig. 7   Fig. 8

slowly and turn the hand, bringing its back to the front. Roll the ball toward the wrist and hold it with the tip of the middle finger only (Fig. 8). Make a circular gesture with the right hand, starting from a point above the left wrist and moving the hand outwards over the left fist, then bringing it back underneath toward the left wrist. At the precise moment when the hand is below the ball, release the pressure of the left second finger. The ball drops and you catch it in the right palm, continuing the motion of the right hand and with it pulling the left sleeve back a little. Stretch out the left hand, point to it with the right forefinger, and complete the vanish in the customary manner.

If the moves have been coordinated perfectly, this vanish is one of the most illusive possible.

2d Method. This vanish is similar to the preceding one but is much easier. Hold the ball in the same way, getting it out of the palm and supporting it with the tip of the middle finger as described. Pat the back of the left hand with the right fingers, then turn this hand over·to show its palm; reverse it again and at the same time turn the left hand to bring the ball against the right palm, which instantly grips it. Pat the puffed-out fingers of the left hand with the right fingers and move the left hand away, slowly closing the fingers and rubbing the ball to nothing in the usual way, the right forefinger pointing to the left hand.

The Tip Tilt

Stand with your right side to the front, the left hand held vertically, the palm outwards, and the ball held between the right thumb and middle finger. Place the ball against the left palm (Fig. 9) and, with a quick half turn of the left wrist, re-

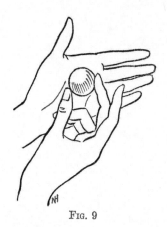

verse the left hand and apparently seize the ball, the left fingers closing on it. In reality, at the precise moment you turn the left hand let the ball drop into the right palm, the left thumb breaking its fall and helping to fix it in the palm. Turn the right hand a little to keep its back to the spectators, and keep your eyes fixed on the left hand as you move it away and annihilate the ball as is customary.

Fig. 9

4. Pretended Throws

The pretended throws are comparatively easy vanishes. You can feign to throw the ball into the air or into the other hand, and the throw can be made with either the back of the hand or the palm toward the spectators.

Into the Air

Stand with your right side to the front and show the ball between the first finger and thumb of the right hand. Drop the hand and make a preliminary gesture of throwing the ball upwards. Repeat the action and, as the hand reaches its lowest point, rapidly palm the ball in the regular palm and bring the hand sharply upwards to shoulder height, separating the fingers, as the motion of the hand is stopped, as if releasing the ball and follow its supposed flight with your eyes. The change over palm, to be described later, can then follow to show both hands empty.

Into the Other Hand

Turn your right side to the spectators and hold the ball between the thumb and fingers of the right hand; place the left hand, palm downwards, about a foot above the right hand. Throw the ball up into the left hand, bringing the two hands almost together in the action. Drop the right hand to its former position and let the ball fall into it from the left hand. Repeat the procedure several times; then, at the last throw, palm the ball in the right hand in the upward movement. Stop the motion of the hand at the same height as in the previous throws, open the right fingers, and immediately afterward close the fingers of the left hand in exactly the same manner as when it really received the ball. Move the hand away, puffed out, and finish the vanish in the usual way.

With the Palm of the Hand to the Front

This vanish can be used only when a dress suit is worn, for it depends on the use of the large pocket, known as the *profonde*, in the tail of the coat. Standing with the left side to the front, the right hand with the ball is brought backwards in the preliminary action of the throw and the ball is dropped into the coat pocket, the pretended throw being made with the empty hand as in the first throw, "Into the Air." After a certain amount of practice the ball can actually be thrown to the rear and into the pocket, so that there is no stoppage at all in the whole action.

5. SECRET TRANSFERS FROM ONE HAND TO THE OTHER

The Horizontal Change Over Palm

Stand with the right side to the front, the left hand open with its palm outwards, the fingers pointing to the left; the right hand has the ball palmed in the regular palm and the

tips of its fingers touch the left wrist (Fig. 10). Swing round
to the right to bring the hands to a similar position on the
right, with the palm of the right hand to the front (Fig. 11);
when the tips of the fingers of both hands meet in front of the
body, relax the pressure of the right palm and grip the ball

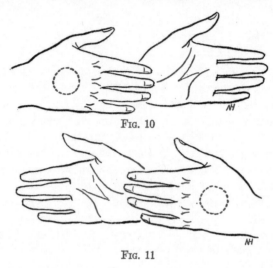

FIG. 10

FIG. 11

in the left palm. At the completion of the movement the spectators see the palm of the right hand and the back of the left,
so that both sides of each hand have been shown in turn.
This change over sleight is a very easy one and therein lies
its danger. Many performers abuse it by overdoing it.

The Vertical Change Over Palm

Take the same position of the body and the left hand; but
hold the right hand, with the ball in the regular palm, with the
back of the hand to the front and the fingers pointing upwards
(Fig. 12). Pass the right hand, with the fingers spread apart,
against the palm of the left hand from the top to the bottom;
then reverse the left hand and make the same movement
against its back. Turn the left hand, bringing its palm against
the ball, grip it there and reverse the hand, at the same time
turn the right-hand palm outwards (Fig. 13). Both sides of
the two hands have thus been shown in succession.

To return the ball to the right hand, turn the hand, bringing its back to the front; reverse the left hand, bringing the ball

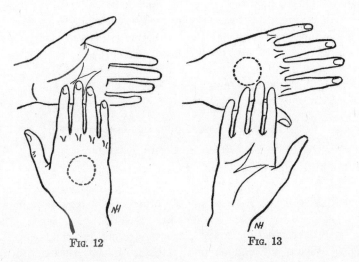

Fig. 12   Fig. 13

against the right palm; grip it there and stroke the left palm with the right fingers.

ACCESSORIES

The only indispensable accessories for billiard-ball manipulations are the ball holders. Of these there are two kinds: holders

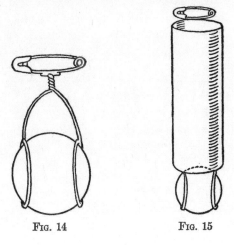

Fig. 14   Fig. 15

for single balls, and holders from which a number of balls can be taken one at a time. The single-ball holders are the more useful, since they can be placed in different positions without bulging the clothing, whereas the holder for a number of balls is bulky and the steal has to be made always at the same spot. The choice between the two must be left to individual preference. Both holders are made in different designs. Figs. 14 and 15 show those most generally in use. They can be obtained at any magic store.

TRICKS WITH BILLIARD BALLS

1. PASSAGE OF A BALL THROUGH THE KNEE

With Solid Balls Only

Two balls are required: one held openly between the thumb and fingers of the right hand, the other in the regular palm in the same hand. Show the left hand empty, take the visible ball with the left thumb and fingers, and, making a turn to the right, execute the change over palm with the concealed ball. Show the right hand empty and repeat the change over palm in turning again to the left, thus bringing the balls back to their original positions in the right hand. Take the visible ball between the tips of the thumb and fingers of the left hand and place the hands, one on each side of the right knee, the backs of the hands to the front. Make a motion of throwing the ball from the left hand through the knee and tap the ball on its side. Repeat the action, quickly palming the ball by bending the fingers upwards, and a moment later produce the ball in the right hand by letting it roll into view at the tips of the fingers.

Place both knees together and, by reversing the movements, pass the ball from the right hand through the knees into the left hand. Finally show the right hand, holding the visible ball only; take the ball with the left hand, executing the change over palm with the duplicate ball, and show all parts of that hand.

With Two Balls and a Shell

In this method you have a ball covered with a shell in the right hand and a single ball in the left. Hold the balls in each hand between the forefinger and thumb on each side of the knees. Make a throwing motion with the left hand and palm the ball in that hand in the regular palm; at the same moment lift the ball from the shell with the right second finger to show, apparently, two balls in that hand.

Repeat the movements in reverse fashion by pulling the ball back into the shell with the right middle finger and allowing the ball in the left hand to roll to the fingertips again, showing one ball in each hand. This is another easy but effective move that performers very often ruin by overdoing it.

Through the Knee and Leg Downwards

This trick is done while seated. Place a chair well down and on the right of the platform and seat yourself well forward, with the knees about a foot apart. Show the ball between the thumb and forefinger of the right hand, in position for the French drop sleight. First actually take the ball in the left hand and show it. Replace it in the right hand and show the left hand empty. Take it again with the left hand; but this time execute the sleight and raise the left hand, closed and puffed out as if it held the ball. Crumble the fingers together a trifle; then strike the fist sharply down on the left knee, opening the fingers at the last moment as if to force the ball into the knee. Lower the right hand at once, but not hurriedly, to the left ankle; nip the lower front edge of the bottom of the trouser leg between the thumb on the outside and the fingers inside; let the ball fall to the fingertips and push it up inside the trousers leg as you turn the hand over toward the front. Retain the ball inside the cloth by the part pinched between the thumb and fingers. Move the left hand down; show it empty; and with it turn back the bottom of the trousers leg, letting the ball drop out into the hand.

When this trick is neatly performed, the effect is that the right hand is used merely to turn back the cuff of the trousers to enable the left hand to take the ball out more easily. The trick is well worth the practice necessary to do it perfectly.

2. COLOR CHANGES

As these are very numerous, it will be possible only to describe some typical methods which will enable the student to work out others for himself. The instantaneous change in the color of a billiard ball is one of the prettiest effects possible.

Using Two Solid Balls

1st Method. Stand with your right side to the front, both hands on the left side of the body and held vertically, the left hand with its palm to the front. In the exact spot for the regular palm in this hand you hold, for example, a red ball with the tip of the right middle finger. This right hand has its back outwards and in its palm a ball of a different color, white for example. At this point the spectators see the red ball, the inside of the left hand, and the back of the right hand. It is necessary now to prove that you are using one ball only, the red. To do this, swing round to the right, rolling the red ball to the tips of the fingers as you turn; transfer the white ball to the left palm and roll the red ball against the right palm, supporting it with the tip of the left middle finger. You have thus shown both sides of the hands and the white ball. Repeat the operation the reverse way in turning again to the left.

To make the color change, instead of rolling the red ball to the tips of the fingers and transferring the white ball from palm to palm, retain both balls in their respective palms as you make the turn to the right and bring the tips of the left middle fingers onto the white ball to hold it against the right palm. By then repeating the first movement with the red ball instead of the white, transferring it from palm to palm, you can show that you have the white ball only in your hands.

2d Method. Stand with your right side to the front and show a white ball, for example, between the thumb and forefinger of the left hand, the palm of the hand to the front, the fingers pointing toward the front. In the right hand you have a ball in the regular palm. Bring this hand over the left hand so that its side rests just above the white ball. Move the right hand downwards, rolling the white ball from the tips of the left thumb and fingers into its palm and leaving the red ball in its place in the left hand.

The effect should be that the mere action of passing the right hand over the ball has changed its color, and care must be taken

that the balls do not "talk" in the action. After the color change
has been made, the change over palm can be executed to prove
that one ball only has been used.

Using a Shell

With one ball and a shell. Stand with your right side to the
front and show a red ball in the left hand, encircled by the thumb
and forefinger. This is really a white ball covered with a red
shell; but if care is taken to cover the junction of the shell and
the ball with the thumb and forefinger and the shell is held
squarely to the front, no one will have any suspicion of the real
state of affairs. Show the right hand empty and pass it in front
of the left hand several times as a feint. At the third passage,
palm off the shell in the right hand and show the white ball.

In making the palm the right hand must pass over the left
at exactly the same tempo as it did in making the feints; there
must be no stoppage or hesitation. Show the white ball on all
sides; then, in making a turn to the right, take it in the right
hand, making the change over palm with the shell to the left
palm; then show the right hand and the ball freely.

With two solid balls and a shell, changing the color of one.
(1) Stand with the right side to the front and show two balls—
white, for example—in your left hand; in reality you have a
white shell between the thumb and first finger and a white ball
between the first and second fingers. Steal a red ball from the
bottom of the vest, or from a holder, palming it in the regular
palm. Bring the right hand over to the left hand under pretense
of adjusting the upper ball—the solid one—and, in so doing, slip
the red ball from the right palm behind and into the white shell.
Be careful to keep the shell squarely to the front. Show the right
hand empty with a casual gesture and pass it downwards in
front of the two balls. This is the feint. Repeat the action and,
this time, palm off the shell from the lower ball, thus effecting
the color change. Take the upper (white) ball with the right
hand, at the same time slipping the shell over it; knock the two
balls together, apparently proving that you have two solid balls
only.

(2) This is one of the prettiest color changes of a billiard ball
possible. Hold a white ball and a white shell with a red ball in-

serted behind it, exactly as in the preceding color change. Place
the right hand a little below the left and directly underneath it.
Move the left hand down a little, release the red ball from behind the white shell, and instantly insert the white ball in the
white shell by the aid of the left middle finger. A few trials
before a mirror will show that a perfect illusion is created of
the white ball changing to red as it drops into the right hand.
Finally knock the two balls together to prove that they are solid
and show the hands are empty otherwise.

3. The Multiplication of Billiard Balls

Before explaining the methods of multiplying the balls, which
is the finest trick possible with billiard balls, it is necessary to
detail several methods of producing the first ball and disposing
of the last one.

Production of the First Ball

The simplest possible method is to enter with a ball palmed
in the right hand, show both hands empty by means of the change
over palm, and then catch the ball in the air—or produce it from
the back of the knee or elbow, or even from the back of the
left hand.

If, however, the trick is to be done in the middle of your program, the ball can be secreted under your vest. In this case the
accepted method of production is to face front; show the right
hand empty in making a slight turn to the right; then turn to
the left and make the same demonstration with the left hand,
twiddling the fingers and turning the hand back and forth to
show both sides. While all eyes, including your own, are on this
hand, quietly drop the right hand to the bottom of the vest and
steal the ball, either by simply drawing in the stomach and letting the ball drop into the hand or by pressing the base of the
thumb on it through the cloth and so forcing it into the hand.
The change over palm can then be made and the ball produced
as desired.

A very good method is with the wand. You have the ball
hidden behind a crumpled silk handkerchief on your table, the
wand lying beside it. Pick up the wand openly, and the ball
secretly, in the palm of your right hand, your right side being

toward the spectators. Show the left hand empty and place the wand against the tips of the left fingers in the position for holding it suspended as explained in Chapter I. Then bring the hands together to transfer the wand to the same position at the tips of the right fingers; turn to the right and, in doing so, transfer the ball to the palm of the left hand. After showing the suspension effect with the right hand, transfer the wand to the left hand and the ball to the palm of the right hand in again turning to the left. Hold the end of the wand with the left hand, run the right hand along it, and produce the ball from the upper end.

This production of the ball comes as a complete surprise and is very effective. The attention of the spectators is so taken up with the supposed magnetic effect that they have no suspicion that anything can be hidden in the hands.

Secretly Disposing of the Last Ball

An easy method is to pretend to place the ball in the left hand, really palming it in the right, and, while making the motions of pulverizing it with the left fingers and under the pretense of pulling up the left sleeve, place the right hand near the left shoulder and drop the palmed ball into the outside coat pocket.

When full dress is worn, the vanish by the pretended throw with the drop into the *profonde* can be used. This has been explained above.

The following is a subtle and deceptive method. Palm the ball in the right hand, apparently placing it in the left; then produce it from behind the left knee. Again place the ball in the left hand, in reality this time. Pretend to vanish it—moving the fingers as usual and opening them widely but keeping the back of the hand to the front, of course. At once point to the left knee with the right forefinger; with that hand pretend to take the ball from the back of the knee, showing the hand puffed out. At the same moment drop the ball from the left hand into the left outside coat pocket. Rather rapidly, pretend to put the supposed ball into the left hand and close the left fingers on it. Raise the hand; make the usual pulverizing motions; and finally open the left hand, showing that the ball has vanished. Then show that the right hand also is empty.

4. THE THREE BALLS TRICK

Preparation. This very interesting trick can be worked before the Excelsior four balls trick (see page 103) with excellent results. Two balls and one shell are required, and you prepare by placing one ball under the vest on the right-hand side and the other ball with the shell in the upper left vest pocket.

Method. Begin by producing the ball from the vest by one of the methods already explained; make several passes with it;

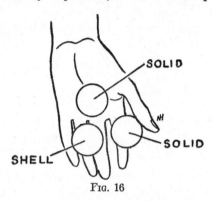

Fig. 16

then pretend to put it in the left hand and make it travel up the sleeve. Thrust the right hand under the coat and take the ball and shell together from the vest pocket, keeping the first ball palmed. Place the ball and shell on the open left hand, supporting them between the thumb and forefinger as one ball, keeping the other fingers bent in a little. Announce that you will produce a second ball by cutting this one in half. Pretend to do this by placing the right hand vertically across the left hand, drop the palmed ball behind the visible ball, and draw the right hand away as if actually cutting the ball. Show the two balls as the result of this halving operation. Then say that you will catch a third ball in the air. Let it be seen that your right hand is empty; make a pretense of catching a ball, holding the hand puffed out, and feign to place it with the other two in the left hand—in reality, under cover of the two hands, you simply left the shell and place it alongside the solid balls. Display the three as three solid balls (Fig. 16).

To vanish the balls, pretend to take the ball last produced;

in reality, roll it under the shell and remove the hand empty but puffed out as if it held the ball. Crumble this to nothing in the usual way.

Take the ball and shell in the right hand and knock the ball against the other to prove that the balls are solid. Replace the shell only, keeping the ball palmed; then say that you will pass one ball up your sleeve. Close the left hand, bringing the shell over the ball, and produce the palmed ball from the armpit under the coat. Pretend to pass the ball the reverse way, put the ball in the right hand under the coat, drop it into the breast pocket, and with a circular wave of the left hand separate the ball and the shell. Apparently take one of these two balls; really slip the shell over the solid and move the right hand away empty, but puffed out. Make the vanish as usual.

Call attention to the one ball that remains; in reality, one ball and the shell. To get rid of the shell ask the spectators if they wish the ball to vanish visibly or invisibly. The greater number will demand a visible vanish; so you place the ball and the shell openly in your breast pocket, a visible vanish, then bring out the ball only. Finally you vanish this ball by one or other of the methods already explained.

5. THE EXCELSIOR BILLIARD BALL TRICK

Effect. The effect of this startling trick is the appearance of four solid balls, one by one, between the fingers of one hand.

Preparation. Four solid balls and a shell are required, all being of the same color. To prepare, place two balls under the vest on the right side, the ball and shell in the upper left vest pocket; enter with the fourth ball palmed or, if necessary, obtain it from the table in picking up the wand in the manner previously explained.

Method. After producing the ball, make various passes, vanishes, and recoveries, using the sleights that have been explained. Then with your right side to the front, pretend to make the ball travel up your sleeve; show the left hand empty; thrust your right hand under the coat; and bring out the ball and shell from the vest pocket, retaining the ball in your palm. Place the ball and shell as one ball between the thumb and forefinger of the left hand, the shell to the front. Turn the hand to show the palm empty; in reversing it again place the middle finger on the side of the ball and pull it out of the shell smartly, so that it appears in the space between the first and second fingers with the shell remaining in its position between the thumb and forefinger.

Apparently the left hand now holds two balls and, to prove this to the satisfaction of the spectators, it is necessary to turn the shell while turning the hand to show the other side of the balls. To do this, place the tip of the left third finger on the middle of the shell and quickly turn the shell as the hand is reversed. Then under cover of the turning of the hand to its original position, the same finger pulls the convex side of the shell to the front again.

Bring the right hand over to take the ball from between the first and second fingers, and in doing so slip the palmed ball into the shell. Remove the upper ball and knock it against the lower one to prove conclusively by the sound that they are solid. Place the second finger alongside the forefinger and put the ball in the right hand in the space between the second and third fingers. Casually show the right hand empty, and let it drop quietly to a position opposite and close to the bottom of the vest. Turn the left hand over to show the palm and, in reversing it again, pull the ball from the shell with the second finger into the space between the first and second fingers exactly as was done to produce the second ball. At the same moment, with the right hand steal one of the balls from under the vest; then raise this hand a little and point with the forefinger at the three balls now showing in the left hand. It should not be necessary to insist that the eyes must be directed to the left hand throughout.

Move the right hand over to the left hand and remove the two upper balls, seizing the opportunity of inserting the palmed ball in the shell as before. Knock the balls together to prove them solid.

Again drop the left second finger against the side of the forefinger and place one ball between the second and third fingers and the other ball between the third and fourth fingers. Make the production of the fourth ball in the same way as before, turning the left hand to show the palm, then turning it over again and pulling the ball out of the shell into the same position between the first and second fingers. Profit by the surprise caused by this production to palm the last ball from the vest. Insert this ball in the shell under cover of taking the ball between the first and second fingers and knock it against the other three balls. Replace this ball, and in so doing palm off the shell with the right hand. You can then knock all four of the balls on the table, or let them fall one by one onto a tray, the resulting sound proving conclusively that they are solid. A very effective finish, when working on the stage, is to throw the balls to the floor one by one, letting them roll off between the wings.

The drawback to this method is the fact that each new ball appears in the same spot, the space between the first and second fingers, although this is disguised to a certain extent by placing the second finger beside the forefinger each time. The correct, but very difficult, procedure is to replace the second ball between the first and second fingers and then, as the hand is turned over, to roll it up between the second and third fingers and immediately after pull the ball from the shell with the second finger. In the case of the last ball, two balls have to be rolled upwards before the ball is pulled out of the shell—a difficult operation, but the student should not be content until he has mastered it.

6. THE MULTIPLICATION TO EIGHT BALLS, FOUR BALLS IN EACH HAND

Effect. This effect, the final flowering of the multiplying ball trick, can be accomplished successfully only after the four ball trick has been mastered with each hand.

Preparation. To prepare for the trick, place a ball and shell in the upper left vest pocket; two balls under the vest, one near the middle and the other to the right; two more, one of which is covered with a shell, in the right trousers pocket; and the last ball in a holder under the edge of the coat on the right-hand side.

Begin by producing the first ball; make various passes with it, finally as if passing it up the left sleeve but really retaining it palmed in the right hand. Thrust this hand under the coat and bring out the ball and shell from the vest pocket, keeping the first ball palmed.

Proceed with the multiplication of the balls in the left hand, up to the stage at which you show three solid balls and the shell as being four balls (Fig. 17). After a momentary pause to allow the effect to register with the audience, with an upward wave of the hand and a downward action of the left middle finger lodge the ball B in the shell A, vanishing it. Show your right hand empty and thrust it into the trousers pocket, palm one ball, and bring out the other ball and shell together between the thumb and forefinger.

With a wave of the right hand pull the ball out of the shell with the middle finger and show two balls in that hand, taking care of the angles so that no part of the palmed ball becomes

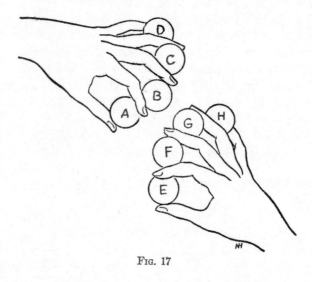

FIG. 17

visible in the operation. Then turn the hand over, closing the fingers, and drop the ball F back into the shell; the spectators, seeing the other solid ball in the palm of the hand, imagine that the ball has simply changed its position. Transfer this last ball to B in the left hand.

The position now is this: You have four balls in the left hand, one being covered with a shell; and in the right hand a ball E, also covered with a shell. Now double this ball and show six balls in the two hands.

Move the right hand up to the mouth and pretend to put the ball at F into it, really pulling it back into the shell E. Make a gesture of swallowing the ball, first pushing out your cheek with the tip of the tongue; then, with the three free fingers of the right hand, recover the last ball from the vest. Place this ball between the second and third fingers of the right hand at G; with the third and fourth fingers take the ball B from the left hand, making the position of the balls as follows: in the left hand a ball and shell at A, a solid ball at C and another at D; in the right hand a ball and shell at E, a solid ball at G and another at H.

The final movement is to lift, simultaneously, the balls from the shells with the middle fingers of each hand, under cover of the usual turn of the hands. A more effective climax for an exit —four balls in each hand—can hardly be wished for.

II. GOLF BALLS

The manipulation of golf balls is a still more recent innovation. It was the happy thought of Mr. Henry Gordien, the clever Minneapolis magician, of making the balls of soft rubber that brought them into their own. Mr. L. Ireland adopted the idea, added the double clinging shell feature, and worked out clever routines with the balls thus prepared, thereby presenting the profession with one of the best tricks in the whole field of sleight of hand. These rubber balls are an exact imitation of the real article: the surface will neither crack nor peel and can be cleaned when necessary; the clinging nature of the rubber makes their handling a matter of ease and pleasure; their small size facilitates manipulations; and the use of the two shells, which can be made to adhere to the ball, permitting it to be thrown in the air safely, makes possible some astonishing effects.

All the sleights and manipulations that have been explained in the preceding section in connection with billiard balls are applicable to golf balls; there are, however, certain sleights which can be done only with golf balls. These will be explained first.

1. VANISH FROM THE BACK OF THE RIGHT FINGERS

Stand with your left side to the front, the right arm extended, the fingers pointing almost directly to the rear, the ball resting on the backs of the fingers near their tips, the hand palm downwards. Bring the left hand over, holding it vertically, the thumb downwards and the fingers joined, the back of the hand to yourself and the spectators (Fig. 18). Encircle the right wrist with the thumb and fingers, and slide the hand outwards as if to grasp the ball. As soon as it is hidden by the left hand, bend the two middle fingers of the right hand; grip the ball by its sides between the first and fourth fingers; pass the bent fingers above the ball; extend them and immediately bend all the fingers inward, press-

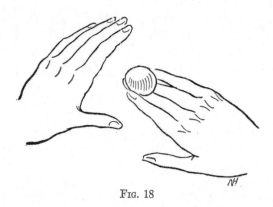

Fig. 18

ing the ball into the palm. Grip the ball in the palm and at once stretch the fingers out again. The whole movement must be completed before the left hand reaches the tips of the right fingers, from which it is then carried away, puffed out as if it held the ball. Complete the vanish in the usual way.

Instead of placing the ball on the back of the right hand with the left, it is much more graceful to hold it in the right hand, toss it in the air, turn the hand, and catch it in the desired position. The transference from the back of the hand to the palm must be done rapidly, and this move, while very difficult with a billiard ball, is comparatively easy with a golf ball.

2. Secret Transfer from One Hand to the Other

Stand with your right side to the front, a golf ball in the regular palm in the right hand, the right forefinger pointing to and almost touching the palm of the left hand—which you hold vertically, the thumb upwards and the fingers joined. Close the last three fingers of the right hand on the palm and grip the ball between the tips of the third and fourth fingers (Fig. 19). Make a turn to the right and, as the left hand passes in front of the right, rapidly extend the last three fingers of the latter and place the ball in the palm of the left hand (Fig. 20). At the end of the turn the left forefinger points to the right palm and

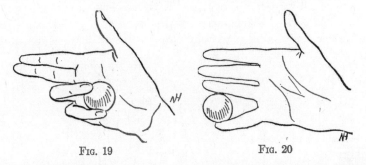

FIG. 19   FIG. 20

the ball is palmed in the left hand, the last three fingers closed on it in readiness to repeat the move in the reverse way under cover of a turn to the left. This is one of the most useful sleights; it must be done with equal facility with either hand.

3. TRANSFER OF THE BALL FROM ONE HAND TO THE OTHER, USING BOTH SIDES OF THE HANDS

Stand facing the audience, the hands at the height of the chin, the backs to the front, the fingers separated and pointing upwards, the little fingers about six inches apart and about a foot in front of the face (Fig. 21).

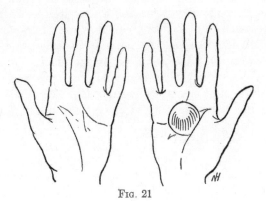

FIG. 21

To place the ball on the back of the left hand so that the palms of the hands can be shown, bring the hands together, one against the other, with the left hand partly in front so that the palmed ball is applied to the hollow which lies below the back of the left thumb fork between the tendons of the thumb and first finger; hold it at this spot with the tip of the right thumb. Separate the hands, the palms now to the front, by the length of the right thumb and place the tip of the left thumb in the fork of the right thumb (Fig. 22).

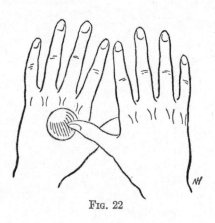

FIG. 22

To pass the ball back to the palm of the right hand, incline the hands toward one another; turn the right hand a little in advance of the left; and bring it down to take the ball, supported by the thumb up to that moment, in its palm. Then turn the hands on one another, bringing their backs to the front, and move them apart to their original positions. The move can be repeated. It should be done rather quickly and without dwelling on the position when the palms are to the front.

Properly done the sleight is a good one with golf balls; but unfortunately many operators use it with billiard balls, with the inevitable result that the spectators on the sides see the ball.

4. To Make a Ball Multiply in the Air

This surprising result is brought about by very simple means but requires careful execution. Stand with your right side to the front and hold the ball and shell between the thumb and first finger, the shell to the front. Pull the ball free from the shell and toss both together into the air, giving them an inward spin as they leave the hand by jerking the forefinger and wrist toward the body. The movement is hard to describe but is practically the same as the return spin one gives to a hoop to make it return after being thrown out. The spin will keep the shell in the same plane, its convex side to the front, and it will separate from the ball at the top of the flight as if the ball had suddenly become two balls. Catch the ball in the right hand and the shell in the left.

The shell should first be squeezed tightly on the ball, so that both can be tossed and caught several times before the shell is loosened. To complete the illusion a second ball should be palmed in the left hand, so that it can be squeezed tightly into the shell when the latter is caught. Two solid balls are then shown, one in each hand.

5. Transfer of the Shell, Held Between the Thumb and Finger, to the Rear Finger Hold

Because of the small size of the shell it can be held in the front finger grip and the thumb grip (Fig. 23), and also in the

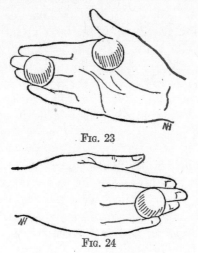

Fig. 23

Fig. 24

same positions at the back of the hand (Fig. 24). The movements required for utilizing these holds are very similar to those with a coin. I shall describe one vanish only.

Stand with your left side to the spectators, the right arm half extended to the right, the palm of the hand to the front; and hold the shell—its convex side to the onlookers, who suppose it

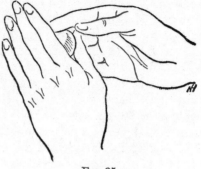

FIG. 25

to be a solid ball—between the tips of the thumb and middle finger. Bring the left hand over, its back to the front; pass its thumb under and behind the shell; and place the fingers in front,

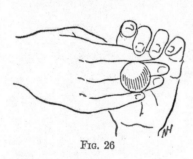

FIG. 26

holding them close together as if to take the ball (Fig. 25). As soon as the left hand hides the shell, grip its sides between the first and fourth fingers of the right hand; bend the two middle fingers underneath it and extend them in front of it—thus making the shell revolve to the back of the fingers, which retain it in the rear finger hold (Fig. 26).

Move the left hand away, its fingers puffed out as if holding the supposed ball, crumbling them preparatory to the usual vanish. Hold the right hand stationary for a moment or two, to allow the inside of the hand to be seen empty; then drop it to the side, letting it go behind the hip for an instant; in that instant reverse the shell to the front of the hand, turn to the left, and bring the hand up with its forefinger pointing to the left hand as that hand completes the vanish and is shown empty.

1. Production of Four Balls Without Using the Shell

Preparation. Prepare by placing three balls under your coat on the right-hand side, either in the cloth container or in single holders—whichever is preferred.

Method. After making several vanishes and recoveries with a single ball, apparently take it with the right hand but really leave it palmed in the left. Make the usual vanish with the right hand, turn the left side to the front, and produce the ball from the back of the left knee with the left hand. At the same moment steal the second ball with the right hand from the holder.

Turn to the left; show the visible ball in the left hand and point to it with the right forefinger, the hands assuming the position for the secret transfer described above. Execute the sleight in turning to the right and taking the visible ball between the right thumb and forefinger. Toss it into the air and catch it with the right hand, so that all parts of the ball and the hand can be seen.

Keeping your left side to the spectators, replace the ball in the left hand between the thumb and forefinger. Jerk the left hand forward suddenly; release the palmed ball and let it roll down between the first and second fingers, gripping it with the tips of those fingers. At the moment this second ball appears, steal the third ball from the holder with the right hand and palm it. Turn to the left, exhibit the two balls in the left hand, and point to them with the right forefinger.

The production of the third and fourth balls between the second and third fingers and the third and fourth is simply a repetition of the same movements, each ball being transferred to the left palm under cover of the turn to the right as the right hand takes the last ball that has appeared. Balls of four different colors can be used, and this enhances the effect.

2. Production of Four Balls, Using the Shell

Preparation. Prepare by placing a ball in each of your lower vest pockets.

Method. To begin, you show a ball and a shell in the right hand. Squeeze the shell on the ball tightly; toss and catch them as one ball. Take the ball between the right thumb and fore-finger at the junction of the ball and shell, the latter being nearest to the spectators. Turn the right hand to show the inside of the hand and take the opportunity to loosen the shell. Turn the hand over and pull the ball out of the shell sharply with the second finger, thus showing apparently two balls. Turn the hand again to show the other side, reversing the shell with the third finger, as already explained in the billiard-ball section of this chapter (see page 104).

Turn the hand, again bringing its back to the spectators, re-peating the move with the shell and third finger. Make a pre-tense of taking the upper ball with the left hand, really returning it to the shell with the second finger of the right hand under cover of the left. Remove this hand puffed out and pretend to snap the ball up your left sleeve. Show the hand empty and bring out the ball from your left vest pocket; this ball will appear to the audience to be the one which just passed up your sleeve.

Turn your left side to the front and place this ball between the right second and third fingers, keeping the second finger alongside the first finger. Reverse the right hand to show the palm; then turn it again and rapidly pull the ball from the shell into the space between the first and second fingers, thus showing, apparently, three solid balls.

In the same way as before, pretend to take the ball from be-tween the first and second fingers with the left hand, in reality pulling it back into the shell. Remove the left hand puffed out, and this time make a pretense of throwing the ball into the right sleeve. Show all parts of both hands, squeeze the shell onto its ball, and toss the balls from hand to hand. Replace the balls in the right hand in the same positions as before and, while the left hand takes the ball from the right vest pocket, loosen the ball from the shell. Place this third ball between the third and fourth fingers, show the inside of the right hand, turn it over, and once more pull the ball from the shell to its former position. You thus show four balls in the right hand; in reality, of course, three balls and a shell.

3. PRODUCTION OF THREE SOLID BALLS WITH ONE HAND

Preparation. Prepare by placing one ball, with two shells inclosing it, in one of your vest pockets and one solid ball in a holder on the right-hand side under your coat.

Method. After various passes with a third ball, vanish it from the left hand, retaining it palmed in the right. Show the left hand empty and with it take the double-shelled ball from the vest pocket. Toss it into the air with the left hand to prove it is solid and that you have one ball only. Hold it in the usual position between the left thumb and finger at the junction of the shells and, in turning the hand to show the interior, loosen the front shell—that nearest to the spectators. Show the palm of the hand; then, turning it to bring the back of the hand to the front, pull the ball and the second shell up into the space between the first and second fingers with the help of the second finger.

At the moment this second ball appears, steal the third solid ball from the holder with the right hand and hold it in the finger palm. You thus hold two balls in the right hand, one in the regular palm, and one in the finger palm.

Loosen the ball from the second shell with the third finger and, with an upward circular movement of the left hand, quickly pull the ball out of the second shell into the space between the second and third fingers, thus showing three balls.

Bring the right hand over to take the uppermost ball—the solid ball—and in so doing slip the two palmed balls into the shells, giving them a squeeze with the fingers so that they will adhere to the balls. Remove the uppermost ball with the right hand and toss it into the air, catching it again with the same hand. Then toss the other two balls, with the shells attached to them, from the left hand to the right, proving conclusively that three solid balls have been produced in one hand.

4. The Production of Eight Balls

The directions already given for the production of eight billiard balls in the two hands (see page 105) apply equally to golf balls, and will be found comparatively easy to do. Once the various sleights and passes have been mastered, the operator will find it an intriguing study to work out combinations of manipulations and productions to suit his own ideas. One warning must be sounded and this applies to the manipulation of all small objects. The one fault common to many performers is that of holding the hands too close to the body, with the result that when a turn to either side is made the article in use is completely hidden from the spectators. Of course, under these conditions you can do some wonderful moves; but they will be wonderful to yourself alone. Hold the hands well away from the body and make sure that everyone can see the effect of every move. Use rather deliberate actions and beware of fast moves; you can easily confuse the spectators. It is quite another thing to make your passes so smoothly and naturally that they will appear to be genuine.

III. SPONGE-BALL MANIPULATIONS

The quite recent use of balls made of sponge has introduced the entirely new principle of compressibility in the manipulation of balls. Two or even three sponge balls can be squeezed together to give them the appearance of one ball only, and the application of this principle has led to the invention of a number of novel effects. For close, intimate work in the parlor or club there are few tricks to compare with a good routine of sponge-ball manipulations.

We will consider first the materials, then the sleights, and finally the tricks and routines for which sponge balls are necessary.

THE MATERIALS

The balls must be made from very soft, natural sponge; the artificial rubber sponges are unsuitable, not being sufficiently compressible. Different sizes of balls, from three-fourths of an inch to two inches in diameter are used, according to the requirements of the several routines. Four balls of the two-inch variety and three of the three-quarter-inch size will be found sufficient for most purposes. The best way to make them is to cut a good-quality soft sponge into squares of about the sizes required, then clip off the corners and the angles with sharp scissors to make them spherical. There is no need to have them perfectly round, but all the balls of each set should be about the same size. Sponge balls can also be obtained at the magic stores.

1. THE THUMB GRIP

The ball is held by clipping a small part of the surface in the fork at the base of the thumb (Fig. 1). To place it in this position, hold the ball between the first joints of the forefinger and thumb; bend the forefinger, bringing its tip against the top of

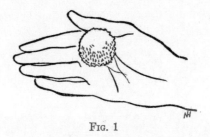

FIG. 1

the ball; and push it into the fork of the thumb, gripping it there by pressing the lower joint of the thumb against it. Immediately afterward extend the thumb to its former position.

2. THE FINGER PALM

In this case the ball is held against the palm of the hand with the second, third, and fourth fingers, the forefinger being stretched out. To place the ball in this position, grip a small portion of

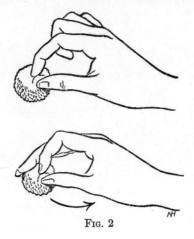

FIG. 2

the surface between the thumb and forefinger (Fig. 2), extend the other three fingers over the ball, grip it with the tips of the second and third fingers, close the last three fingers and carry the ball against the palm of the hand—holding it there by the pressure of these fingers, which retain their grip on the ball. The thumb and the forefinger remain stretched out.

To use this method of palming to vanish a ball, take it between the thumb and forefinger of the right hand and show it. Move the right hand toward the left hand, held palm upwards;

Fig. 3

place the ball at the roots of the left fingers and close them slowly. As soon as they hide it, grip it with the tips of the right second and third fingers; close them, carrying the ball against the palm of the hand. Retain it there by pressure of these fingers and at the same moment complete the closing of the left fingers on the right thumb and forefinger, now empty. Withdraw the thumb and then slowly pull away the forefinger (Fig. 3).

3. The Fist Vanish

Clench the left fist, thumb upwards, and place a ball on top of it (Fig. 4). With the right fist and second fingers apparently push the ball right into the fist; in reality, close the left second finger tightly and compress the ball into the smallest possible compass against it, hold the ball thus compressed by bending the left forefinger around it, and move the thumb over the top. To all appearances the ball has been pushed into the fist; but, if the pressure of the forefinger is relaxed and the thumb moved aside, the ball will instantly spring up to its original position on the top of the fist.

The sleight is used thus: Place a ball, A, on top of the left fist and push it down as explained in the preceding paragraph. Pick up a second ball, B, show it, and apparently place it on the top of the left fist; but at the moment that the right hand arrives over the fist, palm B in the right hand and, at the same instant, allow A to spring

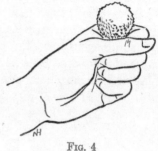

Fig. 4

up. Properly timed the illusion is perfect, and when A is pushed down the spectators think there are two balls in the fist. The procedure can be continued until four balls have been pushed in apparently, when in reality the hand contains one ball only.

Skillful performers apply this sleight to solid balls. In such case, instead of the ball retaking its place on top of the fist automatically by reason of its elasticity, it is squeezed up by the pressure of the left second and first fingers—a much more difficult operation.

4. To Pick Up and Hold Two Balls as One

With a ball palmed in the thumb palm. We will call the palmed ball A; pick up a second ball, B, by placing the joined fingers over it, lifting it with the thumb underneath; close the fingers on both balls, bringing them together; then bend the thumb and press its tip against A, squeezing A onto B and at the same time opening the fingers (Fig. 5). The two balls will thus

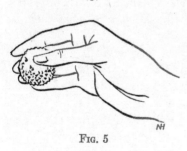

Fig. 5

be held as one between the thumb and the second joints of the second and third fingers.

With the ball held in the finger palm. Call the ball in the palm A and the ball to be added to it B. As you reach out to pick up B with the right hand, extend the second and third fingers, carrying A with them, over B until the inner side of A touches the outer side of B; then press the thumb against the inner side of B, squeeze the two balls tightly together, turn the hand over, and show the two balls as one.

The foregoing are the only special sleights required in the manipulation of sponge balls. The ordinary sleights, already explained in connection with billiard balls (see Chapter V), can also be used when the operator becomes accustomed to the different feel of the sponge balls.

TRICKS AND ROUTINES

The routines which follow will serve to show the possibilities of sponge-ball manipulation. When the student has learned the sleights and has become accustomed to the novel technique required in handling the sponge balls, he will have little difficulty in working out combinations for himself.

1. PASS WITH TWO BALLS

Show two balls and begin by offering them for examination. Let one be chosen; take it and really place it in your left hand, with exactly the same action as when you palm a ball. Pick up the second ball with the right hand and put it on the palm of a spectator's hand; keep your thumb pressed on it; slip your fingers under his and, with them, close his hand on the ball. This is merely a feint, and you take the balls again and put them on the table.

Pick up one ball and put it in your left hand; this time, however, you palm the ball by the finger palm, in the right hand. Close the left hand, keeping it puffed out a little. Pick up the second ball, adding the palmed ball to it as in the second part of sleight 4. Show the two as one and place them on the spectator's hand in the manner described. In this way you hold the balls securely with your thumb while you close the spectator's hand with your fingers, thus preventing a premature expansion of the two balls.

It only remains to order the ball to pass from your hand to the spectator's; pretend to throw it, opening the left hand and showing it empty. The spectator opens his hand and two balls roll out.

2. PASS WITH THREE BALLS

Have a third ball under the vest and fourth ball in the right-hand coat pocket. Take advantage of the surprise caused by the appearance of the two balls in the spectator's hand (see first pass) to steal the third ball from the vest, finger palming it in the right hand. Pick up one of the two balls with that hand, adding the palmed ball to it, and, as in the preceding pass, put the two balls as one in the spectator's hand. Take the remaining ball and pretend to place it in your left hand, really palming it. Command the ball to pass from your hand to his, show your hand empty, and again the spectator finds he holds two balls.

Announce that you will use three balls. Thrust your right hand into the coat pocket and bring out the fourth ball, keeping the other ball palmed. Place one ball in the spectator's hand. Take a second ball, adding the palmed ball to it; place the two as one with the first one in the spectator's hand, closing it with your fingers as before. Take the last ball and feign to put it in your left hand, really palming it. Order the ball to pass; open your left hand, showing it empty, and three balls roll out of the spectator's hand when he opens it.

3. PASS WITH SMALL BALLS

Have three small balls in your right-hand coat pocket.

Pick up one ball, adding the palmed ball; show the two as one and place them in your left hand, closing the fingers on the balls. Take another with the right hand and push it into the left fist. Pick up the third ball as you say, "This one I will put in my pocket"; do this, but in reality palm it and bring it out again hidden in the hand. Open the left hand and roll out three balls.

Once more pick up a ball and drop it openly into the left hand. Seize a second ball, adding the palmed ball, and put the two as one in the left hand, closing the fingers on two balls apparently but really on three. Put the third ball in the pocket, dropping it this time and finger palming a small ball. Roll out three balls from the left hand.

Pick up one with the right hand, adding the small ball, and put the two as one in your left hand. Take another ball and push it into the same hand. Place the remaining ball in the pocket, dropping it and finger palming a second small ball. Open the left hand and roll out two large balls and one small. You have been gradually increasing the pace and now you work quite fast.

Repeat the same procedure to get one large ball and two small balls in the left hand. Pick up the large ball, put it in your pocket, and finger palm the third small ball. Then roll out one large ball and two small ones from the left hand.

Pick up one small ball, adding the palmed small ball to it, and place them in the left hand as one ball; then place the second small ball with them. Pick up the last large ball, put it in your pocket, and bring the hand out empty. Roll out three small balls from the left hand and show both hands empty.

4. VANISHING THE THREE SMALL BALLS

Clench the left fist, holding it thumb upwards. Place a small ball on it and apparently push it right into the fist, really executing sleight 3. Pick up a second ball and, in pretending to place it on top of the fist, palm it and release the first ball, letting it return to the top of the fist. Hold the palmed ball with the right little finger only against the palm.

Bring the right hand over to push the ball into the fist, nip it off with the tips of the second and third fingers, bend them into the palm, and push the forefinger only into the left fist. Pick up the third ball with the thumb and forefinger and put it in your pocket, dropping the two palmed balls with it. Open the left hand and show both hands empty.

5. COFFEE CUPS AND BALLS

An impromptu series of cup and ball passes can be worked very easily with three coffee cups and four sponge balls.

Palm one ball and lay the other three on the table. Show the empty coffee cups and place them in a row, mouth downwards. Put a ball on each cup. Clench the left fist; take the ball from the first cup and push it into the fist, using sleight 3; then lift the cup with the right hand to show there is nothing under it, and release the palmed ball in putting the cup down. Take the ball from the second cup; pretend to place it on the left fist, palming it and letting the first ball spring up in its place. Lift the second cup, showing it empty, and load the palmed ball under it in the usual way. Push the ball back into the fist as before. Proceed in exactly the same way to load the third ball under the third cup.

The position now is this—there is one ball under each cup and the fourth ball is on the left fist, which the spectators think contains two balls. Slope the fist and let the ball roll off onto the table as if by accident. Pick it up with the right hand and pretend to push it into the left fist, in reality palming it in the right hand. Hold the left fist over the first cup, order one ball to pass, and open the little finger. Move the hand over the second cup, order the second ball to pass through the cup, and open the third finger. Repeat the procedure with the third cup and the second finger. Keep the first finger and thumb closed for a moment or two; then throw them open, proving the hand quite empty. Lift the cups, revealing the balls beneath them, and load the palmed ball under one of the cups in readiness for a new move.

Other passes will readily suggest themselves; indeed, sponge balls are excellent to use while the necessary skill is being developed for the execution of the real cups and balls feats.

IV. THE CUPS AND BALLS

"The Noble and Antique Plaie of the Cuppes and Balles" is well called the king of tricks. It has had a run not of hundreds but of thousands of years, a run that appears likely to continue indefinitely. The reason is not far to seek. The trick has everything that a perfect feat of magic should have—a simple plot, appearances, vanishes and reappearances, changes of place and size, multiplications, amusing interludes, and an astounding climax—and all this with the use of the simplest possible materials: three goblets and some balls.

It has been said that no one should consider himself a magician if he cannot work the cups and balls, which is not strictly true; the converse, however, does hold good—anyone who can perform the cups and balls skillfully is a good magician. The reason that the trick is passed up by many is probably because the explanations of it are cluttered up with too many passes and sleights and interminable routines, with the result that neophytes are frightened away at the very start. The fact is that the trick is simple and direct; the indispensable sleights are but few and not difficult. On the other hand, a successful presentation does call for a ready flow of patter and, even to a greater extent than in most conjuring tricks, the action must be fitted to the word and the word to the action.

The necessary materials will be considered first, then the sleights and flourishes, and finally the routines.

THE MATERIALS

1. THE CUPS

Three of these are required; they should be about four and one-half inches in height and three inches in diameter at the mouth. These cups can be obtained at any magic store.

2. THE BALLS

Balls made of cork, blackened and about three-fourths of an inch in diameter, are still the best for general use. If the operator has very dry hands it is a good plan to soak the balls in glycerine for several hours, wipe them carefully, and let them dry. One application will last for a long time. The number of balls required varies with the routines used.

3. THE MAGIC WAND

This is not prepared in any way but should be considered indispensable, by the beginner at any rate. Its use lends authority to the trick; it aids in concealing the balls, by giving a pretext for closing the hand; finally it covers those awkward moments when the performer does not know what to do with his hands.

4. A SMALL TABLE WITH A THICK CLOTH

If the latter is not obtainable, an excellent substitute is a thick, white, Turkish towel spread over the table, which allows not only for ease in picking up the balls but also for displaying them to the best advantage.

5. GIMMICKS

Several double-headed thumbtacks, made by soldering the heads of two thumbtacks together (Fig. 1), and also several safety pins with ordinary pins soldered on the closed ends (Fig. 2) will be found very useful.

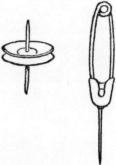

6. LARGE BALLS

Three large balls or, as is generally preferred now, an orange, an apple, and a potato—or any other suitable fruit or vegetable small enough to enter the mouth of a cup and large enough to be wedged inside when forced toward the bottom.

FIGS. 1 and 2

THE SLEIGHTS

1. THE FINGER PALM

The ball is held at the base of the little finger by bending the finger slightly (Fig. 3). To place the ball in this position, hold

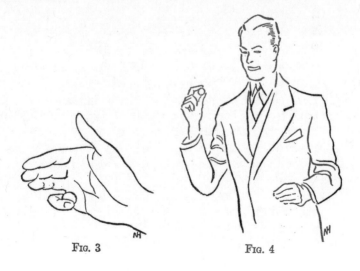

FIG. 3   FIG. 4

it between the first joint of the thumb and the second joint of the forefinger, the palm of the hand to the front, the arm extended at about the height of the shoulder (Fig. 4).

In turning the hand palm downwards roll the ball with the thumb over the first three fingers to the base of the little finger and bend that finger to retain the ball, immediately replacing the thumb in its original position. When executed perfectly the sleight becomes one movement only and is done in a flash, but no attempt at speed should be made at the outset. The old adage "Make haste slowly" applies with particular force to all sleights. To produce the ball from this palm you have simply to reverse the movements of the thumb and the fingers.

2. THE REGULAR PALM

Hold the ball between the tips of the thumb and forefinger and roll it with the thumb over the tips of the second and third

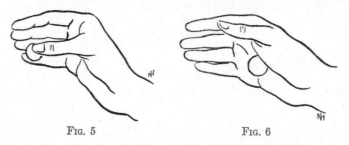

FIG. 5   FIG. 6

fingers until it arrives at the tips of the third and fourth fingers, which separate slightly to receive it (Fig. 5) and then grip it. The instant the ball is thus held, move the thumb back to its first position against the first finger and, simultaneously, close the third and fourth fingers into the palm, carrying the ball with them and pressing it into the regular palming position (Fig. 6).

In this case also the ball is produced at the fingertips by making exactly the same movements of the fingers and the thumb in the reverse order.

These are the only methods of palming that are necessary; indeed, many skilled performers use the finger palm only, but there is a decided advantage in being able to vary one's methods. The regular palm permits the fingers to be separated when it is advisable to do so in order to throw the spectators off the track.

3. To Introduce a Ball Under One of the Cups

Three methods of doing this follow.

With the ball in the finger palm. Seize the cup with the thumb and forefinger (of the hand that holds the ball secretly) between the two projecting moldings, mouth downwards, and lift it to show that there is nothing under it. In setting the cup down again, a moment before its front edge reaches the table release the ball, which is then covered by the cup invisibly. The move is a very easy one, but great care must be taken to make it naturally without precipitation.

With the ball in the regular palm. Grasp the cup as in the preceding move, at the same moment bending the third and fourth

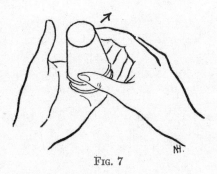

Fig. 7

fingers into the palm; grip the ball between the tips of these two fingers and, at the moment when you replace the cup on the table, extend them rapidly and leave the ball under the cup.

Using either method of palming the ball. (1) Show the ball in the right hand, in the correct position for executing the palm; move the hand toward the left hand, palming the ball in transit; place the tips of the thumb and first two fingers on the palm of the left hand, held half closed. Drop the left hand slightly, as if receiving the ball, and hold it with the fingers almost closed. Place the back of the left hand on the table and take a cup in the right hand. Put this mouth downwards on the palm of the left hand, opening the fingers in such a way that the spectators cannot see that the palm is empty. Slide the cup over the palm and the extended fingers, the nails touching the table, and onto the table as if carrying the ball along with it (Fig. 7). The move should be made slowly with the utmost simplicity and naturalness.

(2) In this case the ball is apparently deposited directly under the cup. Show the ball in the right hand and, in moving the hand toward a cup, palm it; lift the cup with the left hand just enough to allow the thumb and forefinger to be placed on the table below it, as if to deposit the ball; tilt the cup a little forward so that its front edge will reach the table first; remove the right hand and put the cup down with the left hand. Here again there must be no hurry, but an exact imitation of the real deposit of a ball under the cup.

4. To Introduce a Ball Between Two Cups

Hold a ball palmed in the finger palm in the right hand; lift a cup with that hand by the rim between the thumb and forefinger and, in placing it over another cup, give the hand a slight upward jerk, at the same time releasing the ball and bringing the cup down on top of the other cup rather quickly. The ball will thus be lodged on the top of the lower cup.

5. To Produce a Ball from the End of the Wand

With a ball palmed in the finger palm in the right hand, take hold of the wand with the same hand so that its lower end protrudes from the little-finger side of the hand. Seize this end with the left hand and slide the right hand along the wand to the other end, the back of the hand toward the spectators. At the precise moment that the right hand leaves the upper end of the wand, produce the ball at the thumb and fingers as if it had been squeezed out of the wand. To apparently return the ball into the wand, simply reverse the movements.

6. To Load a Large Ball or Fruit Under a Cup

In lifting a cup with the right hand to show a ball just passed under it, turn slightly to the left and with the left hand take the large ball or fruit from the left coat pocket. Fix your whole attention on the ball just uncovered; put the cup in your left hand, which comes up to meet it—its back to the front and capping the ball or fruit, which you then retain in the cup with the help of the little finger. Leave the cup in the left hand, and with the right hand quickly pick up the ball just uncovered and show it. In the meantime with the fingers of the left hand force the ball upwards, wedge it in the cup, and put the cup mouth upwards on the table.

Load the second cup in the same way but, for the third one, reverse the movements of the hands; that is to say, lift the cup with the left hand and load it with the right hand, which has taken the necessary article from the right coat pocket. The position, then, is this—there are three small balls visible on the table and three cups, supposed to be empty, mouth upwards. Pocket the three balls and turn the cups mouth downwards, lightly in order not to dislodge their contents. Raise the two outer cups with the right and left hands, as you remark, "Nothing here, nor here. You see the cups are really empty at last"; replace them with a slight tap to free the large ball or fruit. "And nothing here," you continue as you lift the middle cup and put it down in the same way. Finally pronounce your mystic formula; lift the cups quickly, revealing the contents, and lay them down with the mouths toward the spectators.

THE FLOURISHES

1. To Make One Cup Pass Through the Other

Take two cups, mouths upwards, one in each hand. Bring the cup in the right hand directly over and six or eight inches above that in the left hand. Move the right hand down sharply, releasing its cup so that it falls into the other. The shock will cause the second cup to fall from the left fingers, which release it and catch the first cup in exactly the same position, so that the first cup takes the place of the second in the most natural manner. Continue the downward movement of the right hand and catch the second cup before it reaches the table.

2. To Push the Wand Through the Bottom of a Cup

Hold the cup mouth downwards in the left hand and push the wand into it with the right hand, knocking the end against the bottom several times. Then turn the cup mouth upwards, holding it perpendicularly by the rim between the left thumb and forefinger. Insert the end of the wand in the fork of the thumb, between the side of the cup and the hand, and push it down until it protrudes below the cup. Take hold of this end with the right hand and pull the wand away downwards. Smartly done it appears that the wand has passed through the bottom of the cup (Fig. 8).

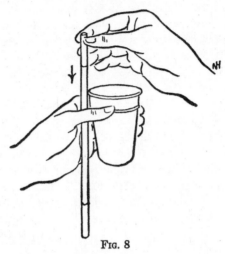

FIG. 8

3. To Show that a Cup Is Deeper Inside than Out

Hold the cup mouth downwards and push the wand into it as if to measure its depth with the thumb; but, in fact, hold the wand obliquely so that its end touches the bottom on the side opposite to the right thumb. Mark the spot on the wand with the thumb, withdraw the wand, and apply it to the outside of the cup—its end will protrude slightly over the bottom. This can be accentuated by secretly sliding the tip of the thumb a fraction of an inch further down in withdrawing the wand from the cup.

4. To Vanish a Ball Placed Between Two Cups

The three cups, which we will call A, B, C, being turned mouth downwards, place a ball on A, cover it with B, and over both place C. To prove that the ball has vanished, take hold of A with the left hand and lift all three, sloping them a little toward the front by inserting the left fingers into A. Lift off C and place it mouth downwards on the table; lift off B with a little upward jerk of the hands and clap it down on top of C—the ball being carried along with the cup is now between C and B and appears to have vanished. Clap A on top of the other two and repeat the movements *ad libitum*.

The name given to this flourish, "Galloping Post," arose from the sound made by its rapid repetition, which resembles that made by the hoofs of a galloping horse.

1. PREPARATION

Set the three cups mouth downwards on the table in a row; one ball on a thumbtack gimmick under the table about the

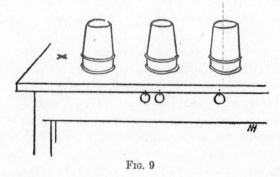

FIG. 9

middle; three balls on similar gimmicks under the rear edge of the table, two of them close together (Fig. 9); an apple and an orange in the left outside coat pocket, a potato in the right outside coat pocket; one ball on a pin gimmick under the edge of the coat on the right-hand side; the magic wand in hand.

2. FLOURISHES

Begin by calling attention to the wand and the cups; show apparently that the cups are deeper inside than outside; then pass the wand through the bottom of one, and lay the wand on the table so that its end protrudes over the rear edge of the table immediately above the single ball impaled on the gimmick. Execute the passing of one cup through the other; then place the cup in the right hand on the table and take the wand in that hand, stealing the ball in the process. In the meantime hold up the cup in the left hand, calling the general attention to it. Place this cup on the table.

3. Production of the Balls

Arrange the three cups in a row, mouth downwards; produce the palmed ball from the wand, show it, and lay the wand down on the table.

Place the ball in the left hand with the right; pick up cup A; and scrape the ball off the left palm onto the table, using exactly the same action as in sleight 3, "Using either method of palming the ball (1)" (see page 127).

Steal the ball from the edge of the coat and produce it from the wand; feign to put it under cup B, really palming it as in sleight 3, "Using either method of palming the ball (2)" (see page 127).

Again produce the palmed ball from the wand and feign to place it under cup C, palming it as before. Put the wand down with its end protruding over the edge of the table just above the two balls on the gimmicks. Casually put your hands in your pockets and drop the palmed ball as you ask, "How would you take a ball from under a cup? Like this?" Lift cup A with the left hand, pick up the ball with the right hand, and put the cup down with the left. "That would be very easy," you say. "Watch how I do it." Lift cup A with the left hand and feign to put the ball under it with the right hand, palming it.

Pick up the wand with the right hand, at the same time stealing the two balls from under the edge of the table; keep the three balls concealed by holding the wand in the hand. Make circular passes with the wand over cup A, tap it with the wand, and call attention to an imaginary ball on its tip. Pretend to remove this but really roll one of the three balls to the tips of the thumb and forefinger as you say, "Here's one"; put the ball on the table and knock the cup over with the wand, "And nothing here."

Repeat the same maneuver to produce the balls from cups B and C. Replace the cups in line; put two balls to one side of the table and the third in front of cup C.

4. A Ball Passes from Cup to Cup

Feign to put the ball under cup C, palming it. Lift B to show there is nothing there and replace it, leaving the ball under it. Lift cup A, showing nothing there either, and replace it. Pretend to take the ball from cup C on the tip of the wand and pass it under cup B.

Lift C, showing it empty; then lift B with the left hand, showing the ball, and pick it up with the right hand. Feign to replace the ball under B and lift A to show there is nothing under it, at the same time releasing the ball as you put the cup down. Repeat the passes with the wand; lift the cups to prove that the journey from B to C has been made.

Feign to put the ball under a cup and cover the cup with the other two, retaining the ball palmed. Strike the cups with the wand and lift all three, showing that the ball has vanished. "It's gone right through the table," you say as you pass your right hand under the table and bring up the palmed ball as if taken from below.

Feign to place the ball in the left hand and from there under A, palming it. Lift B and jerk the ball up as you cover A with B, leaving the ball between the two cups. Place C over the other two.

Order the ball to mount one story through the bottom of A. Lift all three and show that the ball has gone, then take off B and C and show the ball on A.

Again pretend to place the ball under A; cover A with B; then, in placing C over these two, jerk the ball upwards so that it arrives between B and C. Order the ball to go up two flights, lift all three to prove it has departed, then take off C and show the ball on B.

Realign the cups. Pretend to put the ball under A; cover this with B, jerking the ball up between A and B; then place C over both. Now execute flourish 4, "Galloping Post," rapidly to prove that the ball has vanished.

Place the cups in line and let the ball drop invisibly under B by jerking the hands upwards slightly as you lift B off and put it down rather quickly. Pretend to catch the missing ball from the air on the tip of the wand and pass it under B. Lift

B and show the ball. Lift A and C to show there is nothing under them.

Pretend to place the ball in the left hand; palm it in the right and take the wand in that hand. Press the left hand, palm downwards, on the table over the spot where a ball is impaled on a gimmick underneath. Open the hand slowly and press it flat as if to force the ball through the table. Lift the left hand and show it empty. Pass that hand under the table, retrieve the ball from the gimmick, and bring it up into view.

You now have three balls visible on the table and one ball palmed in the right hand.

5. MULTIPLICATION

Place the balls in line and cover each with a cup. Lift A, and in putting it down leave the palmed ball under it. Pick up the ball just uncovered and put it in your pocket, really palming it.

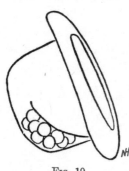

Raise B and load the palmed ball in replacing it. Take the second ball; apparently put it in your pocket, but palm it as before. Lift C and leave the palmed ball under it, again pretending to place the third ball in the pocket but really palming it. Return to A and repeat the same maneuver.

Continue this apparent multiplication for five rounds of the three cups, gradually increasing the pace until for the final round you are working as rapidly as you possibly can. In putting the last ball in your pocket, drop it there, seize the orange, and work up to the climax production of fruit, exactly as described in sleight 6, by loading the apple, the orange, and the potato into the cups and finally revealing them.

FIG. 10

A bowler hat with a compartment holding fifteen balls can be used as a receptacle for the balls as they are produced and apparently placed in it. A half-double bottom provides the necessary hiding place (Fig. 10) and, if the hat is turned quickly to the position shown in the figure, this will never be noticed.

When the hat is turned over the opposite way, the balls will roll out.

It is essential that the trick be accompanied throughout by lively patter, and it must not be dragged out; four or five minutes is ample time to devote to it. Finally, the omission of the use of the wand and the flourishes detracts very greatly from the effect.

VI

EXPERIMENTS WITH EGGS

"As innocent as a new-laid egg."
William Schwenck Gilbert—Engaged.

THE magician, not being quite so innocent as he professes to be, seldom uses new-laid eggs; in fact, only on such occasions as he finds it necessary to break the egg to prove that it is real. For ordinary purposes artificial eggs of ivorine or celluloid (obtainable from the magic shops) are preferable. Even better than these are real eggs prepared by having the contents blown out, the shells being then strengthened by pasting several layers of white paper strips on them. When the strips are thoroughly dry the surface is rubbed smooth with fine emery paper, with the result that the finished article looks like an egg, will not break if accidentally dropped, and will last for an indefinite time.

I. MANIPULATIONS

The manipulation of eggs follows closely that of balls. As the sleights already described for balls are applicable to eggs, it is not necessary to repeat them. Because of the difference in shape some little practice will be necessary to handle them neatly, but the adept in ball manipulation will have little difficulty. The series of moves which follow will serve as an example from which other routines can be arranged.

Four eggs are required and they should be rather small, since one has to be retained in the mouth temporarily. Prepare by placing one egg in the vest pocket on the right-hand side and two more under the vest on the left side. Presuming that you have changed some article into an egg, proceed with the following moves:

(1) Pretend to place the egg in your left hand, vanish it, and produce it from your left elbow.

Note that when vanishing the egg the hand must not be opened immediately and shown empty. Close the left fingers to the same extent that they would be if they really held the egg; move the hand upwards diagonally to the left; close the fingers on the palm slowly, working them as if rubbing the egg to nothing; then open them one by one, beginning with the little finger.

Again, in producing the egg from any particular spot apply the hand there; then draw it back so that the egg appears at the fingertips. Seize the egg between the thumb and fingers, and pull it away as if a slight effort is required to remove it.

(2) Place the egg in the mouth and move the hand upwards as if forcing it in; really take it in the palm and at once push out the cheek with the tongue, strike the swelling with the tips of the fingers, and pretend to swallow the egg. Place both hands flat on the stomach; then turn up the edge of the vest, at the same time pushing the egg up under it with the right little finger. Hold the egg in view for a moment or two by pressing the right hand against the vest; then let it fall into the left hand.

(3) Repeat the swallowing sleight and produce the egg from behind the right ear.

(4) Place the egg in the mouth with exactly the same movements as before, retain it there, and squeeze the egg out of the right vest pocket with the right hand.

(5) Pretend to place the egg in the left hand, slap that hand against the outside of the left knee, and produce the palmed egg from behind the right knee.

(6) Pretend to take the egg with the left hand; place this hand behind the back, strike it against the middle of the back, and bring it forward empty. Then take the egg from the top of the vest with the right hand.

(7) Pretend to put the egg in the left sleeve; raise the left arm and shake it as if letting the egg slide down to the left shoulder; wiggle the shoulders and let the right arm hang down, allowing the sleeve to come down over the right wrist as far as possible. Then raise the right hand, back to front, toward the left; with the left hand take hold of the bottom of the right sleeve and draw it over the egg; then let the egg roll into sight

at the tips of the right fingers. The effect is that the egg put into one sleeve rolls out of the other.

(8) Apparently place the egg in the left hand; bang that hand down on your head; instantly show the egg in your mouth between your teeth (Fig. 1), and at the same moment palm an egg from the vest in the left hand.

FIG. 1

(9) Pretend to take the egg from the mouth with the right hand, really letting it slip back into the mouth, and show the palmed egg.

(10) Take the egg from the right hand with the left and transfer the second egg from the left palm to the right palm. Place the egg on a plate with the left hand. Tap stomach with right fingertips and show egg in mouth; at the same moment palm the remaining egg from the vest.

(11) Repeat moves 9 and 10; place the second egg on the plate with the left hand.

(12) Tap stomach; show egg between the teeth and pretend to take it with the right hand, showing the palmed egg; take egg with the left hand and put it on the plate.

(13) Tap stomach once more and show egg in the mouth, let it drop into the hand, and place it with the others. Adjust your vest with a smile of relief, as if you now felt more comfortable.

The moves are not difficult and if the routine is worked smoothly, without hesitation and without haste, the effect will be found all that can be desired. Patter is not necessary, but a light musical accompaniment should be used if possible.

II. TRICKS

1. PRODUCTION OF FOUR EGGS WITH THE USE OF THE HALF SHELL

The production of four eggs between the fingers with the aid of a half shell is made in exactly the same way as with billiard balls, to which reference should be made (see page 103). A little care is necessary in slipping the eggs into the shell, to prevent any sounds. Sets of four eggs and the half shell (Fig. 2) can be obtained at any magic shop.

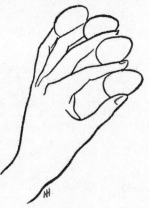

2. EGGS FROM A HANDKERCHIEF

1st Method. In this method an egg is suspended by a thread to the middle of one side of a handkerchief (Fig. 3). A borrowed hat is placed on the table, and the handkerchief is taken by the corners AB and

FIG. 2

stretched out over the hat; then, under pretense of turning back the sleeves, the handkerchief is laid down, the egg going into the hat and the rest falling on the table in front. The corners CD are then seized, and the handkerchief is again held up and

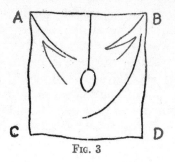

FIG. 3

stretched out; thus both sides have been shown. Once more it is laid down, this time for the sleeves to be pulled down again. The corners AB are again taken, and when the handkerchief is stretched out the egg is again brought behind it.

The handkerchief is now folded over the egg by taking AB in one hand and CD in the other. The opening of AB being held just over the hat and the corners CD being raised, the egg rolls out visibly into the hat. The handkerchief is again spread out by the corners AB and lifted by CD as before, and the process begins anew. Finally the thread is broken, the single egg is palmed, and the supposed contents of the hat thrown to the audience, who, preparing for an avalanche of eggs, are surprised when nothing at all comes out.

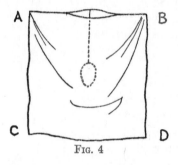

Fig. 4

2d Method. The trick is a good one, although rather well known. The improved method which follows puts a new complexion on it. In this case the handkerchief is a double one, with the edges sewn together all round except for about six inches in the middle of the side AB (Fig. 4). The egg is attached to the middle of this opening by a thread that does not reach quite halfway down. To begin with, the handkerchief is shown freely on both sides, crumpled up, and tossed in the air; then it is folded, the corners AB and CD together as before, and the egg is allowed to drop into the hat. Both sides are then shown as before, but the handkerchief is lifted by the corner A only; the other three corners hang down and the egg rests in the folds behind B, where the hand takes it and palms it in seizing the corner B. It is shown on both sides, well away from the hat; in folding it the egg is allowed to drop from the palm, and the production is made again. The action is continued as long as desired.

3d Method. A further improvement is the loading of a number of eggs into the hat before beginning the production from the handkerchief. For methods of loading, reference should be made to Chapter XV on hat loads.

3. Cigarette Paper Changed to an Egg

The trick is a very old one. Some twenty years ago it was revived by a magician who made a hit with it; it became the rage and every magician had to do it. Then it was forgotten again. Recently it was rediscovered, again it made a hit, and again every magician has to do it. This follow-the-leader complex is one of the great faults of magicians. It is a pity it is not more widely recognized that the secret and the mechanics of a trick are entirely a secondary matter. It is the presentation, the personality of the man behind it, that makes a trick successful. This trick is a case in point. Gracefully presented and perfectly handled, well timed and with appropriate music, it is a beautiful thing; otherwise it is just another trick.

Effect. A cigarette paper is shown; crumpled into a ball; bounced on a fan until it gradually swells into an egg—which is broken, proving it to be a real egg.

1st Method. The trick depends upon the substitution of the inner skin of an egg for the cigarette paper. This is generally done by having the prepared skin in the mouth and making the change in pretending to moisten the paper at the lips. There is no need to actually chew it; and again there is no absolute necessity for making the change at the mouth, which is not a particularly graceful gesture. The skin can be picked up behind the cigarette paper and the exchange made in rolling the paper into a ball. It can then be moistened by dipping it into a glass of water, and the cigarette paper can be dropped unnoticed when taking the fan.

The skin is then placed on the open fan and bounced; the air enters and it gradually assumes the shape of an egg. It is essential that this bouncing be done gracefully, in time with the music and not with stiff, awkward gestures. The real egg, which is to be substituted for the egg skin, is placed at the top of the outside left breast pocket. When the skin is fully distended, it is rolled from the fan onto the left hand, the fan is placed under the left arm and, in passing, the egg is squeezed out of the pocket into the right palm. The right hand takes the inflated skin and presses it against the side of the real egg, which is then shown and broken into a glass.

2d Method. This steal can be made perfectly with adequate practice, but the least hesitation ruins it. An easier method is to have the egg under the vest on the right-hand side. When the inflated skin is rolled off the fan, the right hand drops naturally to the bottom of the vest at the point where the egg lies hidden; the fan points to the left hand and all eyes are fixed on that hand, giving ample opportunity to take the real egg with the fingers of the right hand.

4. An Exposure and a Climax

Effect. A silk changes places with an egg and vice versa, the method is exposed, the spectators see how they have been fooled, and then the climax leaves them more in the dark than ever.

Accessories. A real egg, a hollow egg (Fig. 5), three small red silks, one large red silk, a bottomless glass, and an ordinary glass.

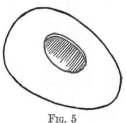

Fig. 5

Preparation. Roll one of the small red silks into a ball, one end protruding and the other tucked into a fold; place the large red silk on the table with the balled red silk on it hidden by a fold; put the hollow egg and a small red silk in the bottomless glass on the table; tuck the third red silk into your collar at the back and the real egg into your right trousers pocket at the top, the pocket itself being screwed up to hold it there.

Method. Stand with the table to your left; take the small red silk from the glass, show it, and throw it over your left shoulder; then remove the egg from the glass, show its good side, put it in your left hand; take the bottomless glass in your right hand, letting it stand on the palm, and put the egg into it. With the left hand pick up the large red silk, with the smaller one in its folds; with it cover the glass and the egg, at the same time letting the small silk drop in. Drape the large silk round the glass; lift both off the right hand, leaving the hollow egg in the right palm; and put the covered glass on the table.

With the right hand holding the hollow egg palmed, take the red silk from your shoulder and show it hanging from the finger-tips. Turn to the left and show the left hand empty. Bring it over to take the silk and turn to the right, making the change over with the egg; then show the right hand empty. Explain the changes of position that are to be made, bring the hands to-gether, wave them up and down, and gradually work the silk into the hollow egg.

When the whole of the silk is inside the egg, show it lying on the palm of the right hand; with the left hand remove the silk covering the glass, seize the corner of the balled silk and jerk it out to its full length. Display the articles thus, the egg in one hand and the silk in the other. Throw the silk over your left shoulder.

Now proceed with the exposure. Take the egg in the left hand, turn it and show the hole and the silk inside; at the same moment hook the real egg out of the trousers pocket with the right thumb and palm it. Draw the silk out of the egg; then push it in again and hold the egg in the left hand, with the hole showing the silk toward the audience. Bring the right hand over to the left as if merely to turn the egg around to show its good side, palm the hollow egg, and leave the good one in its place. With the right hand take the red silk from your left shoulder and push it into your trousers pocket, leaving the egg there as well.

Approach the table; ask the spectators if they thoroughly understand the trick. Then slowly turn the egg, showing all parts of it; break it into the ordinary glass; and, finally, pull the red silk from the back of your collar.

5. THE EGG BAG

Effect. In its older form the trick consisted of the production of a number of eggs from a bag continually shown to be empty. The secret lay in the fact that one side, being double, concealed a row of pockets which held the eggs; the mouths of the bags being closed with elastic, the eggs could be squeezed out at

will to fall into the bag proper. The modern egg bag is a much
simpler affair, but it provides for some bewildering effects.

Preparation. The bag is a small one, about twelve inches deep
by about eight inches wide; one side is double, but the extra
piece is sewn to the bottom of the bag only halfway across it.
Thus a secret pocket is obtained, from which the egg can be
made to roll into the bag by tilting one side (Fig. 6). The
routine that follows should be taken merely as an example from
which to work up one for yourself, because the trick allows for
many effective variations.

Method. Begin by showing the bag; turn it inside out and
back again several times, to convince the onlookers that it is
just a plain little bag. The pocket will not show and the procedure will seem quite fair. Show the egg; hold the bag mouth
downwards, put the egg in it (secretly slipping it into the
pocket), and bring the hand out half closed. Turn your right

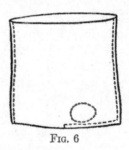

Fig. 6

side away from the audience and furtively thrust your right
hand into the trousers pocket. Continue, taking no notice of
any challenges from the spectators, by ordering the egg to vanish;
then shake the bag, turn it inside out and back again, hold the
corner of the bag with the egg, and strike the rest of the bag
against your left hand as if laboring to prove what the spectators think they know already—that the bag is empty.

You will be challenged by cries that the egg is in your pocket,
so you promptly pull out your left trousers pocket and show
it empty. "No, no, the other one!" someone is sure to call out;
and in response you pull out your left vest pocket, in a very
transparent attempt to bluff your way out. This arouses a call

for the right-hand pocket, so you pull out your right-hand vest pocket and show that empty.

By this time all who do not know the trick are sure they have caught you, and they shout for the "right-hand trousers pocket." You hesitate, pretend to be in a difficulty, try to interest them in the bag again. They insist on seeing the pocket, so you draw it out slowly—then dip your hand into the bag and bring out the egg.

So much for the preliminary stage; you proceed now to the pretended explanation. Show the egg, put it in the bag, then bring it out with the little finger holding it against the palm (there is no need to expose the fact that articles can be held in the palm without the aid of the fingers, as too many performers do). That, you explain, was the simple way you made the egg vanish in the first place. Then, you continue, you merely pretended to put it in your pocket; really you brought it out again, holding it as before (and again you show the egg in the palm held by the little finger), and dropped it into the bag when they weren't looking—so that, of course, the egg was in the bag for you to take out after showing your trousers pocket empty. Do all this as you make the explanation, and the spectators laugh at themselves for having been fooled with so simple a trick.

Offer to do it again, so that the trick will be thoroughly understood. Put the egg into the bag—into the secret pocket. Withdraw the hand, half closed as before, and move it toward the trousers pocket; but stop, show it empty, order the egg to vanish, and proceed to turn the bag inside out and outside in, twist it up, strike it on your hand and on the table, spread it on your leg and pat it, and so on—convincing the spectators that the bag is empty. Invite two persons to stand on either side of you. You have the egg in the top corner of the secret pocket and you hold the bag between your hands, one at each side of the mouth. Have them look into the bag, then feel inside and report to the audience that it is perfectly empty. When they have satisfied themselves with the bag, let the egg drop and have them examine your hands and sleeves. This done, hold the bag with the thumbs inside, at each of the top corners—thus leaving the rest of the hands free. You say, "I am going to get the egg back into the bag and plainly the only possible way I can do that is by taking it from one of my pockets, isn't it? Now I want you to try to prevent me from doing that by holding my wrists. If you see me going to my pockets, stop me." Let them grip your wrists tightly.

Pretend to make attempts to get your hands to your pockets, which, of course, they prevent. Get as much amusement as possible out of this; then give up, and suddenly, as if struck by a new idea, say, "One moment please. Did you examine the bag thoroughly? Yes? Every nook and corner? Well, it looks to me as if you didn't make a very thorough search after all, because . . . here is the egg"—dip your hand into the bag and bring out the egg.

I have treated the trick at length because it is one of the best tricks possible if it is presented properly. It requires no special preparation; the bag and the egg can be carried in the pocket, and the trick is equally successful in a small room or on the largest stage; finally, it can be done with people all around you. I have seen the late De Biere create more enthusiasm with his presentation of the egg bag on the huge stage of the New York Hippodrome than was obtained by the biggest illusions presented by magicians who preceded him on the same program.

VII

THE LINKING RINGS

"Untwisting all the chains that tie
The hidden soul of harmony."
John Milton—L'Allegro.

THE linking rings—an old trick but still one of the best, if not the very best. The effect is magical and the plot is simple; the materials are merely large metal rings. No preparation is required; the trick is equally effective in the parlor or on the largest stage, and it can be done when surrounded by spectators. Of what other trick in the confines of conjuring can this be said? Very little sleight of hand, in the strict sense of the word, is necessary, but deftness and a mastery of misdirection are essential. To get the maximum effect from the linking rings, a routine of movements must be practiced until the operator has it literally at his fingertips.

The most convenient size for the rings is from eight to nine inches in diameter, with a thickness of from a quarter to three-eighths of an inch; they should be made of brass, nickel-plated. The set generally used consists of eight rings. The effect of the trick is that the rings are handed out for examination and are found to be perfectly solid; yet at the will of the operator they are linked and unlinked, chains of varying length are made and numerous pretty designs formed, and finally, after being tangled into an intricate mass, the rings once more fall apart singly.

Explanation. The secret of the trick rests upon the fact that one ring, known as the key ring, is cut open; the ends rest far enough apart to allow for the passage of another ring. Two rings are permanently linked into a chain of two; three rings, in the same way, form a chain of three; and two solid, single rings complete the set of eight rings (Fig. 1).

147

The following routine has been devised to enable the beginner to obtain the full effect of the trick without the complication of false counts, secret addition of the key ring, etc., which serve only to bewilder and discourage the neophyte at the outset. The introduction of the key ring is managed so subtly that the spectators are convinced that they have examined every ring and have proved them to be solid and separate.

Routine. Arrange the rings in the left hand by first placing the two singles in the thumb fork, next the chain of two, then the chain of three, and finally the key ring. Grasp them tightly, so that the fingers cover the cut in the key ring and the rings hang down from the hand.

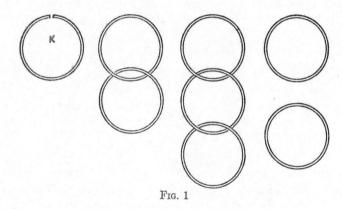

Fig. 1

(1) Show the rings and announce that you have a number of rings all solid and separate. Grasp the outside ring at its lowest point with the right hand; lift it over the left hand, without relaxing the grip of that hand, and let it fall on the left forearm. Do the same with all the rest, one at a time, but do not count them aloud. When the last ring has been folded back, let all the rings fall back into their original position.

(2) Take the rings with the right hand, thus reversing their order; from the tips of the right fingers toward the wrist they now run thus—single, single, chain of two, chain of three, key ring. Announce that you have eight rings, that you will count them one by one, and that you will hand them out for the most stringent examination. Stand with your left side to the specta-

tors and hold the rings up in the right hand, broadside to the spectators. Place the left hand a little below the rings, palm upwards, and drop the first single from the right hand into it, counting "One." Let the left hand drop slightly as it catches the single, showing plainly that it is separate from the rest.

(3) Repeat exactly the same actions with the second single ring, and count "Two."

(4) Bring the left hand up so that the fingers are just above the lowest parts of the rings in the right hand; drop the outside ring of the set of two into the left hand, counting "Three," then the other ring of that set, counting "Four." Close the fingers of the left hand on the four rings and drop it a little below the right-hand rings, showing complete separation from them.

(5) Raise the left hand again to the first position in the preceding paragraph; drop the outer ring of the set of three, counting "Five," then the next one, counting "Six," then the last ring of that set, counting "Seven." Again drop the left hand, showing its rings quite separate from the one ring which remains in the right hand.

(6) Bring the right hand down sharply, clashing the last ring —the key ring—against those in the left hand, counting "Eight," and take all the rings again in the right hand.

(7) Twist the right hand inward and put the rings into the left hand so that the two singles are on the outside; that is, nearest to the left fingertips, the key ring going into the fork of the thumb and nearest to the wrist.

(8) Invite two gentlemen to come forward and assist you by inspecting the rings, standing one on each side of you. Hand a single ring to each of them, and urge them to examine the rings carefully.

(9) When they have satisfied themselves that the rings are solid, change the two rings from the one to the other so that each can check up on the other.

(10) Take the single ring from one man and hand it to the other, telling him to link the two by rubbing them together. Naturally he cannot do this. Take the two rings from him and hand them to the other man, asking him to try. He, too, fails to join the rings. Suggest that he try to do it by striking the rings together. His awkward attempts will probably amuse the

other spectators. In the meantime you have inserted the top joint of the left forefinger between the two rings of the set of two, so that you will be able to let the outside ring drop from the other three fingers and retain the inner one with the forefinger.

(11) Offer to show him how to do it and take one ring from him with the right hand. Stand with your left side to the audience, holding the bunch of rings broadside to them, and strike the single ring down on the others, leaving it on the first joint of the left forefinger and letting the outer ring of the set of two drop off the last three fingers of the left hand. To all appearances you have linked the solid ring into another single ring. Pull out the set of two, leaving the single with the others in the left hand. Give the two linked rings to the same assistant and say, "Here is the ring you examined linked into another solid ring. See if you can take them apart again."

(12) Turn to the other man; take off the single from your left hand and give it to him, remarking, "Here is another single ring, the fourth. Please examine it carefully." Really it is the same ring that was examined before.

(13) Turn again to the man with the set of two and take from him the single ring that he still has. In the meantime you have taken the opportunity of placing the top joint of the left forefinger between the two outside rings of the set of three. Strike the single ring down on the left hand just as you did for the set of two, catching the single on the left forefinger and dropping the outside ring of the set of three. At once take the single again in the right hand, saying, "Here is another solid ring." Pass your left forefinger between the two remaining rings of the three set, strike the single down, catch it on the forefinger, and drop the second ring of the set of three.

(14) Immediately grasp the bottom ring of the set of three and pull the chain away with the right hand, leaving a single and the key in the left hand. Hand the set of three to the man with the single ring and take the single ring from him with the left hand, which will then hold the key and two singles— the key being nearest to the wrist. Twist the three rings toward the right, bringing the key on the outside; take it in the right hand, hold it up toward the assistant, and ask him, "You are

sure that this ring is perfectly solid?" Taking it to be the one he just examined, he replies, "Yes." Hold up the two singles in the left hand, saying, "Here are the last two rings. You have examined six rings; these two make the complete set of eight. Look them over very carefully." Give them to the man with the set of two, which you take from him.

(15) Take the set of two with the rings folded together, not hanging in a chain. Hold them up in the left hand, blow on them, and let one ring drop; at the same moment bring up the right hand with the key ring and slip it onto the top ring, making a chain of three rings. Of course, the linking of the two rings is mere bluff; but the assistant is busy examining the singles and to the audience it appears that you have again linked two solid rings.

If the work has been done cleanly and smoothly up to this point, the audience will be satisfied that every ring has been examined and the rest of the routine will be easy to manage.

(16) Take the set of three, folded together; hold the rings up in the left hand, blow on them, and let them fall one by one, linked. Mere bluff again, but it impresses the audience.

(17) Face the spectators, holding a chain of three rings in each hand—the hands being about fifteen inches apart. Swing the hands and the chains from side to side, gradually bringing the hands closer together until you can slip the top ring of the three set into the key ring, the opening in which is covered by the right forefinger; draw them apart, slowly at first and then with a little jerk, and show that the chains are linked together.

(18) Grasp the bottom ring of the chain of three with the left hand, raise it, and show a chain of six rings. Drop the top ring and grasp the next ring with the same hand; hold the rings across your body and announce, "A watch chain."

(19) Drop this ring and take the top ring of the set of three again in the same hand. Swing the two sets of three as before, gradually bringing the hands closer until you can unlink the chains at the key ring—just the reverse of the previous action. This done, bring the left hand just above the right hand so that one chain is behind the other; then slowly raise one hand and lower the other till the two chains clear one another, the effect being that all the rings pass through one another.

(20) Gather up the rings of the set of three and let them fall onto the left arm at the elbow. With the left hand take hold of the top ring of the set of two; with the right hand pass the key downwards, unlinking it at the top and passing it down behind as if it passed through both rings and were detached at the bottom of the lower ring.

(21) Hand the set of two to one of the assistants and let the set of three slide down into the left hand; hold the rings up, blow on them, and let them fall in a chain. Bluff again, but the spectators do not realize it. As the second ring falls, bring the right hand up with the key and link it into the top ring, making a chain of four.

(22) Link the lowest ring into the key ring and show a single at the top and bottom and two rings in the middle. Fold the bottom ring up to the key and show two sets of two linked into one another. Spin the lower two by drawing them sharply toward the body with the left hand.

(23) As they spin, insert the left hand between them; seize the lower end of the rear ring in the right hand and pull the

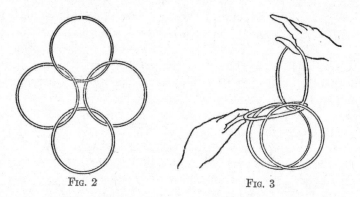

Fig. 2   Fig. 3

rings rapidly apart with a jerk, forming Fig. 2. Rest the opening of the key ring in the fork of the right thumb and hold the lowest ring up horizontally to form a garden seat (Fig. 3). Fold the bottom ring up to the top ring, not linking it, to form a globe (Fig. 4). Announce the "opening of the flower" and let the two top rings slip slowly apart until they open out into the photo frame (Fig. 5). Pull the top ring down over the side ring and form the Ace of Clubs, holding up the left thumb to represent the stalk (Fig. 6).

Between each of these figures it is necessary to make a slight pause to enable the spectators to appreciate the patterns, but from this point you gradually increase the pace.

(24) Let all the rings except the key fall from your left hand. Seize the lowest ring with the right hand, jerk the rings around, and slip this ring into the key ring. Turn to the man holding the set of two; take these two rings in the right hand, strike them several times from below against the rings hanging from the key, then slip them smartly through the opening. Keep the

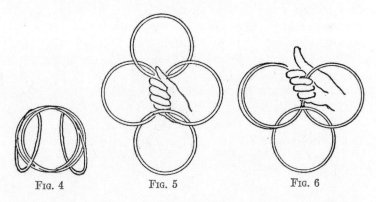

FIG. 4   FIG. 5   FIG. 6

rings jangling with the left hand. Take one of the singles in the right hand, toss it into the air so that in falling it will land across the key, hook the left forefinger over it and it will fall through the opening and join the others on the key ring. Do the same with the second single ring.

(25) Now with the right hand grasp one of the rings, still holding the key with the left hand, and jerk the rings about, making them appear to be in an inextricable tangle. Swing round to the right, drop the ring from the right hand and take the key in that hand, grip all the other rings with the left hand, press them evenly with the left thumb, swing round to the left and pass all the rings through the opening of the key ring, press it against the others, and grasp all the rings with the right hand.

(26) Turn again to the right, hold the rings up in the right

hand, and repeat the count as at the beginning of the routine. Bow and carry the rings off.

SYNOPSIS

Show rings; fold over onto left forearm.
Count. Get two spectators to assist.
Hand single to each, then change them over.
Give both to one, then the other.
Take a single back; link set of two.
Hand set to assistant, also the single.
Take the other single, and link set of three.
Hand out set of three; take back single.
Switch key; hand out two singles.
Take set of two; link key.
Take set of three; pretend to link.
Swing two chains of three; link, making chain of six.
Make watch chain.
Swing and unlink the two sets of three.
Take key off set of two and hand out.
Link key to set of three, making chain of four.
Link 1–2–1, then 2–2.
Pull into frame figure; then sphere, opening of flower, photo frame, ace of clubs.
Link all into key.
Jangle the rings.
Unlink key and count.

VIII

SILKS AND SORCERY

"Fetch me the handkerchief."
Shakespeare—Othello.

I T IS probable that the modern handkerchief is identical with the "swat-cloth" worn on the left side in Saxon times and carried in the hand in the Middle Ages. The word "handkerchief" first appears in 1512, in a list of the Earl of Northumberland's linen. The entry reads: "All manner of kerchiefs, breast kerchiefs, hand kerchiefs and head kerchiefs." It is passing strange, therefore, seeing that handkerchiefs have been in common use for well over four hundred years, that it was not until the later years of the last century that any extensive use of them was made by magicians. Up to that time there were only a few isolated tricks, such as "the handkerchief burnt and restored" and "the vanishing handkerchief" of Robert-Houdin (the first application of the sleeve pull) ; and the use of silk handkerchiefs, apart from serving as covers for apparatus, was entirely unknown. It remained for Buatier de Kolta to apply silks to complete tricks in themselves. His lead was quickly followed, and to such an extent that tricks and manipulations with silks now form a very important branch of the art of magic.

The reason for this is not far to seek: their varied and brilliant colors provide pleasing and beautiful effects and they can be folded and packed in such small compass that their subsequent expansion to full size appears marvelous. It is not surprising, therefore, that several of the most successful magic acts of today make use of silks alone, and rarely does one see a magic act that does not include at least one trick with silks.

We shall consider first the materials; then methods of folding, productions, vanishes, tricks with silks; finally the knots, ties, and flourishes.

155

I. THE MATERIALS

The silk should be of the finest quality and the hems of the separate handkerchiefs must be made as narrow as possible. For this reason it is advisable to purchase handkerchiefs from the magical stores. Prices, of course, vary with the size and quality, but it is always advisable to buy the very best. For ordinary purposes the handkerchief should be at least fifteen inches square and for stage or platform work eighteen inches square. Much of the effect is lost if smaller sizes are used. With regard to colors, modern dyeing art has reached such a degree of perfection that almost any color or combination of colors can be obtained, and even reproductions of playing cards and comic figures—such as Mickey Mouse, etc.—are now available in most effective designs.

When several colored silks are used in combination, great care should be taken to avoid the colors clashing. If the performer has not made a study of colors he should consult an artist when arranging any such combination. The following will serve as an example in which brilliant colors blend effectively: three handkerchiefs, emerald green, scarlet, and gold; the gold handkerchief bordered with green, the red bordered with gold, and the green bordered with red.

It must always be remembered that a great part of the success of a conjuring trick lies in pleasing the eye of the spectator, and if the materials used are dingy, dirty, and crumpled (alas, too often the case) the best handkerchief trick ever invented will fail to please.

II. METHODS OF FOLDING SILKS

1. SINGLE SILKS

(1) Spread the silk flat on the table and fold the four corners to the middle (Fig. 1); do the same with the four corners of the square thus made. Repeat the operation, and do it a fourth time. A small compact bundle is thus obtained, which can be impaled on the point of a long pin—or better, a needle—under the edge of the coat or vest. It can then readily be pulled away

by the fingers and palmed when required. This method should be used when loading a silk into a tube of any kind, the bundle being pushed in with the folded corners on the top.

(2) Fold three corners to the middle as in Fig. 2. Fold the sides AB and CD to the middle. Repeat the folding operation twice;

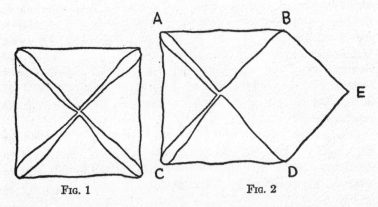

FIG. 1   FIG. 2

then fold one side over the other, making a band. Roll this up tightly, beginning at the end opposite to E. Secure the bundle with a pin or needle as in (1).

(3) Fold two diagonal corners to the middle; fold these doubled portions in half and repeat until, by folding one over the other, you obtain a band about one and one-half inches wide. Then fold about two inches of the end at the right back on the band and turn the extreme corner upwards at a right angle. Roll the band very tightly, beginning at this doubled end, up to the left end. Finally tuck the corner of this end into the folds, thus forming a kind of turban— with a corner projecting from the middle, which can be drawn out when it is necessary to develop the silk (Fig. 3).

FIG. 3

With a little care a silk thus rolled can be manipulated like a ball and palmed with perfect safety. It can also be finger palmed at the front or back of the hand by means of the projecting corner. By gripping this corner and jerking the silk sharply, it will instantly expand to its full extent.

(4) Begin by making a fold about one and one-half inches in width at one corner; turn the silk over and make another fold of the same width; turn the silk and make a third fold. Repeat the operation until the silk has been folded completely, accordion fashion. Start at one end of the band thus made and fold over about two inches; turn the silk over and fold again; continue in this way with accordion folds up to the other end. A square bundle results, and you can make this secure either by tying it crosswise with a weak thread or by pasting a narrow band of tissue paper of the same color round it (Fig. 4). The thread or band can be easily broken with the fingers, which retain hold of the last corner. A quick shake will then cause the silk to expand instantly.

This method should always be used for very large silks or flags, with the first folds made along the whole of one side. Two small beads sewn into the last two corners will enable you to seize them quickly without fumbling.

2. SEVERAL SILKS, TO BE PRODUCED ALL AT ONCE

(1) First fold each silk in half from one corner to the corner diagonally opposite, then lay them one over the other, star

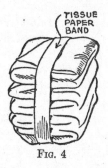

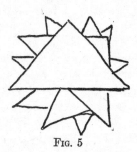

FIG. 4   FIG. 5

fashion as in Fig. 5. Fold the ends into the middle, beginning with the lowest silk and continuing with the next in order. Keep on folding inwards in this way until a compact bundle is obtained, and secure this with a weak thread tied crosswise. To develop the silks seize the bundle by the side opposite the folded ends; break the thread and shake the silks, letting them expand over the hand.

(2) Fold each silk diagonally as in 1 (3) (above), place them on one another, and turn the right hand ends in about two inches (with the extreme tips turned up). Roll the silks into a tight ball and tuck the loose ends into a fold. Develop them in the same way as in 1 (3) for a single silk.

3. SEVERAL SILKS, TO BE PRODUCED SINGLY

(1) Spread one silk out flat and place a second silk on it, also spread out. Fold the corners of this second silk into the

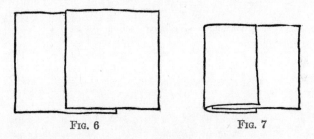

FIG. 6   FIG. 7

middle and the corners of the smaller square thus obtained also into the middle. Spread a third silk over this and fold it in the same way; continue the same procedure until all the silks have been folded. Turn this bundle of folded silks over on the first one, which has remained spread out; fold its corners over the bundle and secure the last corner with a pin.

The bundle having been loaded—we will suppose, into a hat—remove the pin; unfold the covering silk; and take out the other silks one by one, shaking them so that they will develop fully in the process.

(2) Spread the first silk flat on the table and spread the second over it so that it overlaps halfway (Fig. 6). Fold the free half of the first over the second (Fig. 7). Lay a third silk over these, overlapping on the opposite side; then fold the free half of the second over it. Continue the same procedure with the remaining silks. In making the production from a receptacle, when the top silk is lifted away the second one is automatically made ready for seizure, and so on.

It should be noted that all these folds can be made more neatly and rapidly by having an assistant to hold the folds as they are made. Finally, fold all silks at the last possible moment before they have to be used.

III. PRODUCTIONS

1. PRODUCTION OF A SINGLE SILK

(1) A silk rolled into a compact parcel by methods 1(3) or 1(4), can be secreted in various parts of the performer's clothing, from which it can be taken secretly, palmed, and produced apparently from the air. For example, the balled silk can be tucked in a fold of the left sleeve, the opening of the fold being toward the wrist. Pull the right sleeve back a little with the left hand, showing the right hand empty; then pull back the left sleeve with the right hand, showing the left hand empty and at the same time stealing the silk with the right hand. Make the change over palm (as with a ball) in turning to the right and make a pretended catch in the air with the right hand, closing it. Transfer the supposed catch to the left hand, rub the left fingers on the left palm for a moment, nip the projecting corner of the silk with the fingers, and suddenly jerk it free, showing the silk hanging from the fingertips.

(2) Again, the balled silk can be placed under the vest a little toward the right or left, according to which hand is to steal it. For example, if the left hand is to take the silk, press the left elbow against the side and hold the forearm bent to bring the hand just opposite the point at which the silk is vested. Turn to the left, making a pretended catch in the air, high up, with the right hand, and at the same moment steal the silk with the left hand. The change over follows and you produce the silk.

(3) A very pretty production of a silk from the vest can be made with a fan. Roll a sheet of paper into a tube and hold it in the left hand. Pick up the fan with the right hand, open it, and hold it waist high so that the right fingers are close to the vested silk. Raise the tube to your eye to look through it at the spectators, and at the same moment steal the silk with the right fingers behind the fan. Hold the tube vertically and fan its upper end as you free the fold in the balled silk

so that it will expand. Let it fall into the tube and catch it on the fan as it emerges at the lower end.

(4) You can also set the balled silk on the table behind some small object; as you pick up some article from the table with the right hand, drawing marked attention to it, quietly steal the silk with the left hand and palm it. Or you may have it on a small wire holder behind the top rail of a chair and steal it while casually moving the chair a little to one side; or again, in placing an article on the seat of the chair with one hand steal the silk with the other.

(5) A very effective production can be made in this way. A tiny slit is made in the seam of the trouser leg, just wide enough for a silk to be pulled through. A long narrow pocket of black silk is sewn to this inside the trousers and a silk is pushed inside it. To the upper corner of the silk an inch of strong thread is attached with a small black bead on the end. The bead will hang just outside the pocket and can be found instantly with the fingers. When required, the silk is jerked out so rapidly that its appearance is instantaneous. The use of half silks—that is, silks which have been cut in half diagonally— is recommended for this production, as they take up only half the space, yet when held up by one corner they appear to be whole.

I have seen this effect used by a performer with marked success, in this way: at the close of each trick he would rapidly pull a silk, each one a different color, from various parts of his clothing.

(6) A thread can be very useful for getting a silk into the hand invisibly. The following will serve as an example from which other methods can be devised.

Fold a silk by the accordion-pleat method and tie a fairly strong black thread around it crosswise, leaving a free length of about fifteen inches. Tie the end of this to a vest button and place the silk in the left vest pocket. Stand facing the spectators; pull the sleeves back a little; and place the hands, backs outwards, flat against the vest, the fingers pointing downwards. Thrust the hands down, engage the left thumb in the thread loop, then, holding the thread by pressing the thumb against the side of the hand, turn both hands upwards to show the palms. Place the tips of the fingers together, pointing towards the front and a little towards the left, and stretch the arms out quickly. The silk will be dragged from the pocket against the left palm, the hand remaining wide open. Show the palm of the right hand and, in making a turn to the left, bring the right just over the left hand; engage the right thumb under the thread and draw the silk against the right palm at once, showing both sides of the left hand. It only remains to break the thread and produce the silk.

(7) A silk can be rolled around the end of the wand, the free end being tucked into one of the folds. In this case the wand is set on the table with the loaded end behind some small article. Pick it up by that end with the right hand. Show the left hand empty and clench it. Tap the fist with the wand, open it, and appear surprised that there is nothing there. Take the wand with the left hand by the free end, sliding it out of the right hand (which retains and closes on the silk). Now tap the right hand with the wand and open the hand, revealing the silk.

This method can be used with good effect in connection with the vanishing wand, already described. Wrap the silk around the end of the wand to be produced from under the coat and bring it out with the right hand concealing the silk. This is then produced as an introduction to a trick with silks.

There are a great number of gimmicks for the production of silks, some with lugs to permit them to be held at the front or back of the hand, others with loops of fine wire or catgut by means of which they can be suspended from the thumb on either side of the hand. Generally speaking, it will be found that to manipulate these articles successfully is very much harder than to produce a silk by the methods described above, and there is the additional difficulty of having to get rid of the gimmick afterward. Should the reader desire to experiment with any of these, they can be obtained at any magic store.

2. PRODUCTION OF A NUMBER OF SILKS
From the Sleeves.

We will suppose that you have produced a white silk and wish to produce a number of others of different colors.

Preparation. Spread another white silk of the same size on the table; then take three or four others, also of the same size; fold each one lengthwise by the diagonal fold and place them on one another. Seize them by the ends with both hands and twist and twirl them into a tight roll. Lay this on the first silk as shown in Fig. 8. Fold the corner B over to C and then roll the whole up to C. The colored silks will be kept safely in the white silk as long as the corners at A are held tightly. Prepare two rolls in this way; take one in each hand by the corners at A; then don your coat, retaining your hold on the silks and drawing them down each sleeve until the ends A are near the ends of the sleeves at the inner sides of the wrists.

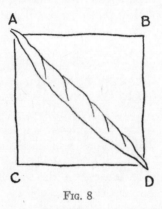

Fig. 8

Method. After producing the first silk by one or other of the methods already explained, hold it up in the right hand and stroke it downwards with the left hand. Bring the left hand up to repeat the action and with the tips of the right fingers, under cover of the right hand, grip the corners A of the load in the left sleeve. Hold the right hand motionless as before and again stroke the silks downwards with the left hand. The onward sweep will cause the load to be pulled out of the left seeve. The moment the load is clear, seize its lower end and the lower end of the first white silk and twirl them with both hands. It will appear to the spectators that one silk only is in view. Release the grip of the left hand and take the single silk in that hand by one corner, showing a white silk in each hand—one apparently pulled out of the other. Throw this over the left arm; with the right hand shake the white silk it holds, causing it to untwist and reveal the colored silks inside it. Draw these away one by one with the left hand by their lower corners.

By stroking these with the right hand ample cover is obtained for the production of the second load from the right sleeve. Develop these in the same way. When a number of silks is required for the performance of a trick, it is much more effective, and more magical, to produce them in this way than to have them set prosaically on the table.

From the Vest or Coat

Rolls of silks prepared in the same way can be produced from the vest by being pulled through the openings between the vest buttons. In this case the outer silk must be black or dark purple.

When it is desired to produce a large number of silks under cover of a number already in the hands, fold them diagonally and lay them one on top of the other. Tie a fairly strong thread around the middle of the pile; run a short piece of fine black wire, or horsehair, under the thread; and tie the ends, making a loop. Place this bundle, folded in half, under the dress vest on the left side, tucking the free ends well down and letting the loop protrude over the top of the vest toward the middle. Under cover of displaying the silks, already produced, in front of the body, it is an easy matter to engage the left thumb in the loop; then, by simply stretching the arms outwards and upwards, the load will be dragged out behind the other silks. It is, after that, merely a matter of breaking the thread and developing the silks to make the greatest display possible. The loop is allowed to fall to the floor unnoticed.

When a dress vest is not worn, the same idea can be applied to the coat by having pockets in the sides with vertical openings. The action is practically the same and a load can be obtained from each side of the coat. Some performers prefer to make a bag (Fig. 9) with a piece of black silk by simply pinning it together; the silks are then folded into accordion pleats and pushed into the bag one by one. When this is full it is tied crosswise with thread and the pins removed (Fig. 10). In this case, after the load has been stolen under cover of other silks, the thread is broken and the silks are shaken out one by one, developing, as they are released, with very pretty effect. The black silk is simply let fall with the others and passes for another silk.

It is surprising what a quantity of silks can be concealed on one's person by exercising a little thought and ingenuity, and the stealing of such loads under cover of other silks is very easy. It is strange that the procedure is so much neglected by

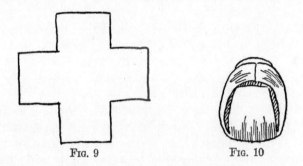

Fig. 9   Fig. 10

magicians. What effect could be prettier than a seemingly endless supply of gorgeous silks welling up spontaneously from the performer's hands?

IV. VANISHES

1. A SINGLE SILK

Face the spectators and show the silk held in the right hand by the extreme corner between the tips of the thumb and forefinger. Throw the silk over the back of the left hand, held palm outwards; draw the top corner through the fork of the left thumb; and press it against the palm of that hand. Twist this corner round several times with the right thumb and fingers and then press the right palm tightly on the folds, the left fingers pointing to the front and the right fingers pointing upwards.

Rub the hands together with a circular motion, with the result that the twisted corner of the silk becomes a nucleus round which the silk rolls itself into a ball; the more tightly the palms are pressed together, the more compact the ball will be. In this process the silk is drawn up into the hands from the back of the left hand with a pretty effect. When the last corner is drawn in between the hands and arrives against the right hand, stop the motion of the hands; turn to the left; palm the balled silk in the right hand, turning its back to the front; and, at the same moment, close the left hand as if it held the silk and move it away—the right hand remaining motionless, with the forefinger pointing at the left hand. At once begin rubbing the left fingers together, as if to reduce it to nothing, and keep your eyes fixed on that hand. Then slowly open the fingers one by one, beginning with the little finger, and prove that the silk has vanished by showing the hand empty. In the meantime the right hand drops quietly to the side and pockets the balled silk.

A good plan is to tuck the wand under the left arm at the start and at the finish take it with the right hand after it has palmed the silk. A tap of the wand on the left hand will afford a plausible reason for the disappearance of the silk. Until the knack of rolling the silk is acquired, it is advisable to sew a bead, or a little piece of tissue paper, of the same color as the silk, to the corner; this makes the subsequent balling of the silk much easier.

The same process can be used to roll the silk up from the middle; it is spread over the left hand, the center of the silk coming against the middle of the left palm. With the right fingers twist a small portion of the middle to form a nucleus and then apply the rotary motion of the hands as before. The result is that the silk is drawn into the hands from all sides at once with pretty effect. The vanish is completed in the same way as with the corner roll.

2. VANISH OF SILK AND CHANGE TO BILLIARD BALL, EGG, LEMON, ETC.

It is often necessary to cause the apparent change of a silk into a billiard ball, an egg, or some other small object. Such articles are hollow and the silk is simply tucked in through a hole in the side. Suppose, for instance, it is desired to change a red silk into a red billiard ball. The ball is palmed in the left hand, while the right hand displays the silk; the hands are then brought together, with the silk hanging to the front from the fingertips. Under cover of an up-and-down movement of the hands, directed toward the left, the fingers of the left hand, masked by the right hand, push the silk into the ball. When it is all in, the hands are separated and the ball is shown lying on the palm of the left hand.

A much more effective method is to palm the ball in the right hand; then spread the silk over the left hand, at the same time pushing the middle of the silk into the opening of the ball with the left thumb. Press the ball tightly against the left palm and make the usual rotary motion of the hands; the silk will then be drawn rapidly inside the ball. This method is much more rapid and much prettier than the first.

3. For Several Silks

The best and most popular method of effecting the disappearance of a number of silks, or indeed of a single silk where a

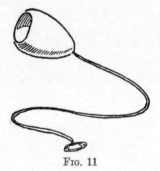

Fig. 11

complete vanish is necessary, is by means of a pull. This is simply a cup attached to a length of cord elastic, so arranged that when the silk (or silks) is pushed into the cup and the latter is released the elastic will pull the whole under the coat (Fig. 11).

To fix the pull, fasten the elastic by means of a loop at the free end to a suspender button on the left side of the body, first passing it through a small loop of elastic sewn at the top of the trousers on the right-hand side; this loop will not only prevent the cup from swinging down into sight under the coat, but will also keep it in a readily accessible position. Arrange the length of the elastic cord so that the cup can be drawn outwards from the body about fifteen inches, with sufficient tension to make it fly back instantly under the coat when it is released.

To use the pull properly, seize a favorable opportunity to take the cup secretly with the left hand and place it at the top of the left trousers pocket. Show the silk in the right hand; pull your sleeves back a little; then roll the silk between the hands as for the sleight-of-hand vanish, but really leave the silk in the left hand. Hold the right hand partly closed and thrust it into the trousers pocket. You will be challenged, or at least there will be knowing looks and whispers amongst the spectators. So you open the left hand, showing the silk, and at the same moment bring the right hand out of the pocket with the cup palmed. Bring the hands together; work the silk into the cup with backward and forward movements of the hands. When it is completely in the receptacle, let this latter slip out of the hands at the moment when they are nearest to the coat, but continue the movements for a few moments; then hold the hands stationary, well away from the body, rub them together, and finally show that they are empty.

Care must be taken to release the pull at such an angle that the cup slips under the side of the coat without disturbing it and slides to the side of the body without the thud too often heard.

V. TRICKS WITH SILKS

1. OBEDIENT SILKS

Effect. Eight silk handkerchiefs of different colors—for example, red, dark blue, yellow, green, white, light blue, violet, and rose—are tied together and displayed in a chain, and the order of the colors is written on a blackboard. Thus red will be 1, dark blue 2, yellow 3, and so on. The silks are then placed in a hat; a spectator is asked to call out any one of the numbers and to say at what number in the chain he wishes it to appear. Suppose, for example, he chooses number six and the color green. The performer lifts out the chain of silks and the green silk is found to be at the sixth place.

Method. The silks are not really knotted together but are attached to one another by snap buttons at the corners, the knots being of the trick variety (see Trick 5, the Sympathetic Silks). After displaying them and checking their positions with the list on the blackboard, the performer gathers them into a bundle by first bringing the lower end of the last silk—in this case the rose silk—against the top corner of the first silk of the chain—the red one—and in doing so fastens the two together, thus forming the silks into an endless chain.

When the spectator calls a number and a color, all the artist has to do is to count back, from the number the color occupies, to the number called and separate the chain at that point. For example, in the case given above—number six and green color—the backward count of six arrives at the violet color; therefore, the separation must be made between the violet and the light blue silks. The performer seizes the violet silk and, in bringing the bunch out of the hat, detaches the light blue silk and holds up the chain, showing the green silk at number six.

For a single repetition, not more, simply attach these last two again by their snap buttons and proceed in exactly the same way as before, with a new number and a different silk.

2. The Silk Cut in Half and Restored

Effect. A silk is pushed into a paper tube in such a way that its ends protrude at each side. The tube is cut fairly in half and the halves are separated, one end of the silk showing in each. The two parts of the tube are placed together and the silk is pulled out whole, as at first.

Articles required. A thumb tip, prepared by gluing inside it, a fairly large corner of a silk of the same color as the silk to be used in the trick, a sheet of paper about five inches square, a pair of scissors, and a silk. Place the tip in a position from which it can be taken secretly when it is required.

Method. Get the tip on your right thumb secretly and pick up the paper between the thumb and fingers, the thumb at the back and hiding the tip. Show both sides of the paper by lifting the bottom with the left hand up to the right hand and at the same time releasing the top. Roll the paper into a tube around the thumb tightly and leave the tip inside, being careful not to let any part of the silk inside it show. Place an elastic band round the middle of the tube.

Hold the tube vertically in the right hand by the lower end, preventing the tip from dropping out by placing the little finger under the mouth. Push the silk in at the top with the left hand until about two inches of the last corner protrude, but prevent any part of the silk going past the middle of the tube by pressing the tip of the right thumb against the paper at the back. Insert the forefinger in the other end and pull out the corner from the tip. Thus to all appearances the silk passes right through the tube, a corner being visible at each end.

Take the scissors in the right hand, pinch the paper tube tightly with the left fingers and thumb at a point between the middle and the thumb tip, and cut the tube in half. Show the parts separate, one in each hand, with the ends showing the protruding corners toward the spectators. Put them together again; push the fake corner in with the right thumb, at the same time stealing the thumb tip; then pull the silk out from the other end with the left hand, showing it whole as at first. Open out the two parts of the paper, keeping the right thumb behind; roll them up with the tip; and put them aside or pocket them. Or you may put the silk momentarily in your left outside coat pocket while you show the papers and tear them up; the tip, of course, drops into the pocket.

3. A Cigarette Changes into a Silk

Effect. A lighted cigarette changes instantly into a silk.

Preparation. Sew a cigarette vanisher, without the elastic, into the hem of a silk handkerchief so that the mouth of the vanisher is at one side of a corner. Fold the silk by method 1(3), so that the vanisher projects at the center of the roll and the free end of the silk is tucked into one of the folds. Place it in your outside left coat pocket with a box of matches.

Method. Show a cigarette, or borrow one; put it in your mouth with the right hand; get the matches with the left hand and at the same time palm the silk. Light the cigarette and puff on it; drop the matches into the pocket without replacing

the left hand in it. Clench the left hand so that the mouth of
the vanisher is pointing upwards; then push the cigarette into
the left fist, lighted end first. When it is right inside the
vanisher, take hold of that corner of the silk with the right
hand, open the left hand, and instantly jerk the right hand
upwards. The silk will expand immediately, leaving no trace
of the cigarette.

The trick is an excellent one for making the passage from
cigarettes to silks, or as an interlude at any stage of the routine.

4. THE TWENTIETH CENTURY SILK

Effect. An easy but effective method of this favorite trick.
Two silks are knotted together and dropped into a hat; a
third silk is vanished and appears between the first two. The
chain of three silks is then vanished and the three are found
in the hat separate, as at first.

Articles required. Six silks—two red, two green, and two
white—a hat, which can be borrowed; and a handkerchief pull.

Preparation. Tie one white silk between a red and a green
and roll the three in a compact bundle, which will unroll
quickly when taken by one end and shaken. If you use your
own hat, place this bundle under the sweatband and set the
hat on the table, crown downwards. The duplicate set of silks
may be lying on your table or be taken from those you have
produced magically.

Method. If you borrow a hat you must have the knotted
silks under your vest and load the little bundle under the
sweatband as you return to your table. In either case you show
the hat empty by grasping it with the fingers inside, covering
the spot at which the bundle is hidden; then set the hat down,
mouth upwards. In doing this lift the sweatband with the tips
of your fingers so that the bundle will fall inside. Show the
duplicate red and green silks and tie them together with the
fake knot (see trick 5, the Sympathetic Silks) and drop them
into the hat beside the bundle.

Pick up the white silk and vanish by rolling it up in the
left hand and palming it in the right hand. Tap the left hand
with the wand and show it empty. Thrust the right hand into
the hat and drop the palmed white silk; seize the corner

of the knotted bundle and jerk it out, showing the white silk
tied between the red and the green silks.

Finally vanish these three with the handkerchief pull; show
your hands empty; take up the hat, turn it over, and let the
three separate silks—red, white, and green—drop from it onto
the table.

5. The Sympathetic Silks

The trick in which knots are made to travel apparently from
one set of silks to another was first described by Hatton and
Plate in *Magicians' Tricks*. Of recent years it has become a
prime favorite with magicians generally. While there are many
variations in detail, the effect remains the same.

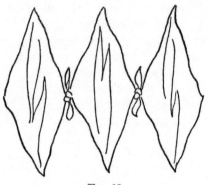

Fig. 12

Effect. The performer counts six large silk handkerchiefs one
by one; he lays three aside and ties the other three together.
The knots are ordered to pass from one set to the other and
this is shown to have taken place. The knotted set is given to
a spectator to untie the knots, to prove that they are genuine;
then he ties them together again. The other set is then found
to be tied in the same manner. Finally the spectator unties his
set and the other set is also found to have become separated.

Articles required. Six large silks, at least eighteen inches square,
all of the same color, the more striking the better; two small
rubber bands; a fan; and two chairs.

Preparation. Tie three of the silks together with small double knots and arrange them as shown in Fig. 12; then put them together so that the knots are hidden in the folds. Place these with the other three over the back of a chair on your right, in such a way that you can pick up the three knotted silks at once without disturbing their arrangement. Lay the fan on the seat of the same chair and put one rubber band on the tip of each middle finger, the second being merely a reserve in case of accident.

Method. The six silks must first be placed in the left hand in such a way that they can be counted, apparently, as six

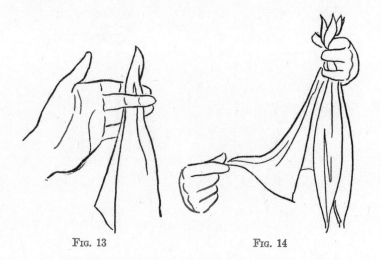

Fig. 13   Fig. 14

separate silks. To do this pick up one silk and put it in the left hand, slipping the left middle finger in front as in Fig. 13. Take the three knotted silks, place the ends between the left third and fourth fingers, bend the second and third fingers in, and grip the ends between the forefinger and thumb; finally put the two remaining separate silks between the left thumb and forefinger.

To count them, take hold of one of the separate silks just below the left thumb with the right hand, run the hand down to the lower end, pull the silk away by that end, separate the hands about two feet, and count "One" (Fig. 14).

Take the top corner of the second separate silk, pull it away the same distance, and count "Two." Hold these two silks as in Fig. 15.

Place the ends of these two between the thumb and fore-finger of the left hand; grasp the ends of the three knotted silks with the right hand and draw them away, counting "Three." Slip the right forefinger in front of them, so that they are held between the first and second fingers (Fig. 16).

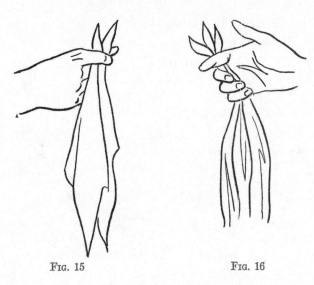

FIG. 15   FIG. 16

Complete the count by taking the three singles, one by one, between the right thumb and forefinger, separating the hands each time and counting "Four, five, six."

The count must be made at the same tempo throughout and there must be no hesitation at the moment when the two singles are substituted for the three knotted ones.

Take the three singles from between the right thumb and fore-finger and place them over the right arm. Run the left hand down the other set to the middle, double them in half, and lay them on the seat of the chair at the right.

Go over to the chair on the left; put one of the singles on the seat and show the other two, one in each hand, holding them about two inches from the top corners. These two must now be tied with a false knot. Place the corner in the right hand crosswise over the corner in the left hand and hold both corners with the tip of the left thumb (Fig. 17). With the right hand turn the corner of the left-hand silk over the other under the left thumb tip (Fig. 18); then grasp the remaining corner and

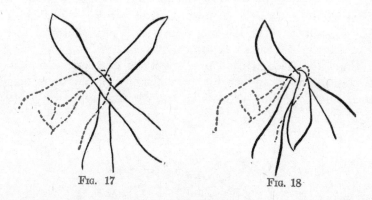

FIG. 17   FIG. 18

its silk with the right hand so that the two corners are looped together, pull them tightly, and then put the left thumb on the point of junction. In doing this simulate the action of tying a knot; really the corners are simply doubled one over the other. Now tie the corners with a single knot and pull it very tight (Fig. 19). Take hold of the opposite corner of one silk and let the two hang down; they will appear to be firmly tied, but a shake will cause them to fall apart.

FIG. 19

Take the third silk from the chair and make the same false knot, attaching it to the upper one of the other two. Display the chain and lower the silks onto the seat of the chair. Explain what you are about to do—that is, to make the knots pass from one set of silks to the other—and with the fan pretend to waft them from one chair to the other. Then, without showing any result, pretend that you have succeeded and remark that it is much harder to send the knots back to their original positions. Fan again and lift the first silk of the set on the left-hand chair high enough to show the first knot; then let it fall back on the seat.

This pretense will arouse some laughter; so, to convince the audience that the knots really did pass, repeat the fan pantomime. Then seize the loose corner of the upper silk on the right-hand chair, jerk it upwards, and display the chain of knotted silks. Go to the other chair and jerk the silks there upwards, in the same way, and they fall apart.

Hand the knotted silks to a spectator and have him untie the knots to prove that they are genuine. While he is doing this, take the other three silks by the ends; slip the rubber

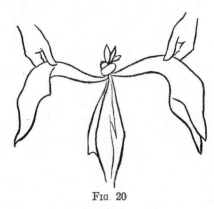

Fig. 20

band off your middle finger over the ends; and then gather them in a loose bundle in your right hand, holding the hand stretched out with the silks on its palm.

Instruct the spectator to take his three silks, now separate, by their ends; tie them together with a single knot and hold the other ends of two of them, with the third hanging down between them (Fig. 20). Toss your bundle in the air, catch the silks as they drop, and display them apparently tied in the same way. Bundle them up again, seizing the opportunity of slipping the rubber band off, and place them on the seat of one of the chairs. Retrieve the knotted silks from the spectator, openly untie the knot holding them together, and order the set on the chair to follow suit. Lift these one by one and show the magic has worked.

The trick comes to a natural conclusion at this point; the climax has been reached and the effect has not been overdone. But some performers continue by apparently tying all six by means of another rubber band, then again showing them separate, and so on. These additions drag out the trick too much and increase the danger of discovery of the means employed. It is a wise magician who knows when to stop.

6. DYEING THE SILKS

The dyeing of silk handkerchiefs by simply passing them through a paper tube, invented by David Devant a number of years ago, is still one of the best tricks with silks. The original method has been described so often that I will content myself with the explanation of some recent modifications.

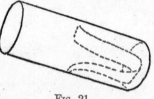

FIG. 21

The special gimmick, a small metal tube with a tape as long as itself fastened across it at the middle, is still used (Fig. 21). Silks pushed in at one end are prevented by the tape from emerging at the other end. If, however, other silks are pushed in at the opposite side, the first silks will be forced out and the new ones will take their place inside the tube. By having the gimmick made with a gutter along one side, large enough to take the performer's wand easily, the paper tube can be proved to be empty after the gimmick has been loaded in—at any rate, by magician's logic. He takes his own handkerchief from his pocket—a small one, by the way—pushes it into the gutter, and with his wand pushes it right through the paper tube. The silks to be dyed go into the gimmick itself, with the usual result.

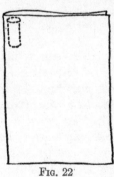

FIG. 22

Another method is to have the gimmick just large enough to take two medium-sized silks. This is concealed in the fold of a full sheet of a tabloid newspaper, at the back (Fig. 22). The doubled sheet is shown as a single sheet only, the gimmick being held in place with the fingers between the two thicknesses of the paper. This is rolled into a tube which can be shown with its mouth toward the spectators, the fingers inside hiding the bulge caused by the gimmick. Three silks are shown and two are apparently pushed into the tube, really into the gimmick between the two thicknesses of the paper; as soon as the second is safely home and the two colored silks have been pushed out, the gimmick is allowed to slide into the hand and is disposed of in taking the third silk. This one is simply wrapped around the paper tube to keep it from unrolling.

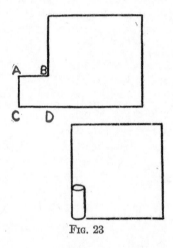

FIG. 23

In due course the dyed silks are extracted, the silk round the tube is removed, and the paper tube torn to little pieces. As a final touch the performer pulls this last silk through his hand and it changes color. This is simply another use of the well-known color-changing handkerchief.

The latest development of the trick is a self-contained tube and gimmick combined. A sheet of very thin black cardboard, about ten by twelve inches is cut into the shape shown in Fig. 23. The part ABCD is rolled into a tube and the edge AC is glued to the main sheet. The usual tape is then fixed in the middle of this tube. The tube is rolled up with the sheet around it and kept in that condition so that whenever it is opened out and then released it will automatically roll itself around the gimmicked part. The method of working is sufficiently obvious. The tube is loaded with silks in the usual way; when the sheet is unrolled toward the audience, the fingers hide the gimmicked section and the spectators naturally think they see the whole sheet. This is then again rolled round the small tube, the silks are pushed in, the colored silks emerge, and once more the sheet is unrolled and shown free from guile.

7. PRODUCTION OF SILKS FROM THE HANDKERCHIEF BALL

This is the prettiest and most effective method of producing silks. One would be justified in saying that it is the prettiest effect in the whole range of sleight-of-hand magic; yet it is almost entirely neglected, or done so badly that the effect is spoiled. This may be from failure to get a clear understanding of the essential parts of the manipulations necessary. If the reader will try the moves with the articles in his hands, the following explanation should make the matter quite clear.

Materials. The hollow balls, which should be large enough to contain four fifteen-inch silks, can be obtained at any magic store. They are painted flesh color and have a hole for the insertion of the silks. An ordinary rubber ball will serve the purpose; but the metal balls have a slightly larger capacity, owing to the thinness of their material. In either case the surface should be slightly roughened to aid in palming them.

Preparation. Load the ball by taking a silk by one corner and pushing the opposite diagonal corner inside the ball first, then the rest of the silk; when the last corner is arrived at, take the second silk by one corner, place this corner against that of the first, and fold one over the other in such a way that when the second silk is pulled out it will cause the corner of the first to protrude a little from the hole in the ball. Push in the rest of the second silk in the same way, engaging its last corner with a corner of the third silk, and follow the same procedure with it and the last silk.

Method. Thus prepared, the ball is manipulated in the following manner; but it must always be borne in mind that it is not a case of manipulating a billiard ball, as the audience should not have the slightest suspicion that you have anything in your hands. In making the necessary moves the hands should be shown empty only in the perfectly natural stroking of the silks as they are produced and without calling marked attention to them. This is a most important point. Many manipulators would seem to wish the spectators to know that they have a ball in their hands in order to accentuate their cleverness in concealing it. Such a course destroys the illusion, which is that the silks materialize from the air.

Palm the ball in the right hand with the hole outwards. The change over palm can be made, if desired; but if the ball has

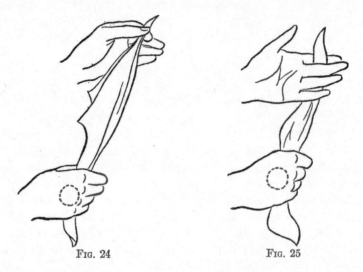

FIG. 24   FIG. 25

been stolen from the vest or elsewhere imperceptibly, this is not necessary. Fix your gaze on a point in the air a little to your left (you have your right side to the front), about as high as you can reach with your left hand; then suddenly reach out with that hand and pretend to catch a silk handkerchief by one corner between the tips of the thumb and forefinger. Hold the hand as if a real silk were hanging down from it and look it up and down as if admiring the beauty of its color. With the right hand stroke this imaginary silk from top to bottom twice. At the third stroke nip the protruding end of the last silk loaded into the ball and move the right hand down with exactly the same motion as before. The result is that this silk is dragged out of the ball (Fig. 24), but the effect to the spectators is that a silk already in the left hand has suddenly become visible to them. The left hand must be kept perfectly still, and if the move is made properly there will be no suspicion that the silk comes from the right hand.

The ball has now to be transferred invisibly to the left hand. To do this, move the last three fingers of the left hand in front of the silk and release the thumb so that the silk hangs behind these three fingers, its top corner being gripped between the first and second fingers and protruding in front of the hand

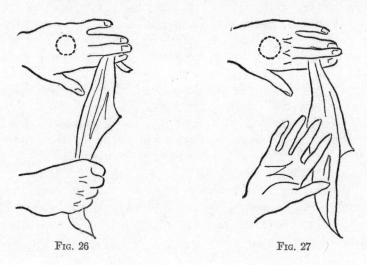

FIG. 26   FIG. 27

(Fig. 25). Now stroke the visible silk, from the tips of the left thumb and fingers to its lowest corner, twice. As the right hand comes over the left hand to do this a third time, bend the left fingers in front of those of the right hand and turn the hand inwards so that for a moment the palm of the left hand is brought behind the palm of the right hand. In that moment the ball is transferred to the left palm; the left hand turns over completely, bringing its back to the front; the silk falls to the position shown in Fig. 26; and the right hand again strokes it from top to bottom, turning naturally at the end of the stroke to show its palm (Fig. 27).

The left hand now has its back turned squarely to the spectators and both sides of both hands have been brought into view with perfectly natural actions. To return the ball to the right hand, bring it up to stroke the silk a third time and at the moment that it covers the left hand bend the left fingers in and turn the hand over inwards; the silk slips over the fingers into the position shown in Fig. 25, the palms meet, the ball is taken into the right palm, the left hand turns its palm to the front, and the right hand continues its stroking of the silk. The position now is once more that shown in Fig. 25.

Continue the production of the remaining silks in the same way, keeping them in the left hand and stroking them just as you did the single silk. From first to last the only movement made by the left hand is the turn from front to back and from back to front, the up-and-down movements being made by the right hand only. By using half silks—that is, silks cut in half diagonally—five or more can be loaded into the hollow ball, but the first silk should be one of full size.

When the supply of silks in the first ball is exhausted, it can be dropped and a second ball palmed in placing the silks on the back of a chair, one silk being retained for beginning the production from the second ball.

By using the silks produced by this method as cover, the operator can proceed to the production of a large number at once, by means of the methods already explained, or employ them for a set trick.

VI. KNOTS, TIES, AND FLOURISHES

For the acquisition of that deft, graceful manner of handling articles so necessary for the proper presentation of magic, there is no better method than the practice of the knot flourishes with silk handkerchiefs. In fact, these flourishes serve a double purpose, for the use of some of them in the course of an act with silks makes a pleasing interlude; indeed, a very interesting and entertaining act can be arranged with these flourishes alone.

Large silks, at least eighteen inches square, should be used and, in the early stages of practice, after twirling them rope fashion, small rubber bands should be passed over them to the middle to keep the twisted folds together.

1. THE INSTANTANEOUS KNOT

Grasp the silk about five inches from one end in the right hand and hold it up in front of you. Place the left hand just below the right hand, the thumb and fingers encircling the silk, and run that hand down the silk to a point about five inches from the other end; grip the silk there and turn the left hand over inwards. Hold the silk at each end by pressing the thumbs against the sides of the hands and open the fingers (Fig. 28).

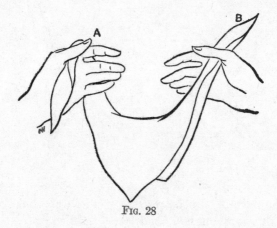

FIG. 28

Bring the hands together, turning them over inwards. Grip end A between the right second and third fingers and, at the same time, end B with the fingers of the left hand by bending them into the left palm; draw the hands apart and a knot is tied in the middle of the silk.

As soon as the action is thoroughly understood, practice it under cover of a swing of the whole body from right to left. Display the silk, as in Fig. 26, with your left side to the front; swing round to the left, moving the right hand faster than the left so that they come together in the middle of the swing, where the exchange of the ends is made; then move the left hand away faster than the right. At once begin to twirl the silk between the hands; then draw it taut and the knot becomes visible.

Smoothly and quickly done, the turn of the body completely

covers the meeting of the hands and the knot appears instantaneously.

2. Instantaneous Knot on One Arm

Hold the silk, stretched out in front of you, by the ends, between the tips of the forefinger and thumb of each hand.

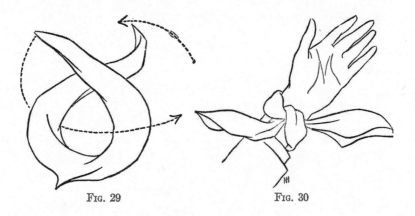

FIG. 29   FIG. 30

With an upward, circular sweep of the right hand, outward and back toward the left hand, twist the body of the silk into a loop (Fig. 29). Thrust the left hand through this loop to its full length and bring the right hand back to the left shoulder. The moment the knot forms on the left forearm, drop the ends and stretch the left arm out to the left (Fig. 30).

3. One Hand Knot

Hold the right hand vertically, palm outwards, and lay the middle of the silk over the fork of the thumb, letting the part at the front of the hand pass between the third and fourth fingers (Fig. 31). Turn the hand so that the fingers point to the floor and the back of the hand is uppermost; then seize B between the tips of the first and second fingers, the little finger keeping A out of the way. Jerk the hand downwards, throwing the loop off the back of the hand, and the knot forms in the middle of the silk.

The action is covered by a quick downward movement of the hand, followed at once by an upward throw—tossing the silk into the air. Catch it by one corner as it falls.

4. DOUBLE LOOP KNOT

Hold the silk as in Fig. 28 but with the hands near the middle, about six inches apart. Grip the silk in exactly the same way as for the instantaneous knot but do not pull the ends through, leaving two loops as shown in Fig. 32.

FIG. 31

5. VANISHING LOOP KNOTS

After displaying the double knot slip the two first fingers of each hand through their respective loops from above, nip the ends (one in each hand), and pull them through the loops, as shown by the dotted lines, under the pretense of making an even more intricate knot. In reality this action unties the knot if the silk is pulled taut. By pulling on the ends, however, until the two loops merge into

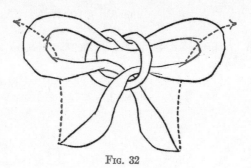

FIG. 32

the other folds, to all appearances a very large knot is made. Display this; then hold the silk by one end with the left hand and pass the right hand down its full length, causing the folds to dissolve under cover of that hand.

An amusing effect can be obtained by having an actual knot of the same material under the vest. While displaying the large knot, palm the loose knot from the vest with the right hand. Pass this hand down the silk, dissolving the apparent knot, and show the loose knot as having been pulled bodily from the silk.

6. The Vanishing Knot

Hold the silk by one end (A), between the first and second fingers of the left hand, so that it falls in front of the hand, the corner protruding at the back. Close the third and fourth fingers on the silk; take the lower end (B) with the right hand, place it

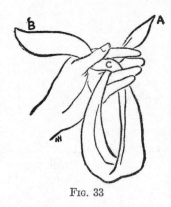

Fig. 33

in the fork of the left thumb, and drop the second finger on it at C (Fig. 33).

Pass the right hand through the loop; grip the end A and pull it through the loop, but keep the second finger firmly on the part C—so that the apparent knot forms around the loop held back by this finger. Pull the second finger out of the loop it held and hold the silk by the end B in the left hand. A pull on the end A, or a simple shake, will cause the knot to vanish.

7. Upsetting a Square Knot

This is a very useful principle and it is surprising how many performers do not know it. Fig. 34 shows a double knot—the regular square or reef knot—in the formation of which the ends always lie parallel with the body of the silk. If you grip the silk at the point C with one hand and the end A with the other, the knot will "upset" and AC will be pulled out straight with two loops round it (Fig. 35). A very slight pull will slip these free and the knot is untied. The same result follows if the pull is made at D and B, the end BD coming out straight with two loops round it.

If, in tying the second knot, the ends A and B are passed the opposite way—that is to say, A going under the loop and B above it—the resulting knot is called a "granny" and the

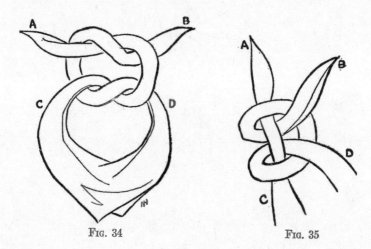

FIG. 34   FIG. 35

ends will lie at right angles instead of parallel to the body of the silk. To upset such a knot, take hold of the silk to the left of the knot with the left hand and the end that points toward the body with the right hand and pull as before.

The best way to learn this "upsetting," but simple, principle is to make the knots by tying the ends of two differently colored handkerchiefs together.

8. THE KNOT THAT UNTIES ITSELF

There are several methods of working this popular effect. For example, sew a black silk thread about twenty-four inches long to one corner of a silk handkerchief and make a large knot at the free end. When ready to show the trick, take the silk from your pocket and execute several of the flourish knots, such as the instantaneous knot and the vanishing knot, with which the attached thread will not interfere. Then take it by the unprepared end with the left hand, the thread hanging down from the diagonally opposite corner. With the right hand tie a single knot with the thread end and bring the thread through

Fig. 36

the bight with its free end hanging down on the opposite side (Fig. 36).

Now stroke the silk downwards with the right hand and catch the knotted end of the thread between two fingers, holding it tightly. Raise the left hand and lower the right hand, slowly; the attached end will be pulled up by the thread through the bight, untying the knot, and the silk will fall free to its full length.

IX

CONJURING WITH CIGARETTES

"My cigarette! The amulet
That charms afar unrest and sorrow,
The magic wand that, far beyond
Today, can conjure up tomorrow."
Charles Fletcher Lummis—My Cigarette.

APART from a few isolated tricks, the cigarette was little used in magic until recent years. It was only when some bright mind conceived the idea of building manipulations with a lighted cigarette into a complete act that the humble fag came into its own. The act is supposed to have originated in Spain; in any case, it was first presented in Paris by Franz-Klint, a Spanish magician, in 1916. The novelty was received with such favor, by both the public and the magicians, that nowadays one rarely sees a magical performance that does not include a cigarette number.

The subject divides naturally into two parts—unlighted cigarettes and lighted cigarettes.

I. UNLIGHTED CIGARETTES

So many sleights and moves with cigarettes have been invented that the mere enumeration of them would take up too much space. The interest in most of them, however, is confined to the specialist, the basic sleights being comparatively few and the only ones of use to a practical operator. I shall begin by describing the various holds whereby a cigarette is retained in the hand secretly.

SECRET HOLDS

1. THE THUMB GRIP

This consists in holding the cigarette by one end in the fold formed when the thumb is pressed against the side of the hand.

189

It is by far the easiest and most useful hold for the cigarette and also, as we shall see later, for a thimble. The free end should slant toward the base of the little finger and the top joint of the

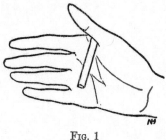

FIG. 1

thumb, separated as far as possible from the first finger. The fingers can be slightly separated, the cigarette being shielded by the palm of the hand (Fig. 1).

2. THE PINCH

In this case the cigarette is held by one end, pinched between the fingers, so that it lies along the line formed by the joining of the fingers, pressure being exerted to flatten the end a little to

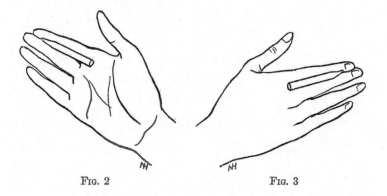

FIG. 2   FIG. 3

prevent exposure of the white paper covering it. The most useful position is between the first and second fingers, at either the front or the back of the hand (Figs. 2 and 3).

3. THE FINGER PALM

The cigarette is held by the pressure of a fingertip on one end, the other end resting against the base of the thumb or the palm of the hand—according to the length of the finger or the cigarette

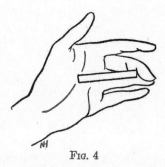

FIG. 4

in use. This hold is most often made with the middle finger, though it can also be made with the first or third (Fig. 4).

PRODUCTIONS FROM THE SECRET HOLDS

1. FROM THE THUMB GRIP

This is done by bending the fingers (the first finger coming above the cigarette and the second below it), gripping the cigarette between them, and carrying it away as they are extended. The bending and subsequent straightening of the fingers, with the cigarette between them, must be done in a flash as the hand reaches up into the air under the pretense of catching a cigarette. The production from the right hand must be made with the right side of the body to the front and from the left hand with the left side nearest to the spectators. As we shall see later, as many as five or six cigarettes can be held in the thumb grip and be produced singly.

2. FROM THE FRONT PINCH

This is a very simple matter. Drop the point of the thumb under the pinched end of the cigarette and push it upwards and forwards against the first finger, so that the cigarette comes into view above the forefinger at a right angle to it; at the same time close the other fingers into the palm. The back of the hand is, of course, to the front (Fig. 5).

For the production from the back pinch, bend the first and second fingers slightly and place the point of the thumb on the pinched end of the cigarette, holding it against the second finger; lift the forefinger and place it in front of the cigarette opposite the thumb, pressing the cigarette upwards into the same position as in the front pinch production.

3. FROM THE FINGER PALM

Bend the first joints of the first and third fingers in a little and grip the end of the cigarette; at the same time bend the thumb under it near the tips of the fingers, press the cigarette upwards, and grip it in exactly the same way as is shown in Fig. 5.

FIG. 5

VANISHES

The difference between the real vanish and the apparent vanish must first be understood. The real vanish takes place when the cigarette is placed in the secret hold in pretending to put it in the other hand; and the apparent vanish, when the hand supposed to contain the cigarette is shown empty. The spectators should have no suspicion that the real vanish has already been made.

1. BY THE THUMB GRIP

Hold the cigarette by its middle at the second joints of the first and second finger of the right hand (Fig. 6). Turn a little toward the left and bring the left hand, its back to the front and the fingers pointing downwards, in front of the right hand, the thumb behind it. Under cover of this screen, close the right fingers and put the cigarette in the thumb grip (Fig. 7), immediately straightening them as the left fingers close and appear to carry away the cigarette.

Move the left hand upwards in a diagonal direction to the left, agitating the fingers on the palm as if crumbling the cigarette to nothing; then open them, one by one, beginning with the little

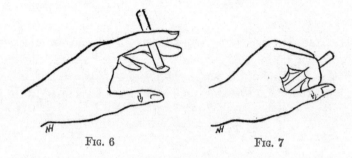

Fig. 6   Fig. 7

finger and show the hand empty. Fix your eyes on the left hand throughout and let the right hand fall naturally to the side.

The following is a new starting point for the thumb grip: Hold the cigarette between the thumb below it and the first three fingers above it, the little finger being free; that is, in the posi-

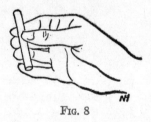

Fig. 8

tion taken before knocking the ash from the tip (Fig. 8). Pass the little finger under the cigarette, release the thumb, and bend the second and third fingers slightly—the result being that the thumb end of the cigarette is levered straight into the thumb grip.

2. Pretended Throw in the Air

Stand with the right side of the body to the front, holding the cigarette in the usual smoking position; drop the hand slightly, preparatory to making the throw, and in the upward motion bend the fingers, place the cigarette in the thumb grip, and immediately straighten and separate them as the hand reaches its highest point. Follow the supposed flight of the cigarette with your eyes.

3. FINGER PALM

(1) Hold the cigarette by the extreme end between the tips of the right thumb and middle finger, the palm being upwards and the first and third fingers beside the middle finger. Place the left hand, palm upwards, under the cigarette (Fig. 9) ; turn it

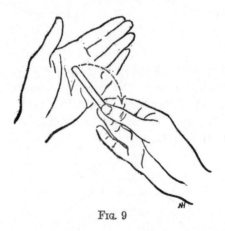

Fig. 9

over inwards as if to grasp the cigarette but really make it tilt back into the right hand, releasing the right thumb and holding the outer end as a fulcrum. Turn the back of the right hand to the front as the cigarette is gripped in the finger palm between the end of the middle finger and the palm. Move the left hand away, closed as if it contained the cigarette, and make the vanish as already explained.

(2) *This method is called the Clasp.* Hold the left hand palm upwards and lay the cigarette across the roots of the fingers. Bring the right hand over, palm upwards, and place it under the left fingers. Move the right hand upwards and inwards and with it close the left fingers on the cigarette, continuing the movement over the left wrist and toward the elbow. This is a feint.

Open the left hand and show the cigarette, then resume the starting position. Again close the left fingers with the right hand; but this time place the tip of the middle finger on the outer end of the cigarette, press its inner end against the palm of the right hand, and carry the cigarette away—moving the right hand toward the left elbow as before. In the meantime close the left hand, move it diagonally upwards, and consummate the vanish as usual (Fig. 10).

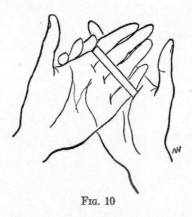

FIG. 10

Variation 1. As the right hand closes the fingers of the left hand and the cigarette is hidden, push its outer end with the left thumb into the thumb grip in the right hand.

Variation 2. Really close the left fingers on the cigarette in the same way, turn the left hand back to front, and move it toward the left. Pass the right hand in front of it, back outwards, and with the left thumb push the cigarette up, making it protrude slightly. Pass the right hand over the left fist; seize the protruding end between the second and third fingers; and carry it away, placing it at the finger palm or thumb grip in the right hand.

4. THE TIP TILT

Take the cigarette by one end between the tips of the left fingers, turned upwards, so that the whole cigarette is visible. With the right hand give it a series of gentle taps to push it down into the left hand; then show it there by turning the palm of the hand to the front. This is a feint. Repeat the operation; but at the moment when the cigarette is about to disappear into the left hand, instead of striking vertically with the tips of the right fingers, give it a slanting blow, which will make it tilt on the fingers of the left hand. It is thus brought into a horizontal position and you seize it by pressing the tip of the right middle finger on the outer end, pushing the inner end against the palm of the right hand (Figs. 11 and 12). Close the left hand, apparently carrying the cigarette away, and complete the vanish.

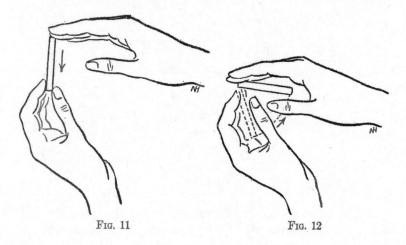

FIG. 11   FIG. 12

5. THE PUSH IN

Take the cigarette between the tips of the thumb and first and second fingers of the right hand; apply the other end to the spot at which the cigarette is to be inserted (Fig. 13). Hold it very lightly and move the fingers along it so that it goes to the inside of the hand as they move forwards, until the end reaches the thumb crotch and you seize it in the thumb grip. Continue to press the fingers on the spot for a moment longer; then straighten them and remove the right hand, with the forefinger extended, pointing. Do not use cigarettes with cork tips or gold bands for this sleight.

To produce the cigarette from any spot after the push in vanish, the action is reversed. Hold the cigarette in the finger palm, apply the tips of the first three fingers to the spot, press the tip of the thumb on the free end, and slide the fingers back along the cigarette to the other end. Hold it thus for a moment, then pull it away with a little jerk.

By means of this sleight a cigarette can be pushed apparently into the back of the left hand and pulled out of the palm, into one ear and out of the other, etc. A favorite method of reproduction is from the mouth, the free end being lightly seized by the lips and the fingers slid back along the cigarette. The illusion is perfect.

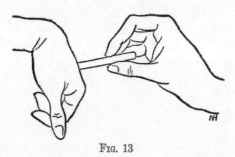

FIG. 13

Finally I mention the vanish made in taking a cigarette from the mouth. Take hold of it near the mouth with the thumb below and the third finger above it, then finger palm it from this position while pretending to place it in the left hand. A clean and easy sleight.

Again, a cigarette can be vanished by balancing it on the ear. Stand with your right side to the front and apparently take the cigarette from the left hand, leaving it there in the thumb grip. Bend the left forearm and pretend to push the cigarette into the point of the elbow; at the same time balance the cigarette on the left ear with the left hand.

TRANSFERS

The idea is to show the hands empty while concealing a cigarette. With a cigarette palmed in the left thumb grip and your left side to the front, show the right hand empty, palm outwards, and point to it with the left forefinger. Turn to the left and, as the tips of the fingers meet in front of the body, seize the free end of the cigarette in the right thumb grip (Fig. 14), complete the turn, and point to the empty left hand with the right forefinger.

The sleight is an easy one and the tendency to abuse it must be resisted.

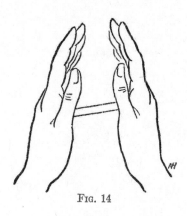

FIG. 14

ACCESSORIES

1. THE FINGER CLIP

This is a half ring of metal with a pin soldered to it (Fig. 15). It fits on the back of the middle finger just below the nail and

FIG. 15

when a cigarette is impaled on the pin it lies along the back of the finger, thus being invisible when the hand is held with its palm to the front. In bending the fingers to make a pretended catch, the cigarette is brought into view, extending from the tips of the fingers. In putting the cigarette into a receptacle, the hand is inserted, the fingers are straightened, and the cigarette is again brought behind the middle finger ready for another catch. Finally the gimmick can be disposed of by letting it fall into the receptacle with the cigarette after the last catch.

2. CIGARETTE DROPPERS

These are reservoirs holding a number of cigarettes, which can be taken from them secretly one by one. The Diestel dropper is the most practical dropper and it can be obtained very reasonably at any magic store. The dropper is placed under the lower edge of the coat, and a light pressure on it through the fabric with the heel of the hand will deliver a cigarette imperceptibly. By having a dropper on each side and using the hands alternately, a seemingly inexhaustible supply of cigarettes can be produced.

3. HOLDER FOR A SINGLE CIGARETTE

Tie a knot in the middle of a small rubber band, making two loops. Fasten a safety pin to one loop and insert a cigarette in the other. The cigarette can then be attached to any part of the clothing you desire.

TRICKS WITH CIGARETTES

1. THE TRAVELING CIGARETTE

Effect. The passage of a cigarette from hand to hand through the right knee and back again, then through both knees.

Method. Two cigarettes are required, both being held in the left hand—one openly, the other in the thumb grip. Show the right hand empty, and take the cigarette with it between the first and second fingers. Lower the hands with their backs to the front and place them one on each side of the right knee, about six inches away. Tap the side of the right knee with the cigarette, then move the hand back to its first position. Repeat the movement; but this time rapidly thumb palm the cigarette and at the same time bring the left hand against the left side of the knee and produce the palmed cigarette between the first and second fingers of that hand. Pause for a moment or two; then repeat the moves the reverse way, apparently sending the cigarette through the knee back to the right hand.

Place the knees together and pass the cigarette across in exactly the same way. This feat is very effective and so easy that there is a temptation to repeat it too often, a fault frequently committed by manipulators.

2. THE MULTIPLYING CIGARETTES

Effect. The successive production of a number of cigarettes from one hand.

Method. Two cigarettes are necessary. Hold one in the right hand in the finger palm and the other, which has been slightly

shortened, in the left hand, lying along the junction of the second and third fingers; the hand is palm upwards and the fingers
pressed together in the shape of a cone and bent at the first

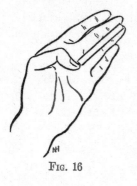

FIG. 16

joints only, sloping a little to the right
(Fig. 16).

Push the cigarette up with the left
thumb to its full length and pretend to
take it with the right hand; in reality allow it to drop behind the left fingers under
cover of the right hand, which then shows
the duplicate cigarette. Place this apparently in the coat pocket, or in a receptacle; but really take it again in the
thumb palm. Repeat the procedure as
many times as desired.

3. DOUBLING A CIGARETTE

Effect. A cigarette is shown and a second one is pulled out of
it. The operation is repeated several times.

Method. Again you require two cigarettes. Palm one in the
right hand, calling this one A; show the other, B, in the left

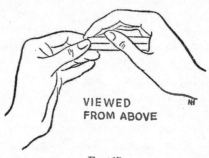

VIEWED
FROM ABOVE

FIG. 17

hand. Take B in the right hand between the thumb and first
finger and show the left hand empty. Again place B in the left
hand and hold it with the thumb above it and the middle finger
below it, so that the cigarette is in a horizontal position pointing
to the right. Bring the right hand over and place A in front of
and parallel to B, gripping its outer end between the tips of the

left thumb and first finger. Release A from the right fingers and hold both with the left thumb and fingers (Fig. 17).

Slide the right fingers back along the two cigarettes; grip the end of B, releasing it from the left hand, and draw it away to the right. Show it and pretend to put it in your coat pocket, really taking it in the finger palm again. The procedure can be repeated *ad libitum*.

4. Novel Cigarette Manufacture

Effect. A cigarette is made from a cigarette paper only and smoked.

Method. Place a cigarette in the rubber-band holder, already described, and fasten it under the edge of your coat, on the left

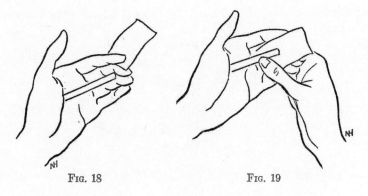

Fig. 18   Fig. 19

hand side, in position to be easily stolen with the left fingers. The cigarette should have a little of the tobacco removed from each end and the paper pressed in.

Show a cigarette paper and, if you are skillful enough, balance it on the bridge of your nose; if not, make several attempts, then deliberately wet one corner and plaster it against the side of your nose. This will certainly get a laugh and give you the opportunity of stealing the planted cigarette with your left hand in the finger palm. Take the paper in the same hand, between the first and second fingers (Fig. 18).

Show the right hand empty, then with that hand slide the bottom of the paper under the top of the cigarette (Fig. 19) and draw the cigarette up behind it with the right thumb. You have then merely to roll the real cigarette in the paper. Being short-ened a little, its ends will not protrude and the rolling can be completed very openly. Screw the ends up a little, as is generally done with a handmade cigarette, and call attention to the perfect way in which you have rolled the paper tube. Pretend to take a pinch of tobacco from your pocket and throw it toward the paper. Strike a match, light the cigarette, and puff on it. This is a charming little feat that is always effective.

5. The Phantom Cigarette

Effect. The performer goes through all the motions of rolling a cigarette in pantomime and a real lighted cigarette suddenly appears in his mouth.

Method. To prepare for the trick, fasten a part of the striking side of a box of safety matches to the inside of your left shoe

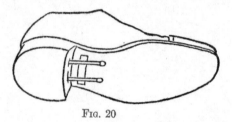

Fig. 20

and between the heel and the sole push two matches, cut down and the ends wedge-shaped (Fig. 20); fasten a cigarette in a rubber-band holder under the left side of your coat.

In all the actions that follow an exact imitation of handling the real articles must be made. In pantomime take out a book of cigarette papers, remove one, put the book back in the vest pocket, smooth the paper with the fingers, make a crease in it to receive the tobacco, take a bag of tobacco from your coat pocket, open its mouth, pour some tobacco onto the paper, close the bag (pulling the draw string with your teeth), replace the bag in the pocket, roll the cigarette, raise it to your mouth to wet the paper and fix it, and put it in your mouth. Take a matchbox from your pocket, take out a match, turn slightly to the left, lift the left foot, bend down and *really* take a match from the heel of your shoe, strike it on the strip of lighting material (shielding the flame with your hand so that the match cannot be seen).

At the same time steal the cigarette with your left hand; bring the lighted match up to your mouth, shielding it with both hands, and under their cover place the cigarette between your lips. Light it and blow out smoke, extinguishing the match. Push the match between the second and third fingers as you show your hands empty, the palms to the front. Puff on the cigarette; then take it in your left hand to show it, drop the right hand to the side, and let the match fall to the floor. If well acted there is no better trick for opening a series of cigarette manipulations.

6. THE CIGARETTE CHASE

This is based on the Miser's Dream (see page 42); but, instead of coins, cigarettes are caught in the air, singly and in quantities, placed in a receptacle, and finally distributed to the audience. With a mastery of the sleights that have been explained and a Diestel dropper on each side a very interesting and effective routine can be presented. Either of the two preceding experiments makes a good opening trick, or, if preferred, the first few catches can be made with the finger clip. As they are caught, the cigarettes should be placed in an opaque receptacle so that an occasional false deposit can be made, the hand being hidden as it again palms the cigarette.

With every cigarette that is caught—or, at least, every other one—some little manipulative feat—such as passing it into one ear and out of the other, into the corner of one eye and making it emerge from the mouth, etc.—should be introduced. They not only make the routine brighter and more intriguing but help to cover the steals. For example, having caught a cigarette with the right hand, you casually show the left hand empty. Push the cigarette into the corner of your right eye and then extract it from your mouth. At the right moment steal a cigarette with the left hand. Place the right-hand cigarette in the left hand, really palming it, and show the one just stolen. Pretend to place this in the receptacle but take it in the thumb grip.

Catch the cigarette in the right hand from the air and work the passage of the cigarette from one hand to the other through the knees. At the last passage leave the visible cigarette in the left hand. Throw this into the receptacle, catch the right-hand fag in the air, and steal another with the left hand, and so on.

By the time you have exhausted the loads in the droppers and the cigarettes from individual holders, the effect on the spectators will be that you have caught a hundred or more. If the cigarettes are to be distributed, a supply should be put in the receptacle beforehand. If a borrowed hat is used for the purpose, it is an easy matter to load the little bundle from the person or the table, as explained in Chapter XV on hat loads. The distribution is always a popular feature.

Once a routine has been worked out, keep strictly to it until it becomes so familiar that you can give your whole attention to the presentation. Beware of working too quickly; rather deliberate moves (which enable the spectator to get the full effect of every manipulation) are the best and, for the same reason, always make a pause for a few moments after each production or vanish for the effect to register.

II. LIGHTED CIGARETTES

In general, the cigarettes used in the lighted cigarette act are butts; that is, half-smoked cigarettes. On occasion, however, full-length cigarettes are used. I will deal first with the principles.

THE SECRET HOLDS

The thumb grip and the pinches remain the principal holds, and of these the thumb grip is the most useful. Four, five, and even six cigarettes can be held by it at the same time and they can be produced one by one. Simply bend the fingers in, insert the tip of the middle finger between the two outer cigarettes, seize the outermost one between the first and second fingers, and then straighten the fingers. The rest follow in the same way.

PRODUCTION OF LIGHTED CIGARETTES

The methods are exactly the same as for unlighted cigarettes.

VANISHES

The same procedure is used for the butts as for unlighted cigarettes, but with the pinches care must be taken to keep the lighted end a little distance from the hand by holding the butt at an angle.

1. SPECIAL VANISH FOR A BUTT

Close the left hand into a fist, the thumb upwards. Place the butt, lighted end downwards, into the opening made by the bent forefinger and hold it with the opposite end protruding. Push it into the fist by little taps with the right hand, tapping first with the middle of the palm and then moving the hand forwards a little and making the final tap as the butt is almost wholly in the fist, take it in the thumb grip and carry it away in the right hand. Turn the left fist over and raise it diagonally to the left, completing the vanish as usual.

TONGUING

It was on the basis of this sleight that the whole act of producing lighted cigarettes from the air was built. As an isolated feat, the tonguing—that is, the vanish or producton of a butt in the mouth—has been used for generations, especially by circus clowns.

The sleight is not a difficult one; confidence is the main requisite, and to attain this confidence practice should first be with an unlighted butt. Place it between the lips; press the point of the tongue on the end; open the mouth and make the butt tilt backwards, using the back of the lower teeth as a fulcrum. The butt will then fall on the tongue, the lighted end projecting over the arch formed by the root of the tongue and not coming into contact with it. The reverse movement will bring the butt, still lighted, back between the lips.

As many as five butts can be tongued at once or singly. For the best results from the sleight, the performer should be able to hold three lighted butts on the tongue and produce them one by one with ease and certainty. The production must be made under cover of the hand, which is placed to the mouth as if to put a cigarette between the lips or to remove one. The spectators should not have the slightest suspicion that a lighted cigarette can be held in the mouth. This is a point too often neglected by magicians; indeed, some of them do the tonguing quite openly to show how clever they are.

A good effect can be obtained in the course of the act by blowing smoke from the apparently empty mouth. To do this, press the unlighted end of the butt against the back of the upper front teeth and exhale strongly. Air is thus forced through the cigarette and the resulting smoke issues from the lips.

A second method of tonguing can be used for a single butt only. It is not somersaulted backwards but is drawn straight back into the mouth. To do this, slide the tongue along the end until it almost reaches the lighted part and then draw it back until the lighted end is behind the front teeth. The advantages of this method are that the mouth need not be opened widely in its execution and that a somewhat longer butt can be used. It is well to have both methods at command.

SWITCHES

1st Method. Steal a dummy butt from a holder or dropper and hold it in the right hand by bending the third and fourth fingers

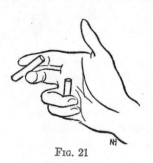

Fig. 21

on it (Fig. 21). Take the lighted butt between the first and second fingers, raise it to the mouth, and puff on it; then throw it to the floor apparently but, really, in making the throw you pass the lighted butt to the thumb grip and release the dummy.

2d Method. Have a dummy in the thumb grip and a lighted butt between the first and second fingers. Carry this to the mouth and take a deep mouthful of smoke; then remove it. Exhale part of the smoke and, as the hand drops, grip the dummy between the second and third fingers, removing it from the thumb crotch, and thumb palm the lighted butt in its place. Raise the dummy to the lips, blow some smoke through it, exhale the rest, and throw the dummy into the receptacle.

By using both hands and getting dummies from holders on each side alternately, very little skill is required to stage an imitation of the cigarette-catching act. The subterfuge may serve until the necessary skill is acquired. Punk should be placed in the receptacle and one or two lighted butts thrown into it to cause the appearance of some smoke from it as the catching goes on.

1st Method. In the course of the act you find you have an unlighted butt. You take a matchbox, only to find it empty; so you rub the butt on the box and it lights up. The secret is simple—the head half of a safety match is inserted in the end of the butt beforehand. The rest follows.

2d Method. While puffing on a cigarette, you are startled by a sudden flash of flame. The preparation for this is equally simple —just a strip of flash paper wrapped around the cigarette. When the fire reaches the prepared paper, there is a sudden flash and nothing is left to show how the flame was produced.

THE CIGARETTE CHASE—CATCHING LIGHTED CIGARETTES IN THE AIR

This is the act which has elevated the manipulation of cigarettes to the dignity of a stage illusion. The routine is very elastic and every performer should arrange a sequence to suit himself. I have already indicated the use of dummy butts; three other routines follow.

1st Routine. The production of a number of lighted cigarettes, full size, without the hands approaching the body.

This method is the simplest possible and is suitable only for the opening of an act. You have five lighted cigarettes thumb palmed in each hand. Make your entry from the right-hand side and catch the five cigarettes in the right hand first, taking a puff or two from each one and then throwing them to the floor. Make a half turn to the left and produce those in the left hand in similar fashion.

Various vanishes and productions can be interspersed between the productions and, if one cigarette be retained in the right hand, the last one in the left hand can be used for the passage through the knees and other passes.

Expert manipulators will probably disdain such a simple method, but I have seen professional magicians obtain great success with it.

2d Routine. The magician shows his hands empty and produces a lighted cigarette. This is manipulated and multiplied to four, all lighted; four more are produced in the other hand and finally a full-sized lighted cigarette appears in his mouth.

Preparation. A rubber cigarette with a red foil tip is held in the mouth; four lighted cigarettes are put in a tank on the coat on the left side, a dummy under the left side of the vest; one lighted butt in a tank in the right vest pocket, another lighted butt in a tank at the foot of the trousers, and one more lighted butt on the finger clip on the middle finger of the right hand.

Method. Enter from the left side of the stage and show the hands empty, the palms to the front. Catch the butt from the clip in the air, detach it, and place it in the mouth with the left hand. Puff on it as the right hand drops to the side and disposes of the clip by pushing the pin into the trousers back of the hip.

Take the cigarette in the right hand and puff on it again, retaining some of the smoke. Vanish it from the left hand, and recover it from behind the right knee with the right hand as the left hand steals the dummy from the vest.

Place the lighted butt in the left hand between the third and fourth fingers and at the same time steal the dummy from that hand with the right fingers. Catch this dummy from the air, place it in the mouth, and puff out the retained smoke.

Push it into the right ear, thumb palming it, and take the lighted butt from the tank in the right vest pocket. Puff on it and retain some smoke in the mouth, then put it between the left second and third fingers.

Catch the dummy in the right hand from the air, place it in your mouth, and puff out some of the retained smoke. Push it into your chin and pull it out of your ear; then puff on it, exhaling the rest of the smoke. Push it into the top of the knee and produce the lighted butt from the tank at the bottom of the trousers leg. Puff on this, again retaining some smoke, and place it between the left first and second fingers.

Catch the dummy from the air, puff out the retained smoke as if coming from it, and place it between the left thumb and first finger. Turn to the right, displaying the four cigarettes between the left fingers, and steal the four lighted cigarettes from the tank on the right side, taking them in the thumb grip.

Produce these from the air one by one, puffing on each one and taking them from the mouth between the right fingers. The first two go between the third and fourth and the second and third fingers. Produce the third, place it in the mouth, puff on it, and leave it there for the moment. Produce the fourth from the air between the second and third fingers; then take the one from the mouth with the thumb and first finger, first taking a deep mouthful of smoke and retaining as much as possible.

Display the four lighted cigarettes in each hand and let the rubber cigarette pop out of the mouth between the lips. Exit puffing the retained smoke from it.

3d Routine. The routine that follows will require a good deal of practice; but it is well worth the practice, for a more effective series of manipulations would be hard to devise.

Effect. The performer enters smoking a butt. He throws this openly to the floor and another instantly appears between his lips. He smokes this and throws it down, shows both hands empty, and catches another. After several more productions of lighted butts, he catches six full-sized lighted cigarettes in rapid succession, then four more without the hand nearing the body. Finally he produces a large pipe from the air and exits smoking it.

Preparation. Place a tank for three full-sized lighted cigarettes under the edge of the coat on each side; at the back of the right hip a tank for four full-sized lighted cigarettes in position to be taken in the thumb grip, all four at once. In your mouth you have three lighted butts. To keep these alight, breathe through the lightly parted lips to give them air. They will burn longer if you light them beforehand and let a little ash form on the ends, then let them go out. Light them again when ready for the act.

Finally you have a fourth butt in your mouth and enter smoking it. Inside the coat, on the right-hand side, fasten a large straight stem pipe in a rubber-band holder by the stem. Fix it so that the bowl can be taken hold of by bending the top joints of the fingers under the edge of the coat.

Method. After entering, puff several times on the butt in the mouth, attracting attention to it. Show your hands casually; take the butt and throw it to the floor, pointing to it. Bring one of the three butts in the mouth between the lips, puff on it, and then point to it. This production can be made without the cover of the hand, since all eyes are attracted to the butt on the floor.

Puff on this one several times, retain some smoke, and then throw it down. Puff out the retained smoke; reach into the smoke with the right hand; pretend to catch a cigarette and place it in the mouth, really bringing the empty hand to the mouth and pushing out the second butt under its cover.

Take several puffs; remove the butt with the left hand, pretend to throw it to the floor, really palming it in the left hand and at the same time making a three-quarter turn to the left, pretending to crush the butt with your left foot. At the same moment push out the third butt between the lips. Turn to face the spectators, puffing it.

Pretend to take this butt from the mouth, really tonguing it; then, with the arms outstretched to each side, pretend to throw it from the right hand to the left hand, which produces the palmed butt. Take this in the right hand and throw it to the floor.

Pretend to catch another with the right hand and put it in the mouth, really bringing the tongued butt between the lips under cover of the hand.

Take a handkerchief from your pocket, at the same time stealing a thumb tip on the right thumb; spread the handkerchief over the left hand; make a well with the right thumb, leaving the thumb tip inside it. Take the butt from the lips and pretend to push it into the well; but really put it into the thumb tip, which you steal away on the thumb.

Shake out the handkerchief to prove the vanish of the butt; replace it in the pocket, getting rid of the butt at the same time; with the left hand steal a lighted cigarette from the tank on the left side. Puff some of the retained smoke toward the left, then turn to the right and puff the remainder to that side as you steal a cigarette with the right hand from the tank on that side. Produce the left-hand cigarette from the air.

Place it in your mouth and puff on it; take it in the right hand and throw it down, while the left hand steals another. Immediately after the throw, produce the cigarette palmed in the right hand. Puff on it, take it in the left hand and throw it to the floor, and catch another with the left hand as the right hand steals one.

Continue in the same way until all six have been caught. The various passes—through the knees, into the ear, and recovery from the mouth, etc.—should be introduced between catches.

While the left hand makes a last move with the last cigarette, rest the right hand casually on the right hip, in a natural position, and quietly steal the four cigarettes from the holder on that side in the thumb grip. Do this while your whole attention is fixed on the left hand and without any perceptible movement of the right fingers. Catch these four in rapid succession and place them between the fingers of the left hand. Display them, turn the right side to the front, put one cigarette in the mouth with the left hand, puff deeply on it and exhale the smoke; at the same moment steal the pipe with the right fingers, bending them over the bowl so that the stem lies back along the hand and the wrist. Puff again but retain as much smoke as possible, take the cigarette from the mouth with the left hand, reach out with the right hand, and produce the pipe. Place it in your mouth and exit puffing out the smoke you retained in the mouth.

X

CIGAR CONJURATIONS

"O, finer far
Than fame, or riches, are
The graceful smoke-wreaths of this free cigar."
George Arnold—Beer.

BECAUSE of the difference in its size, shape, and color, the cigar has not attained the vogue of the cigarette for stage purposes. However, for intimate work, or for parlor and club performances, it can be employed with very fine effect.

As a general rule ordinary cigars are too large to be handled easily unless one has a very large hand and, for this reason, many performers use small, faked cigars of wood, shaped and colored appropriately. These are very easy to handle, but unfortunately they will not bear close inspection and they do not look like real cigars. A genuine cigar can be prepared very easily for manipulative work so that it will last for an indefinite period without deteriorating.

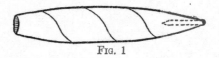

Fɪɢ. 1

Choose a cigar about four inches in length, one that can be held comfortably in the finger palm; that is to say, with one end pressed against the end of the middle finger and the other end against the base of the thumb or the palm. Cut a large wooden safety match in half, sharpen one end, and push this carefully into the point of the cigar. Prepare a strip of brown paper with good library paste and roll it round the cigar spirally, finishing off by covering the match point carefully. Roll the cigar on a table with the palm of the hand to make sure that the paper adheres throughout. When this coat is dry, paste another strip

212

over it in the same way and let this dry thoroughly. Then rub the surface smooth with very fine sandpaper, give the whole cigar a final coat of shellac, and paste a band in the usual position. You will then have a cigar that can be handled easily, thanks to the match point, and that will last indefinitely (Fig. 1).

I. SLEIGHTS

Several of the methods already explained for cigarettes—such as the thumb grip, the finger palm, and the tip tilt—are equally applicable to cigars. There are, however, some special methods peculiar to cigars.

1st Method. Hold the cigar vertically on the left palm, supporting it by placing the right middle finger on the pointed end

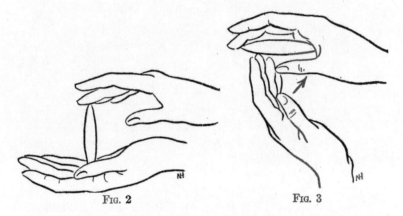

FIG. 2   FIG. 3

(Fig. 2). Move the right hand downwards and the left hand upwards to bring the tips of the two middle fingers together, with the point of the cigar between them, and cause the cigar to tilt up into the right hand, which secures it in the finger palm (Fig. 3). At the same time close the fingers of the left hand, turning the hand over inwards and bringing its back to the front. Move the closed hand away to the left, agitating the fingers, and vanish the cigar in the usual way.

An effective recovery is from the back of the left knee. Apply the right hand to the back of the knee, bend the knee, grip the outer end of the cigar in the bend, slide the fingers back along the cigar to the other end, and pull it into view slowly.

2d Method. Hold the point of the cigar between the thumb and fingers of the right hand and place it on the palm of the left hand (Fig. 4). Close the left fingers on it and push the cigar into the fist with the tip of the right middle finger (Fig. 5) as the hands turn over inwards. At the moment when the left fingers are about to close on the cigar, press on the point with the right middle fingertip and tilt it back into the finger palm in the right

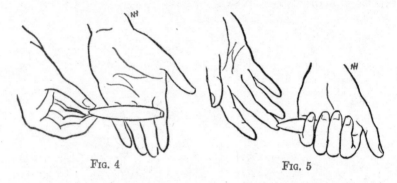

Fig. 4   Fig. 5

hand. Close the left hand completely and move it away, pointing to it with the left forefinger. It should not now be necessary to reiterate that you follow the left hand with your eyes. Complete the vanish in the usual way.

3d Method. Show the palms of the hands empty and place the cigar against the left palm, the hands held vertically, supporting it by the tips of the right fingers; roll it between the hands, the right hand moving outwards and the left hand inwards, bringing the cigar against the right palm supported by the tips of the left fingers. Repeat the action several times and at the third roll seize the end of the cigar in the left thumb grip, continuing the outward movement of the right hand without any hesitation and closing it, apparently on the cigar, as its palm reaches the fingertips of the left hand. Move the right hand away, following it with your eyes, and drop the left hand to the side with a natural gesture. Complete the vanish as usual.

4th Method. Complete vanish in the vest. Hold the cigar by the blunt end between the tips of the right thumb and fore-

finger and place the left hand, closed, against the vest buttons at
one of the openings (Fig. 6). Push the cigar into the left fist,
the point really going into the vest between two of the buttons.
When it is fully inserted under the vest, move the right hand

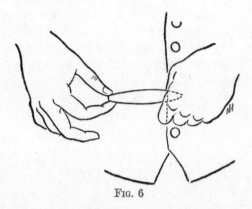

FIG. 6

away and make the vanish from the left hand in the prescribed
manner. Finally show both hands empty.

5th Method. Prepared cigar. Pierce two holes in one of the
prepared cigars and with a fine, flesh-colored thread make two
loops, as shown in Fig. 7, large enough for the insertion of the
top joints of the first and third fingers.
Thus prepared, the cigar can be held
concealed along the middle finger, at
either the front or the back of the
hand, supported by the loops on the
first and third fingers. To produce the
cigar from the back of the hand, for
example, you have only to bend the
top joint of the middle finger under

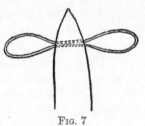

FIG. 7

the point and grip this against the tip of the thumb; the cigar
then extends straight out from the fingers and is apparently
caught from the air. Place it in a hat or other receptacle and, as
soon as the hand is out of sight, pass the end of the middle finger
under the point of the cigar, stretch out the finger, and it will
again be hidden at the back of the hand. Bring this out of the

receptacle with the palm toward the audience and repeat the catch.

An effective "Cigar Chase" can be made by using this cigar only. It is advisable to vary the catches, making some of them with the back of the hand to the front, the action, of course, being just the reverse of that described in the preceding paragraph. Finally the cigar can be palmed, or sleeved, after the last catch and a pretense of throwing the hatful of cigars to the spectators, the hat, of course, proving to be empty. Or again, a supply of cigars can be loaded into the hat beforehand and a real distribution made, which is always a popular feature.

II. TRICKS WITH CIGARS

1. SWALLOWING A CIGAR

Place an unlighted cigar between the lips and show your hands empty. Put the tip of the middle finger of the right hand against the outer end of the cigar, throw the head back a little, push the right hand upwards, release the end from the lips, and press the middle of the cigar against the nose. The lower end is thus brought against the palm of the right hand and you grip the cigar in the finger palm. Remove the hand, carrying the cigar away; close the mouth and make a pretense of swallowing the cigar.

Place both hands flat on the stomach, the fingers of the right hand pointing to the left and those of the left hand to the right, the left fingers slightly overlapping those of the right hand. With the right middle finger push the point of the cigar between two buttons of the vest, rub the stomach with the hands, and with the heel of the right hand push the cigar completely into the left side of the vest. Continue rubbing and gradually separate the hands, finally removing them and letting it be seen that both are empty. Lift the edge of the vest with both hands and bring the cigar out with the right hand.

2. THE PURSE PRODUCTION

A little preparation is necessary. In your left outside coat pocket put two small snap purses, one unprepared and the other with a slit in the bottom into which you push the point of a cigar.

In the right-hand coat pocket, or in a holder under the coat, place a second cigar.

Patter about a special brand of cigar that has a lot of rubber in it and offer to show a sample. With your left hand bring out the purse and the cigar, hiding the latter with the fingers. Open the purse, seize the point of the cigar with the right hand and pull it out with a twisting movement.

Turn to the left and offer the cigar for inspection, at the same time dropping the purse into the left coat pocket and taking the unprepared one. Take the cigar back, open the purse, push the cigar into it; hold both in the left hand and turn to the right to have both examined by a spectator on that side, seizing the opportunity to steal the second cigar.

Face the spectators and hold the purse in the left hand. Open it with the right hand, the back of the hand to the front; push the end of the palmed cigar inside and then apparently extract it, with the same twisting movement you applied to the first one. In reality you grip the end that is inside the purse with the left hand on the outside and then slide the fingers and thumb of the right hand along the cigar to the end, finally pulling it away with a little jerk. Both purse and cigar can then be handed out for inspection.

3. MULTIPLICATION OF CIGARS

The performer shows a cigar in his right hand, holding it upright by the pointed end. He takes it with his left hand and puts it in his pocket. With the right hand he catches another cigar from the air; this also is put in his left pocket. The production of cigars is continued *ad libitum* and finally a distribution of cigars is made, or the pocket is shown to be empty.

To produce this effect you require two cigars: one you show openly in the right hand, held upright by the point between the tips of the thumb and forefinger; the other you have finger palmed in the left hand. Take the visible cigar with the left hand and, as the hands meet in front of the body, bring the tips of the two middle fingers together; press on the point of the cigar with the right middle finger, at the same time releasing the other end from the left palm, and tilt the cigar back into the right hand, which seizes it in the finger palm position (Fig. 8). Put the visible cigar in the left coat pocket and as soon as the left hand is out of sight take the cigar in the finger palm again. Bring the hand out of the pocket with its back to the front, ready for a repetition of the moves.

FIG. 8

Reach out to the left with the right hand and produce the palmed cigar; to do this, bend the fingers slightly, grip the point of the cigar between the tips of the first and second fingers, put the tip of the thumb under the end of the cigar and press upwards. Almost the whole length of the cigar should then be visible above the first finger and at right angles to it. The moves can be repeated as often as you wish, but six or seven catches will be enough.

If you have loaded a number of cigars in your pocket beforehand, you can distribute them after the last catch; but if not, then simply palm the cigars and prove that the whole thing was an illusion by showing the pocket empty.

4. Routine of Cigar Productions and Manipulations

Two cigars only are necessary: one you have finger palmed in the right hand and the other in a holder under the left side of your coat. Begin by borrowing a hat; place it mouth upwards, resting on the backs of two chairs placed back to back on your left.

Produce the cigar palmed in your right hand from the air; at the same time steal the second cigar with the left hand, taking it in the finger palm. Execute the doubling sleight (already explained in connection with cigarettes) and show the two cigars, one in each hand, holding them upright by the points. Pretend to put the one in the left hand into the borrowed hat, but really take it again in the finger palm as soon as the hand is hidden. Repeat the same maneuvers six or seven times; after the last pretended deposit in the hat you will have a cigar openly in the right hand and the other finger palmed in the left.

Next make a pretense of swallowing the cigar, using the sleight already explained, palming it in the right hand and producing the duplicate with the left hand from the point of your shoe. Push this one into your stomach with the left hand and produce the palmed cigar with the right hand from your back, making a three-quarter turn so that the spectators can see you apparently pull it out. At the same time quietly drop the cigar from the left hand into the left coat pocket. Continue by pushing the cigar into one nostril and pulling it out of the other, using the sleights explained.

Pick up the hat with the left hand and proceed to catch cigars from the air after the style of the Miser's Dream (see page 42) with coins. Make a motion of placing the visible cigar in the hat, really finger palming it. Catch it again and make the same moves, enabling you to make some half a dozen more catches. Then change your grip of the cigar to the back finger hold; that is to say, you hold the cigar on the back of the middle finger by pressure on its sides by the first and third fingers. With this hold you can bring the hand out of the hat with its palm to the front. Make the catch from this position by simply bending the fingers, placing the tip of the thumb on the point of the cigar, and then extending the fingers.

After several catches from the back of the hand, make the last few from the front of the hand as before. Finally palm the cigar, take the hat in the right hand, and pretend to throw the cigars from it in a shower over the spectators; but they have vanished— the hat is empty. Or, if the occasion warrants it, you can load a bundle of cigars into the hat at the start and finish with a distribution of them.

XI

THIMBLE THAUMATURGY

"At my fingers' ends . . ."
Shakespeare—Twelfth Night.

THE humble thimble of everyday use is the latest addition to the armory of the magician. Starting from a simple vanish invented by the great English magician, David Devant, the ingenuity of many other performers has added so many sleights and manipulations that thimble magic has become a recognized and important branch of the art. Because of its small size the thimble is not well suited for use on large stages, although some performers have scored great successes in that field; but for the parlor, and for small and medium-sized stages, it is an ideal medium. Quite apart from their effectiveness and popularity with the public, manipulations with thimbles are of the greatest help in developing that suppleness of the fingers so indispensable to the practice of sleight of hand. Anyone interested in magic will be well advised to take up this branch of the art.

The thimbles may be of metal, silver, or steel, of wood or of celluloid, and they may be simply polished or colored—these are matters to be settled by individual fancy. The general consensus of opinion, however, is that a metal thimble, colored bright red, is the best for all ordinary purposes. Thimbles studded with brilliants make a flashy appearance but they should be avoided —at any rate, by the beginner—as they are unsuitable for many sleights. Some performers have their thimbles graded, a different size for each finger; others again have the mouths of the thimbles slightly flattened; the beginner, however, should choose a thimble to fit firmly on the tip of the forefinger and have all the others the same size. By slightly scoring the inside of the rim of the thimbles it will be found that they can be held securely on any finger. Again there are various kinds of faked thimbles; these should be avoided, because they are of no practical use in manipulations.

I. SECRET HOLDS

It is necessary first to study the various positions in which a thimble can be held in the hand secretly. The first and most important is the thumb grip.

1. THE THUMB GRIP

In this position the thimble is held by its rounded end in the fold at the base of the thumb. The correct hold is shown in Fig. 1 and particular note must be taken of the fact that the thimble lies at right angles to the palm and not with its mouth pointing upwards, a mistake that is made too often. When the

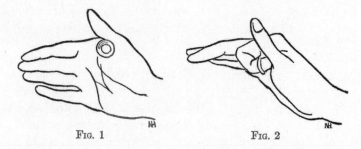

FIG. 1   FIG. 2

thimble is held correctly the top joint of the thumb is well separated from the hand, yet no portion of the thimble is visible from the back.

To place the thimble in this grip, first put it on the tip of the forefinger, bend the finger in, press the rounded end into the angle formed at the base of the thumb, and grip it there by pressing the lower part of the thumb inwards (Fig. 2). Withdraw the tip of the finger; press lightly on the lower edge of the opening to place the thimble at a right angle with the palm of the hand; and extend the finger, aligning it with the others. To recover the thimble from the thumb grip, simply reverse the action. Bend the forefinger, insert its tip deeply in the thimble, and again extend the finger.

Both these actions of the forefinger, placing the thimble in the thumb grip and recovering it, must be done in a flash and to acquire this rapidity is simply a matter of practice. When the starting point is from the tip of the second finger, the action is exactly the same as for the first finger and its execution should be equally rapid. The transfers of the thimble from the third and fourth fingers to the thumb grip require more complicated movements of the fingers, which will come naturally to the student after he learns the other basic sleights.

2. THE REGULAR PALM

The thimble, in this case, is held by the contraction of the muscles of the palm (Fig. 3), as with a coin or any other small object. It is useful mainly for the production of a thimble on the

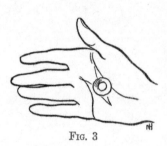

tips of the third or little fingers, and a thimble can be placed in this position from the tip of either of these fingers by simply bending them into the palm.

3. THE FINGER PINCHES

The pinch of a thimble between the fingers can be made between the first and third fingers, or between

FIG. 3

the second and little fingers. The technique is the same in both cases, so that a description of the first, which is the one most often used, will be sufficient.

For the pinch between the first and third fingers, the thimble is held with its opening flat against the upper part of the middle finger by pressing against its sides with the sides of the first and third fingers. It can be held thus at either the front (Fig. 4) or the back (Fig. 5) of the hand.

To place the thimble in this position, starting from the tip of the forefinger, begin by putting it against the side of the middle finger, hold it there with the thumb and remove the fingertip, turn it with the thumb, and grip the opening between the sides of the first and third fingers. The thimble is then at the front pinch. To place it at the rear pinch from the same position on the tip of the forefinger, press the thimble between the tips of the thumb and second finger; withdraw the first finger; grip the sides of the thimble between the first and third fingers; bend the middle finger under the thimble and bring it in front, turning the thimble in so doing. The first and second fingers maintain their grip and the thimble is thus brought to the rear of the second finger, with its opening against the back of that finger. The thimble is then at the rear pinch.

When the thimble is on the tip of the middle finger, it suffices to grip it between the first and third·fingers, then withdraw the tip of the middle finger, straighten that finger and turn the

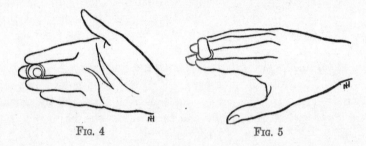

FIG. 4   FIG. 5

thimble in so doing—bringing its opening against the front of the finger. This is the front pinch; to bring it to the rear pinch from the same position, simply bend the middle finger and pass it to the front, turning the thimble at the same time and leaving it at the back of the finger.

At first it may be found necessary to place the thumb on the thimble to steady it, but with a little practice this can be dispensed with. The pinches are very useful and should be done at lightning speed.

II. TRANSFERS FROM THE FRONT TO THE BACK OF THE HAND

1. FROM THE FRONT PINCH TO THE BACK PINCH

Hold the thimble by the pressure of the first and third fingers; bend the middle finger and press its tip against the lower edge of the mouth (Fig. 6), turning the thimble until it is stretched between the other two fingers, mouth downwards. Then pass the middle finger to the front, completing the turning of the thimble to the back of the fingers. The first and third fingers retain their pressure on the sides throughout the movement, which must be done without the aid of the thumb.

To transfer the thimble from the rear pinch to the front pinch,

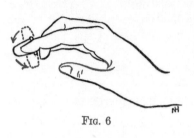

FIG. 6

the action is simply reversed—the middle finger being bent in and turning the thimble in the reverse direction.

2. FROM THE THUMB GRIP TO THE REAR PINCH

The thimble being in the thumb grip, first bend the fingers in and insert the tip of the middle finger in it; lift the fingers, carrying away the thimble, and press the top joints of the first and third fingers against its sides. As the fingers open, withdraw the tip of the middle finger, press it upwards on the inner part of the mouth of the thimble, and bring the finger to the front. Straighten out all the fingers and the thimble will be in the rear pinch.

To transfer the thimble from the rear pinch to the thumb grip, the action is reversed. Bend the fingers inwards, insert the tip of the middle finger in the thimble, and press it into the thumb crotch in the usual manner. These two moves are very useful for showing the back and front of the hand empty while still holding the thimble.

III. VANISHES

1. THE THIMBLE ON THE TIP OF THE FOREFINGER

1st Method. Stand facing the front with the left hand palm upwards, the fingers half closed, the left arm bent, and the left hand a little to the left of the body. Show the thimble on the tip of the right first finger, the other three fingers bent in, the arm extended to the right. Bring the right hand over toward the left palm rather quickly, the back of the hand to the front; the moment before it reaches the left hand, thumb palm the thimble and instantly extend the forefinger again, placing it on the left palm and completely closing the left fingers on it (Fig. 7).

Remove the left fist, simulating a slight effort as if the thimble required a little pull to free it from the forefinger. Hold the right hand still for a moment, showing the forefinger bare; then let it drop naturally to the side. Move the left hand diagonally upwards to the left, agitating the fingers as if crumbling the thimble

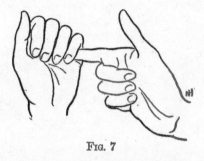

FIG. 7

away; then slowly open the fingers one by one, the little finger first, and show the hand empty.

2d Method. Starting from the same position, place the right forefinger, capped with the thimble, on the left palm, the left fingers stretched out (Fig. 8). Close the left fingers rather slowly and, as soon as they form a screen in front of the right forefinger, rapidly thumb palm the thimble and instantly extend the finger again. Complete the closing of the left fingers and finish the action as in the preceding sleight. The right forefinger must be bent in and extended again in the twinkling of an eye.

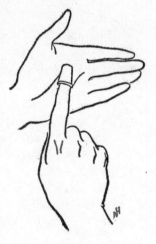

FIG. 8

3d Method. Show the thimble on the tip of the extended right forefinger, the other fingers closed and the thumb separated. Turn the right side of the body to the front and hold the left arm half bent, the hand stretched out with its palm to the front, the fingers pointing to the left, the

thumb upwards. Place the right forefinger against the palm, with
the thimble near the top of the hand but not protruding. Close the
left fingers slowly, so that the thimble is actually in the left hand
but not gripped tightly (Fig. 9).

To make the steal, raise the back of the right hand a little;
bend the right forefinger and withdraw it, placing the thimble in
the thumb grip at once while moving the hand, first toward the
right, then toward the left and downwards—as if to call attention
to the other hand, which you hold still and which is supposed to

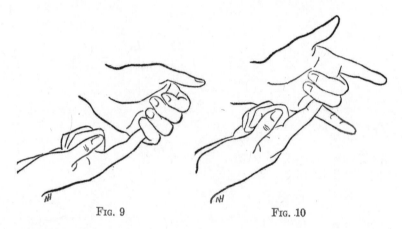

FIG. 9   FIG. .10

contain the thimble. Agitate the left fingers and vanish the
thimble as usual.

Variation. The two middle fingers only of the left hand may
be closed on the thimble (Fig. 10). The withdrawal of the forefinger and the thimble and the final vanish follow, as described
in the preceding paragraph.

It should be noted here that by reversing the action of the forefinger described in the first method, the thimble can be secretly
inserted in the left fist. To do this, show the left hand empty on
all sides, make a pretended catch in the air, and close the left
fingers. Extend the right forefinger, closing the other fingers in;
push it into the fist and immediately bring it out capped with a
thimble. The thimble was picked up from the thumb palm in the

right hand just the moment before the forefinger entered the fist. This is a useful and effective move.

4th Method. Stand facing the spectators, the thimble on the tip of the right forefinger, the back of the hand to the front at the same height as the mouth and about six inches away from it. Pretend to place the thimble in the mouth by raising the wrist, rapidly thumb palming the thimble and putting the bare forefinger in it. Push the cheek out a little with the tongue, then pretend to swallow the thimble as you withdraw the finger.

IV. PRETENDED THROWS INTO THE AIR

1. THE BACK OF THE HAND TO THE FRONT

Stand with the right side of the body to the front and exhibit the thimble on the tip of the right forefinger, the hand being at shoulder height. Drop the hand as if preparing to throw the thimble and, when it reaches the lowest point, rapidly bend the finger and thumb palm the thimble, immediately extend it, and raise the hand quickly to complete the action of throwing. This sleight is also useful in making a pretense of throwing the thimble into a receptacle.

2. FROM THE FRONT OF THE HAND

Stand with the left side to the front, showing the thimble on the tip of the right middle finger, the palm of the hand to the front and the hand held vertically. Move the hand downwards, preparatory to making the throw into the air; as it comes up again, transfer the thimble to the rear pinch. On the completion of the throw, hold the hand still for a moment or two, the fingers pointing upwards, and follow the supposed flight of the thimble with your eyes. Then drop the hand and, under cover of a turn to the right, transfer the thimble to the right thumb grip.

3. VANISH OF FOUR THIMBLES SIMULTANEOUSLY

Stand with your right side to the front and show the back of the right hand at about the height of the left elbow, the fingers extended and each of them capped with a thimble. Drop the hand a little in preparing for the throw, and bend the four fingers into the palm as far as possible (Fig. 11). Then bend the thumb down tightly, bringing its side on top of the thimbles; withdraw the fingers, leaving the thimbles under the thumb, and extend them, widely separated (Fig. 12), in completing the throw.

The sleight is not difficult but it is well to practice it first with thimbles on the first three fingers only, adding the little-finger

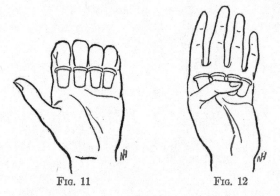

FIG. 11   FIG. 12

thimble when the action has become familiar. It is the most startling of all thimble manipulations and can be done with either hand with equal facility. The thimbles can be reproduced, one by one, after the vanish by simply bending the fingers in turn and picking them up. Apart from its great value as a vanish, the sleight is a most valuable exercise for the fingers.

V. REPRODUCTIONS

1. ON THE TIP OF THE FIRST OR SECOND FINGER

This is merely a matter of bending the finger in and picking up the thimble from the thumb palm. The inward bend and the subsequent extension of the finger with the thimble on its tip must be made literally in a flash.

2. ON THE TIP OF THE THIRD OR FOURTH FINGER

In both these cases the thimble is generally first transferred to the ordinary palm by the second finger and then picked up from the palm by the third or fourth finger as the case may be. The direct transfer from the thumb grip to these fingers requires exceptionally supple fingers.

3. On the Tip of the Thumb

The thimble being at the rear pinch, under cover of a wave of the hand bend the middle finger into the palm and insert the tip of the thumb directly into the thimble. Straighten the thumb immediately and separate it from the fingers as widely as possible.

VI. CONCEALMENT OF THIMBLES

There are so many suitable hiding places on the person that it is rarely necessary to resort to tables or chairs. For example, a thimble can be placed between the buttons of the vest, under the vest, in the vest pockets, in the cuff of the trousers, in the collar of the coat, in the shirt collar, etc. In all cases the thimble

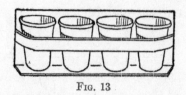

Fig. 13

must be placed with the opening outwards, ready for the insertion of the fingertip.

The only accessory required is a holder for four thimbles. This generally takes the form of a piece of metal with a flange, against which the tops of the thimbles rest, with a piece of broad elastic round it to hold the thimbles in place (Fig. 13). They can be obtained at any magic store. Even these holders can be dispensed with by having loops of elastic to hold the thimbles securely, yet allowing for easy removal, under the vest or lapels, or at the tops of the vest pockets.

VII. TRICKS WITH THIMBLES

1. To Pass a Thimble Through the Right Knee and Back Again, Then Through Both Knees

With a thimble held secretly in the thumb grip in the left hand, stand facing the front and place the hands on each side of the right knee, the backs to the front, the forefingers extended, the other fingers closed on the palms and the right forefinger capped with a thimble. Tap the right forefinger against the side of the knee, then move it back to its original position. This is a feint. Repeat the action, but this time thumb palm the thimble and strike the bare tip of the finger against the side of the knee. A moment later bring the left forefinger against the knee on the other side, rapidly transferring its thimble from the thumb grip to its tip.

Smoothly done, the illusion of the thimble having passed through the knee is perfect. By reversing the action you then make the thimble apparently return to its original position. Continue by joining both knees and make the thimble pass through them from right to left and back again.

In similar fashion you can apparently place a thimble in the mouth and bring it out of the ear; pass it into one ear, through the head, and out of the other ear; and so on according to your own fancy.

2. The Multiplication of One Thimble to Eight

The thimble holder, already mentioned, is required for this very effective trick. Place four thimbles in it and fasten it to the vest under the coat near the right armpit. Arrange three thimbles in different places in your clothing; for example, one may be placed in the left lower vest pocket, one in the cuff of the left trousers leg, and one in your collar at the back of the neck. With another thimble palmed in the right hand, you are ready to perform the trick.

Begin by showing the right hand empty by means of the transfer to the rear pinch, then produce the thimble by apparently catching it in the air on the tip of the second finger. Transfer it to the tip of the forefinger and really place it in the left hand as a feint. Take it again on the right forefinger tip and show it, then pretend to place it in the left hand but palm it in the right. Vanish it from the left hand, then put the right hand behind the head to get the thimble from the collar. The hand being out of sight, it is an easy matter to transfer the palmed thimble from the thumb grip to the tip of the little finger. Press this finger, together with the second and third, tightly into the palm and bring out the thimble from the coat collar on the tip of the forefinger. Be careful to keep the back of the hand to the front, both in putting the hand behind the head and in bringing it forwards again.

Again vanish the visible thimble from the left hand. You can pretend to snap it up the left sleeve, show the hand empty, then take the thimble from the lower left vest pocket on the tip of the right forefinger. As the right hand goes under the coat to the vest pocket, seize the opportunity of transferring the thimble in the thumb crotch to the tip of the third finger; then pull the side of the coat open with the left hand, push the right forefinger into the pocket, and bring the thimble out on its tip. Two fingers of the right hand have been secretly capped with thimbles; keep them bent tightly into the palm of the hand. Vanish the visible thimble by the throw and take the thimble from the trousers cuff, slipping the middle fingertip in the other.

Again pretend to place the visible thimble into the left hand, using a different pass, and pretend to throw it up the right sleeve. Show the left hand empty, then thrust it under the right side of the coat to the armpit. Abstract the four thimbles from the holder on the tips of the fingers; bend the second, third, and fourth fingers into the palm; and bring the hand out with the forefinger extended, a thimble showing on its tip. Be careful to keep the back of the hand towards the spectators.

The position now is that you have four thimbles in each hand, one only being visible, and the multiplication to eight could be made at once. This, however, would be very bad policy, since the production would take place immediately after the left hand had been placed under the coat. It is a standing rule that an interlude of some sort must take place between a steal and a production, so you proceed to pass the thimble from hand to hand. The visible thimble being on the tip of the left forefinger, place the hands a little to the left of the body, the fingers pointing downwards, the forefingers only extended, and the backs of the hands to the front. Move them across the body to a similar position on the right, and in the action palm the thimble on the left forefinger and produce the thumb palmed thimble in the right hand at the right forefinger tip. Hold the hands still for a moment for the effect to register; then move them back to the first position, palming the right-hand thimble and producing the other on the tip of the left forefinger. Once more move the hands to the right side of the body, repeating the effect.

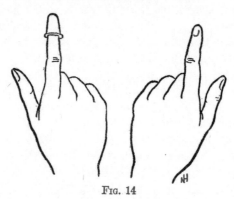

FIG. 14

Now vanish the thimble from the tip of the right forefinger with an upward throw. Hold up both hands, the backs to the front and the forefingers extended upwards, attracting all attention to them (Fig. 14). Bend them down; then sharply ex-

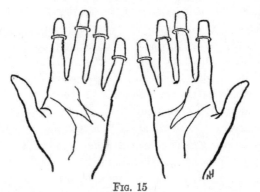

FIG. 15

tend the four right-hand fingers, each capped with a thimble, and separate the fingers widely. Gaze at these for a moment; then look at the left fist and suddenly stretch its fingers upwards in the same way, showing each of them also capped with a thimble (Fig. 15). Turn the hands back and front to show that they are otherwise empty. Have a glass on your table into which you can drop the thimbles.

It must be understood that the various vanishes and recoveries leading up to the multiplication are subject to almost infinite variation, and each performer will arrange them to suit himself; but the final production of the eight thimbles—the most startling effect possible with thimbles—should invariably form the climax to the manipulations. Some performers make the great mistake of continuing with more sleights, thereby greatly lessening the whole effect.

3. An Impromptu Method

The preceding trick makes such a great impression that on occasion one may be asked to do it when not prepared with the necessary holder. In such case seize an opportunity of placing three thimbles in different hiding places, as already explained. Proceed to show some tricks with one thimble; then go on to the various passes up the sleeve and so on, thus getting the last three fingers of the right hand capped with thimbles. After the last vanish, which leaves the forefinger bare, hold the right hand up, back to the front and the forefinger extended. Bend this finger in and ask the spectators on which finger they wish the thimble to reappear. There will be contradictory replies and, in order to give satisfaction to all, suddenly stretch out all four fingers, each one capped with a thimble.

4. The Passage of a Thimble Through a Handkerchief

Show the right hand with a thimble on the tip of the forefinger, the other three fingers being bent into the palm. Take a handkerchief by the middle, the corners hanging down, and put it over the right hand so that its middle will rest on the tip of the forefinger; but as soon as the right hand is hidden, thumb palm the thimble and rapidly extend the finger again to receive the handkerchief on it. Stroke the fabric over the forefinger with the left hand and draw it a little over the finger, so that the greater part falls to the front. As you pass the left hand down a second time, insert the tip of the right second finger into the thimble;

extend the finger and push the thimble into the thumb crotch of the left hand, which carries it away (Fig. 16).

Stroke the forefinger of the right hand once more and leave the thimble from the left thumb crotch on the tip of the right forefinger outside the handkerchief.

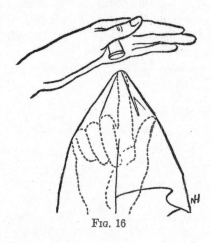

FIG. 16

5. THE PAPER CONE AND THE THIMBLE

This trick introduces a new principle and will serve as a model on which other feats can be based.

Two thimbles, which nest exactly one into the other, are required. Show these on the tip of the forefinger of the right hand as one thimble. Make a little cone with a piece of paper to fit easily over the thimbles and be careful that the edges of its mouth are quite even, so that it will stand upright on the table with no break through which any object inside it might be glimpsed. Place the cone over the right forefinger momentarily, as if to show that it fits; then place it point upwards on the table, apparently empty; in reality you have removed the outer thimble with the cone and set it down inside the cone on the table. This last must be covered with a cloth to avoid any telltale sound.

Announce that the thimble, still visible on the forefinger, is to pass under the cone. Vanish it from the left hand by one of the sleights already explained, carrying the left hand over the cone, agitating the fingers, then opening the hand and showing it empty. Seize the cone by its mouth with the thumb and fingers of the right hand (its back to the front) and lift it, showing the thimble on the table. Take the thimble in the left hand to show it better, drawing all attention to that side, and at the same time let the palmed thimble drop into the cone by relaxing the pressure of the right thumb. Replace the cone on the table, point up, and announce that you will repeat the trick.

Vanish the thimble again, using a different pass. This time pick up the cone by the middle between the first and second fingers of the right hand; point to the thimble, thus revealed, with the left forefinger; turn the cone, mouth upwards, toward the inside of the right hand with the tip of the middle finger and let the thumb palmed thimble drop into the cone. Complete the upward turn of the cone and hold it, mouth upwards, by the point. The move can be made in a moment while all eyes are attracted to the thimble on the table.

Take the cone by the point in the left hand and vanish the thimble from the right forefinger by making a pretended throw into the air. Follow its supposed flight with your eyes and suddenly reach out with the left hand as if to catch the thimble in the cone. Claim that you have succeeded; turn to a spectator on your right, have him hold out his hand (palm upwards), turn the cone over, and let the thimble drop onto his hand. In the meantime you have disposed of the duplicate thimble by dropping it into the right-hand trousers pocket.

FINAL REMARKS

As a general rule, thimble manipulations should be done, without patter, to a light musical accompaniment. Slow, deliberate moves are best, in order that the spectators may be able to follow them without effort and that each surprise may register. The commonest fault is that of working with the hands too close to the body, the head down and the body turned away from the spectators. Remember that if the onlookers cannot see plainly all that you are supposed to be doing they will not be interested and your efforts will fall flat.

In the course of thimble manipulations, opportunities will occur for imperceptibly dropping the thimble into the sleeves, thus making a complete vanish.

XII

THE BIRTH OF FLOWERS

"Roses red and violets blew
And all the sweetest flowres, that in the forrest grew."
Edmund Spenser—The Faerie Queen.

THERE is nothing in the whole realm of magic which is received with greater favor and acclaim by all audiences than the magical production of real flowers. Yet this field is almost totally neglected at the present time, partly because of the greater ease with which feather flowers, so called, and tissue spring flowers can be handled, and partly because of the expense entailed when fresh flowers have to be obtained for every performance. The older magicians realized the value of the production and distribution of real flowers both as a beautiful effect and as a means of stamping their performances on the minds of their patrons. Time and again I have been shown flowers tossed out by Kellar, with his tag attached, kept religiously as souvenirs. No matter what the season or the expense incurred, Kellar included his rose trick in his program, and he always maintained that the trick repaid him handsomely.

I. REAL FLOWERS

1. USING A HAT

Effect. The magician causes a flower to appear in his buttonhole; he grows a bouquet in a tumbler and then produces a number of bouquets from a borrowed hat and distributes them to the spectators.

Preparation. Fasten a black silk thread to a real or artificial rose or carnation; pass the thread through the buttonhole of the lapel, then through an eyelet in the cloth beneath, and attach it to a length of elastic—the other end of which you loop over a suspender button on the left side. The length of the silk must

236

be so adjusted that the flower can be pulled from the lapel to the back of the left armpit without drawing the elastic through the buttonhole.

Place the bouquet, which must be not more than six inches in diameter, on a small wire shelf at the back of your table, the stem pointing upwards (Fig. 1). The small bouquets or nosegays, with stems a little longer than usual, you pack together in a bundle as tightly as possible and pass a rubber band round the

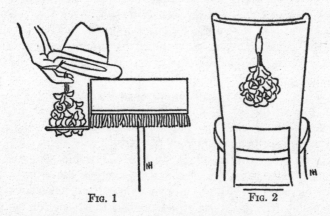

FIG. 1   FIG. 2

stems to keep them in that condition. Pass a strong thread under the rubber band and tie it, making a loop about three inches long. Hang the bundle on the back of a chair on the right-hand side of the stage on a short, stout needle driven into the rail obliquely upwards (Fig. 2). The chair must either be a solid-backed one or have some cover—a large silk handkerchief, for example—thrown over it.

On the table you have a tumbler and a little box, about the size of a pillbox and on the seat of the chair a second small box. These are supposed to contain the seeds for the flowers. Just before entering, draw the flower from your buttonhole back behind the armpit and hold it there by pressing the left upper arm to the side.

Method. Enter wand in hand and announce a demonstration of flower growing by magic, first a single flower. Take the little box from the table and open it; pretend to take a seed, naming the flower you have under your arm, and place it on your lapel.

Wave the wand to the left, then to the right, and strike it smartly against the lapel, at the same time throwing up the left arm and seizing the wand with the left hand. The flower appears instantly; adjust it with the right hand.

Borrow a hat; explaining that as you will use it as a hothouse you require as much room in it as possible, you pull down the sweatband and push out the dent in the crown. Stand behind the table; hold the hat in the left hand—crown upwards, the thumb on the brim, fingers inside with the first and second fingers free—so that the hat comes directly over the bouquet. Lean forwards to take a pinch of the supposed seed from the box with the right hand and place it in the tumbler; at the same moment let the front edge of the brim of the hat touch the rear of the table, grip the stem of the bouquet between the first and second fingers of the left hand, and introduce it into the hat. The moment it is safely inside move the hat away, retaining hold of the stem with the first two fingers; lift the glass with the right hand and move to the center of the stage.

Making the excuse that any draft of air would spoil the experiment, place the hat over the glass, keeping the crown tilted a little forwards—which will make the insertion of the stem of the bouquet into the glass easier and prevent the spectators getting any glimpse of the flowers. A few moments later uncover the glass and reveal the bouquet, a charming surprise. Pretend that a lady requests it and say, "With pleasure, but first allow me to produce a larger quantity." Turn toward the chair on the right as you remark that you want another variety of seeds. Bend down, put the glass and bouquet on the seat of the chair, open the little box with the left hand and pick it up; at the same time your right hand, with the hat held mouth upwards, goes behind the chair and scoops the bundle of flowers off the needle as you straighten up with the box in your left hand. In the whole action keep your attention fixed on your left hand.

Move forwards, pretend to empty the seeds into the hat, wave the wand over it, and use your magic formula; then dip your right hand inside, remove the rubber band, and spread the flowers—giving them the appearance of overflowing the hat. Toss the little nosegays to the ladies and finally present the large one to the lady you previously addressed. Note particularly that each

bouquet should have a little card attached to it with the date
and your name.

With regard to the flower in the buttonhole, there has recently
been introduced a wand with a hollow tip which will hold a small
feather flower with a sharp protruding hook. A downward tap of
the wand engages the hook in the lapel and the flower is instantly
pulled out. Its appearance is so rapid that it is impossible to detect the method.

2. USING A PAPER CONE

Effect. Here again real flowers are produced but by a different
method.

Preparation. Arrange a quantity of flowers into neat buttonhole bouquets with your tags attached. Take some fifteen of these,
press them together into a tight bundle, wrap them round with
a piece of black tissue paper, tie the bundle crosswise with black
thread (not too strong for it must be broken later on), and leave
a loop of about eight inches in length projecting from one side.

Make a large cone with a piece of white tissue paper; cut off
the top level and pack the rest of the flowers into it, filling it
to the brim. Tie a thread around the top about an inch from the
edge, leaving a loop by means of which you can hang it on a
short, stout needle driven into the back of a chair. Between
the point of the cone and the back of the chair fix a piece of thin
black wire about three inches long. If the chair is not one with
a solid back, arrange a silk foulard to conceal the cone. Place
a small basket on the table, and off stage have a piece of stiff
white paper about eighteen by twenty-four inches.

Method. When you are ready to show the trick, place the bundle
of flowers under your left arm, the thread loop to the front;
bend the arm against your chest and slip your left thumb through
the loop. Take the sheet of paper in the same hand and the wand
in the right hand. Go to your table, lay the wand down, and
pick up the basket with the right hand. Announce that you
are about to use the basket, show it empty, and put it on the
seat of the chair. Show the sheet of paper; twirl it round between your hands, showing both sides. Take the upper edge in
the left hand, the thumb behind and fingers in front; move the

hand forwards a little and release the bundle, letting it drop behind the paper (Fig. 3). With the right hand seize the lower right corner; twist it up over the bundle and make a cone, at the same time letting the loop slip off the left thumb and twisting the corner of the cone tightly with that hand. Place the right hand inside, apparently to straighten it out but really to break the thread and crumple up the black tissue, and release the flowers.

Hold the cone up in your left hand and, in time with appropriate music, make motions of catching flowers in the air and throwing them into the cone; at each catch look at the imaginary flower and name it, using the names of those in the cone. Keep

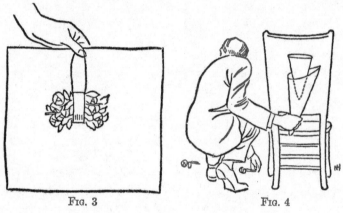

Fig. 3   Fig. 4

shaking the cone to bring the flowers nearer the top and to separate them. When you have made some eight or ten catches, gracefully and realistically, approach the chair and turn the mouth of the cone toward the spectators.

Take the nosegays out, one at a time, and drop them into the basket, contriving to drop several accidentally on the floor. Bring out the black tissue, squeezed into a little ball, with the last flower. Take the cone in the right hand, stoop down to pick up the flowers off the floor, and under cover of the body bring the mouth of the cone just under the point of the flower-filled cone behind the chair. In the act of rising, pick up the basket from the seat of the chair and carry off the cone and loop of thread from the needle (Fig. 4).

Walk forwards as if about to distribute the flowers from the basket, on which you have kept your whole attention; then pretend to realize that more will be required. Put the basket on the table, repeat the catches, and finally show the cone full to overflowing. Empty these flowers into the basket, and in taking out the last squeeze the tissue paper into a ball and drop it into the basket. Open out the paper, show it, and proceed with the distribution.

3. A Flower from the Flame of a Candle

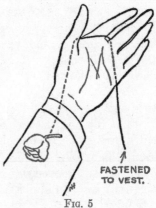

FASTENED TO VEST.

Fig. 5

Cut a rose or a carnation with about two inches of stalk. Near the end of the stalk tie a black silk thread about eighteen inches long; push the flower into the sleeve at the back of the wrist; bring the silk along the back of the hand, over the thumb fork and then between the first and second fingers, and fasten the end to your vest by means of a bent black pin (Fig. 5).

The act of stretching out your hand (after showing it empty) toward the candle flame will pull the flower out of your sleeve to the root of the forefinger; drop the thumb on it and push it to the tips of the fingers, so that it appears to be taken from the flame.

II. FEATHER FLOWERS

The bouquets of feather flowers, so much affected by the average performer, cannot be said to create any illusion. They do not look like real flowers and in too many cases they are presented in so bedraggled a state that they resemble a feather duster more nearly than a flower. I shall give one example only of their use and in this they do create a striking effect.

Preparation. Obtain four medium-sized bouquets and place two in each sleeve in such a way that the ends of the stems come close to the cuffs. Put a much larger bouquet under the vest on the left side, spreading the branches out toward the back with the stem coming midway between the top of the opening of the trousers pocket and the middle of the vest. The only other requirement is a large silk, at least twenty-four inches square.

Method. Show the silk, spreading both sides; twist it and pull it through your left hand to prove it is empty and unprepared. Spread it and place the left hand against the middle, letting the fabric fall down over that hand. With the right hand nip the end of the stem of one of the bouquets in the left sleeve and draw the left hand away, the right hand remaining stationary. Shake the handkerchief and turn the right hand upwards, bringing the bouquet into an upright position; the handkerchief falls down over the right hand.

Seize the visible bouquet with the left hand and at the same time nip, through the handkerchief, the end of one of the bouquets in the right sleeve; withdraw the right hand, keeping the left stationary, and put the first bouquet on your table. Turn the left hand over and display the second bouquet. Continue exactly the same movements to produce the remaining bouquets.

Finally spread the silk, one corner between the right thumb and forefinger (the other three fingers free behind the silk) and the opposite corner in the left hand. Stretch the silk toward the left so that the right hand is brought to the spot where the stem of the large bouquet is hidden. Bow to the audience as though the trick were finished, grip the stem of the large bouquet with the free fingers of the right hand, release the left-hand corner of the silk, and bring the left hand over to the right; as you straighten up, draw the silk and the bouquet very rapidly through the left hand, first downwards, then upwards toward the right. Shake the silk free and turn the right hand upwards, exhibiting the huge bouquet.

III. SPRING FLOWERS

These are so well known there is no necessity to describe them in detail. Briefly, pieces of colored tissue are gummed together in part along the edges and then attached to a piece of split steel spring. This allows them to be folded flat, but when released they open out to the full extent of the spring. They bear little resemblance to any known flower, but their production from a paper cone after the manner of the inventor is a very pretty and effective trick when properly presented. Different grades and sizes of the flowers can be purchased at the magic stores.

There are many methods of loading the flowers into the paper cone imperceptibly, and details of several of the best yet devised follow; but it must be borne in mind that any method by which the operator finds he can achieve the desired end—that is, an imperceptible loading—is the best method for him. A sheet of stiff white paper, about twenty-four inches square, is necessary and a parasol with a spike (in lieu of a ferrule), by which it can be stuck in the floor, is generally used to receive the flowers as they are poured from the cone.

1. FOR ONE VERY LARGE LOAD

Preparation. Put the flowers up in bundles of one hundred and wrap each bundle round twice with green ribbon. Stack some fifteen or more or these bundles on edge and wrap them tightly with a strip of cloth, two inches wide, black on the outside and green inside. Tie the bundle firmly, crosswise, with black thread and leave a loop about eight inches in length.

Method. To perform the trick place the bundle under your coat on the right side, bend the right arm across the chest, slip the right thumb through the thread loop, take the sheet of paper in the right hand and the open parasol in the left hand. Take your position in the center of the stage; stick the parasol in the floor; twirl the paper two or three times between the hands, showing both sides; then grasp the top edge with the right hand—the thumb nearest the body, the fingers on the outside—and the bottom edge with the left hand. Move the right hand forwards a little and allow the bundle to swing, from behind the coat, back of the paper. Seize the lower left-hand corner with the left hand, twist it upwards over the load, let the loop slip off the thumb, and twist the corner of the cone tightly with the right hand. The whole action must be done coolly and deliberately.

After the pretended catching of the flowers from the air, it is necessary only to push one of the packets free and then shake all the packets loose, so that the flowers well upwards in a continuous stream. As many as two thousand flowers can be loaded at once by this method.

2. For Small Loads

Preparation. Make up a load of about one hundred flowers and secure it with a band of green tissue paper passed around the bundle twice. Gum the end of the band and under it pass a black thread. Tie this round the green band, leaving one end about nine inches long and cutting the other end off short. Take two pieces of stiff white paper, twenty-four inches square, and paste them together with three inches of the black thread between them at the middle of one side. When the paper is held up, the bundle of flowers will hang six inches below the bottom edge. Dry the sheets under pressure.

1st Method. To prepare for the trick, lay the sheet on your table so that the load lies at the back on a small wire shelf. Stand behind the table and lift the paper by the two front corners to show the lower side. Show it clear of the table by about three inches at the bottom. Lay it down again flat and smooth it with your hands, a plausible excuse for putting it down; then lift it by the rear corners, thus raising the load behind it. Twist the paper into a cone around the load, hold the apex in the left hand, insert the right hand (under pretense of finishing off the cone) and break the band round the flowers.

After the pantomime catching of flowers in the air and the throwing into the cone, shake them out into the parasol. An easy method of getting a second load is to have it clipped behind a ribbon bow on the handle of the parasol. It is taken in the left hand in the action of holding the parasol steady while the first load is poured out of the cone. This second load is introduced by grasping the cone at the mouth with the left hand to show it empty.

2d Method. In another method a wire clip is used to hold the flowers together, and, projecting at the back of this, is a small lug by means of which the load can be clipped onto the back of the hand. Thus arranged, the first load is placed under the paper at the rear left corner. In picking up the sheet, with your right side to the spectators, clip the load of flowers at the back of the left hand between the second and third fingers. The palm of the left hand is thus seen to be empty and the right hand, which then forms the cone over the left hand, is also palpably empty.

Under cover of the surprise caused by the appearance of the first flowers, a second load can be secured in the same way and inserted under cover of removing the last few flowers of the first load.

3d Method. There is another method in which the cone is self-contained and the loading is avoided. Take two large sheets of dark brown wrapping paper and paste them together after the fashion of the cone for vanishing a silk handkerchief (see page 74). In the open space put three loads of fifty flowers, fastened with bands of green tissue. Show the paper on both sides, make the cone, open the double part under pretense of smoothing the inside, and the rest follows.

Finally, granting that the load has been made imperceptibly, the effect of the trick depends entirely on the operator. If the pretended catching of the flowers is done gracefully, to appropriate music, the subsequent welling forth of apparently innumerable blossoms is a very beautiful thing.

XIII

ROPES AND CORDS

"You shall never want rope enough."
François Rabelais—Works—Book v. Prologue.

TRICKS with ropes, cords, and string have been popular with magicians and the public as far back as our records go, and some of the oldest are still used, with modifications, in present-day magic. The treatment of this subject is divided into three sections: flourish knots, tricks with ropes and cords, and cut and restored rope. It is an extremely difficult task to give a clear explanation of the various moves, twists, coils, etc., which are used in these tricks and it is more than ever necessary that the reader follow the explanations with a rope or cord in hand.

I. FLOURISH KNOTS

The various knots already described at the close of Chapter VIII on silks are also applicable to ropes. The following are practicable with ropes or cords only. The best results will be obtained with a flexible cotton rope about five feet long.

1. Two Simultaneous Knots

Place the rope over the wrists, the hands being about twelve inches apart and the palms upwards, the elbows pressed to the side, and the arms half bent.

Turn the hands over sharply toward the body, engaging the middle of the cord and jerking the two ends of the cord over it (Fig. 1).

Seize one end in each hand, let the loops slide free over the backs of the hands, and then separate the hands. Two knots form, one to the right and one to the left.

246

With a little practice the action can be done with extreme rapidity.

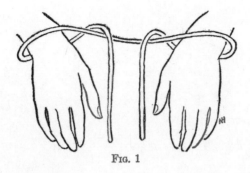

FIG. 1

2. THE SELF-TYING ROPE

The performer holds the rope by one end, the other end hanging down; he jerks the free end upwards and it falls into a knot.

There are two secrets in the performance of this feat: one is to have the free end of the rope weighted, and the other is, to devote the amount of time required to master it. It is for the reader to decide if the effect is worth the time and patience necessary.

3. THE IMPOSSIBLE KNOT

Take one end of the cord in each hand, so that each end protrudes not more than two inches from the fist. Hold the left hand stationary and make the following moves with the right hand, holding its end throughout.

First Effect: Tying a Simple Knot

(1) Pass the right hand over the left wrist from the front of the wrist to the back and downwards, forming the loop C (Fig. 2).

(2) Pass the right hand through the loop C from within outwards and then back through D from without inwards as shown by the arrows (Fig. 2A).

(3) Separate the hands and the cord will be in the position shown in Fig. 3.

(4) Turn both hands downwards as if merely to allow the cords

to slip over them; release the end B and seize the cord at Y, thus regaining hold of B after it has passed through the loop X.

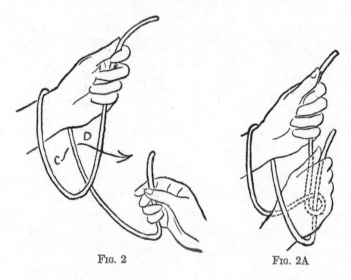

FIG. 2   FIG. 2A

(5) It only remains to stretch the hands wide apart and a knot forms in the middle of the cord. Be careful that at the finish the end B is the same length as before.

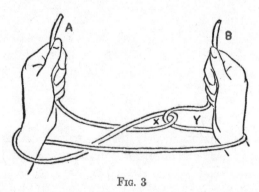

FIG. 3

Second Effect: Tying a Ring on the Cord

All you have to do is to pass the cord through the ring and let it hang in the middle of the cord. A repetition of the moves explained in the first effect will tie the ring on the cord.

Third Effect: A Spectator Holds the Ends of the Cord

Form Fig. 3 with the cord and invite a spectator to take hold of the ends A and B, one end in each hand. Draw your hands away from the cords entirely and instruct the spectator to draw his hands apart. Much to his surprise the knot forms as before.

Fourth Effect: The Ends of the Cord Tied on the Thumbs

As a final and positive proof that the ends are not released or crossed in the action, invite a spectator to tie them to your thumb tips. Once more make Fig. 3, forming it very slowly and inviting the closest inspection; then, holding your hands well apart, let the spectator take the ends off your thumb tips and hold them one in each hand. Again he finds that the mysterious knot forms in the middle of the cord.

This is a very effective trick and to the uninitiated it creates a perfect illusion.

II. TRICKS

1. Spontaneous Knots

Effect. A rope several yards long is coiled, sailor fashion, and put in a small basket. After the necessary magical incantation,

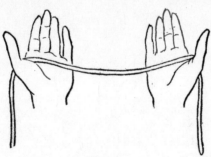

Fig. 4

the magician shows that a dozen or more knots have been tied in it at regular intervals.

Method. The secret lies in the manner of making the coils. Begin by placing the rope over the hands, held palms upwards about eight inches apart, so that one end falls behind the fork of the left thumb and the other end behind the right thumb (Fig. 4).

Close the right hand, grasping the rope, and turn it palm downwards, forming a loop (Fig. 5). Place this loop on the left hand turned to the position shown in Fig. 6. Turn the right hand palm upwards and pass it along the rope to a point which will make a second loop slightly larger than the first. Turn the hand over and carry this second loop to the left hand and place it alongside the first, the left hand remaining stationary. Continue

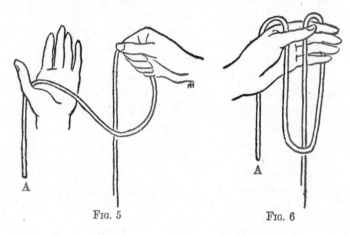

Fig. 5   Fig. 6

making loops in exactly the same way until the other end is reached.

In laying the last loop on the left hand, grip the end A and pull it through all the loops. Place the rope in the basket with the first coil, the smallest, at the bottom and the end A in the middle. It only remains to utter the magic formula, seize the end A, and draw the rope out. Grasp the end A with the left hand and pull the rope upwards through the fist with the right hand. It appears as if the knots actually form in the closed and motionless left hand.

2. THE TRAVELING KNOTS

Effect. By using a second basket prepared with a flap inside, the effect of the knots traveling from one rope to the other can be obtained.

Preparation. Three lengths of rope will be required; coil one in the secret compartment of the basket, place the other two on the backs of two chairs. Put the two baskets on the chair seats.

Method. Begin by taking the rope from the chair which has the faked basket on its seat, and openly tie the same number of knots, at intervals, as you will secretly tie on the other rope. Coil this rope on the left hand in the same way as you will later coil the other. Lay the coils in the prepared basket; release the flap, covering this knotted rope; bring out the end of the unprepared rope, letting it hang in full view over the side of the basket.

Take the rope on the other chair; make the trick coils; put it in the second basket; and in due course draw it out, producing the knots. Hold this up by one end in your left hand; go to the other basket and draw out the unknotted rope with your right hand. Display the ropes thus, one hanging from each hand.

Finally drop both into the faked basket; pick up the second basket, casually turning it so that the spectators can see the inside; put it on top of the other basket and put both aside.

Chung Ling Soo presented the first part of the trick, the formation of the knots, by using a rope long enough to stretch across his stage. Having coiled the rope, he would stand at one side and give the end to an assistant, who, then drew it away to the other side, the knots—some thirty or more—being formed, apparently, in Soo's cupped hands. A brilliant effect.

3. GRANDMOTHER'S NECKLACE

Effect. The origin of this trick is lost in the mists of antiquity, but the fact that it has survived to the present day proves that the principle upon which it is based is a sound one. The plot, as with all the best tricks, is a simple one. Briefly, various articles are tied to the middle of two cords; the ends of the cords are held by two spectators; and the magician removes the articles, leaving the cords still held by the spectators and entirely free from knots.

Method. In the original trick the cords are secretly tied together at the middle with a thread (Fig. 7) and then secretly doubled as in Fig. 8. It follows that any articles threaded on the cords and then tied on will be freed as soon as the thread is broken. In order to disguise this simple solution it is necessary, after the articles have been tied on, to transfer one cord from each side to the other. This is done by tying a single knot with

one cord, under the pretense of making the tying still more secure (Fig. 9). Then, when the cords are pulled taut, they come
out straight as before.

In this form the trick has become so well known that one could
hardly present it, even before a small audience, without being
asked to show the cords separately. Various ingenious methods
of overcoming this difficulty have been devised.

(1) The two parts of a snap button are sewn on the middles
of the cords. Simple pressure of the fingers then suffices to make
the connection, but the method creates another difficulty—the
cords cannot be subjected to close examination.

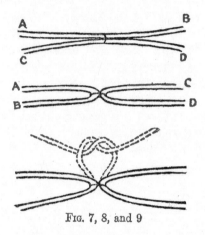

Fig. 7, 8, and 9

(2) A small rubber band, held on the tips of two fingers, can
be slipped over the cords to the middle after they have been
tested separately. The final pull on the cords breaks the band
and it falls to the floor unnoticed.

(3) In place of the rubber band, a small piece of flexible copper or lead wire is pressed round the nail of the left middle finger
and clipped on the middles of the cords at the proper moment.
It will be pulled apart and fall imperceptibly at the finish.

(4) A small handkerchief tied round the middle of the cords
provides a convincing method of working the trick. The knot is
converted into a slipknot in tightening it, the cords are doubled
(as in Fig. 8) under cover of the handkerchief, and a single knot
is then tied with both cords. To remove the various articles that
are threaded and tied on the cords you have simply to pull the

knot in the handkerchief apart; the loops of the cords are thus freed and the rest follows.

(5) By using strong black tapes and a black pin the junction can be made by thrusting the pin through the middle of both tapes. The pin can be carried at the lower edge of the vest until it is required.

(6) The best and simplest method of all is to pass the doubled middle of one cord through the other and bend it over as shown in Fig. 10. The junction is then hidden and kept secure by tying a handkerchief around it tightly.

The final improvement in the trick is in the method of tying the various articles on the cords. Instead of threading them all on at once, a single knot is tied on each one and finally the cords on one side are pushed through one sleeve of a borrowed coat and the cords on the other side through the other sleeve; then the usual single knot is made with one cord. Under cover of the coat the operator first removes the handkerchief, the work of

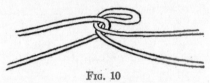

Fig. 10

a moment thanks to the doubling of the cord; then the articles are removed, one by one, by simply untying the knots between them. When the last one has been taken off, the two spectators holding the ends of the cords pull them taut and they come away free and separate, leaving the coat in the operator's hands.

Variations. Two novel presentations of the trick follow purely as examples; each performer should work out his own variation of the theme.

Cords and watch. Two pieces of white sash cord about three-eighths of an inch thick and about five feet in length are required. Invite two spectators to assist you; have them stand one on each side of you and hand each of them a cord to examine. When they are satisfied, take the cords and lay them over the forefinger of your left hand, the ends hanging down evenly on each side. Ask for the loan of a watch, dispatch one of your helpers to get it, and profit by the diversion to double the middles of the cords (Fig. 10). Do this by taking the middle of the outside cord with the right thumb and forefinger; push it through the bend of the other cord and press the left thumb on the junction, hiding it completely.

This done, take a small red silk handkerchief from your pocket; wind it round the junction of the two loops, tightly enough to hold them in position, and surreptitiously pass one end of the silk between the two cords to the right of the junction; then tie it tightly. Take the borrowed watch, pass two ends of the cord through the ring, and slide it up to the silk. Have a single knot tied on this with both cords; then place the middle of the cords, the watch, and the silk behind your neck and have another single knot tied coming under your chin.

Instruct each assistant, in turn, to pass the ends he holds under your vest and out at the armholes on each side; be careful that they are not passed under the suspenders. Finally, as a further complication, have a single knot tied with one cord, thus effecting the necessary crossing of one cord.

Place both hands at the back of your neck, release the doubled cords, slip the watch off and palm it in the right hand. Give the signal to the assistants to pull hard; the ropes come free in front of you with the red silk still tied on the middle, conclusive proof that the cords have passed through your neck. In reality it is on one cord only, so you seize the cords on each side of the silk as you call attention to it, then slide it off with the left hand and hold the ropes in the right hand.

Now pretend to notice that the watch is missing, thrust your hands in the outside coat pockets of the man on the left, drop the watch in one, tap his vest and trousers pockets quickly, then turn and pretend to search the other man. Finally the watch is found by the assistant on the left in his own pocket and all ends well.

Cords and glass tube. A glass tube is required—a large gas chimney serves very well. The working of the trick is the same as in the preceding variation up to the time you have doubled the cords and hold the junction under the left thumb. Hold the cords as shown in Fig. 11 and invite the man on your right to wrap his handkerchief several times round the cord and tie it on tightly. Turn to the man on your left, at the same time sliding your left hand along the cords and covering the junction

with your right thumb. Have him tie his handkerchief on the
cords on that side so that the hidden join is between the two
handkerchiefs. Slide this last over the junction and have a third
handkerchief tied on by the same man; then push the two outside ones against the middle one.

Pass the two ends of the cords on one side through the glass
tube and move it to the middle over the handkerchiefs. Finally
have a single knot tied with one cord as usual. At the word of

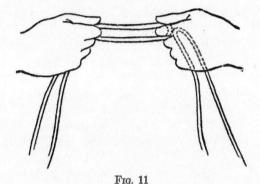

FIG. 11

command the cords are pulled free, the glass tube with the handkerchiefs inside it remaining in your hands.

III. CUT AND RESTORED ROPE

It would be an interesting study to trace the growth of this
trick from the schoolboy trick with string to the rope trick of
the present day, now elevated to the dignity of a stage feat. That,
however, is outside the scope of the present work and I shall
content myself with the explanation of the main principles, variations of which can be worked out by the student himself.

1. THE SLIDING KNOT PRINCIPLE

Preparation. Prepare by tying a short piece of rope round the
rope to be cut, making a double knot which will slide freely.
Cut the ends off short and set the knot about a foot from one
end. Place the rope on a chair so that the knot is hidden by

the chair rail and can be grasped naturally when the rope is picked up.

Method. To perform, approach the chair from the right; pick up the rope by taking hold of the end on the seat with the right hand and grasping the sliding knot with the left hand. Show the rope and jerk it between the hands to prove its strength; then tie the ends together with a double knot and secretly slide the fake knot tightly against the real one. Cut the ends of the real knot off short. Hold the knotted ends in the left hand, slide the right hand down the rope to the middle, and jerk the rope again. Repeat the action, but this time secretly slide the fake knot down to the middle in the right hand. Carry the middle part and the fake knot, hidden in the right hand, up to the left hand, which then grasps them both against the real knot.

Test the double loops by jerking them between the hands and  drop the fake knot, keeping the real knot hidden in the left hand. Take the fake knot in the right hand and jerk the rope again. Pick up the scissors; cut the rope first on one side of the left hand, then on the other. Take the rope in your right hand and put the scissors with the piece cut off in your left coat pocket. Wind the rope round your left hand and slide the fake knot off into your right hand. Apply the usual formula —pull the rope off your left hand and toss it out for examination.

2. WITHOUT PREPARATION

Any rope can be used for this method. Begin by tying the ends together with a square knot; upset it in pretending to tighten it and get the two ends the same length. Cut them off close to the knot. Say that you propose to make a test cut before cutting the rope in half, and cut the part which forms a portion of the knot so that you then have a sliding knot on the remainder of the rope (Fig. 12).

FIG. 12

Seize the lower end and bring it up to the left hand, the back of which is toward the audience. Hold the ends close together between the left thumb and fingers and at the same time grasp the sliding knot secretly with the right hand, drag it down to the middle of the bight, grip this with the knot, and place both in the left hand. Rub the left fingers on the rope and let the knot and the bight fall (Fig. 13). As the cut was made close to the knot, it now appears that the rope has been made whole again. Keep the two ends tightly together in the left hand and again test it by jerking.

You are now prepared to cut the rope in the middle. Pretend to do this by passing the blade of the scissors between the ends under cover of the left hand. Drop one end and display the rope, to all appearance cut in two pieces and tied in the middle. Tie the ends and ask for one of the knots to be chosen. Whichever is selected, you cut away the fake knot completely and all that remains to be done is to untie the remaining knot, show the rope whole, and toss it to the spectators.

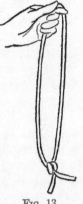

Fig. 13

3. Loop and Sleeve Method

Preparation. Cut a short piece, about ten inches long, from the rope to be used and tie the ends tightly together with thread, making a loop of about five inches in length. Attach a piece of cord elastic to the closed end of the loop; pass the cord up the left sleeve (over the shoulder) and fasten the free end to a suspender botton on the right-hand side, adjusting the length of the pull so that the loop will be drawn up close to the elbow when it is free. Pass a handkerchief through the rope loop and pull the ends down to the cuff. There is nothing unusual in carrying a handkerchief in this manner and it permits you to get the faked loop into your left hand in merely taking the handkerchief from the sleeve.

Method. Coil the rope, about fifteen feet in length, over the left arm and bring it forwards. Invite two spectators to assist; stand them one on each side and give each of them an end of the rope to hold. Have them test its strength, then slacken it so that you will be able to make a loop in the middle. Pull your sleeves back a little; let both hands be seen empty; take hold of the rope in the middle and draw up a small loop, holding it in the left hand projecting over the fist.

Look closely at the loop and say that the rope must be absolutely free from dust or the experiment is likely to fail. Let the right side of the loop fall from the left hand, but retain hold of the rope itself with that hand. With the right hand draw out your handkerchief; pull the faked loop into your left hand and hold it against the rope, covered by the back of the hand and the fingers. Rub the middle of the rope vigorously with the handkerchief; make a pretense of pulling up a loop as before, but in reality seize the fake loop and bring it up above the fist. Put the handkerchief in your coat pocket, bring out the scissors, cut the loop, and show the ends well separated.

Replace the scissors in your pocket; grasp the cut ends with your right hand apparently but really release the hold of the left fingers and let the fake fly up the sleeve, at once making a loose knot with the slack of the rope itself. Rub the middle of this loop between your hands, have the spectators pull the rope taut—the knot is pulled free and the rope is whole.

4. STRETCHING A ROPE

The sleeve is used in this feat also and it makes an excellent introduction to the preceding feat.

Preparation. Take about seven yards of flexible cotton rope, remove your coat, double the rope, grasp the ends with your right hand, and don the garment. Pack the middle of the rope carefully in the right trousers pocket; close the right hand on the ends, holding it so that about two feet of rope protrude from the thumb side of the fist and about eighteen inches from the little-finger side.

Method. Enter with the rope in position. Invite a boy to come up and help you. Place him on your left and give him the longer end to hold. Now propose a tug of war and incite him to pull his hardest against you. Allow the rope to glide very slowly through your right fist until it is stretched out to its full length.

5. PREPARED ROPE

The gimmicks shown in Fig. 14 are used in this method, which has become the standard rope-cutting trick. They are painted

white, and when slipped on the ends of a white rope they are
not noticeable if the rope is kept slightly in motion. They screw
together with a single twist of the fingers and make a stable
junction.

Prepare a piece of rope (the best kind is white cotton rope,
obtainable at any magic shop) about six feet in length, with a
positive gimmick on one end and a negative gimmick on the
other. Do the same with a short piece about eight inches long;
then snap this short piece between the ends of the long piece,
making a circle of the rope. At the point opposite the short

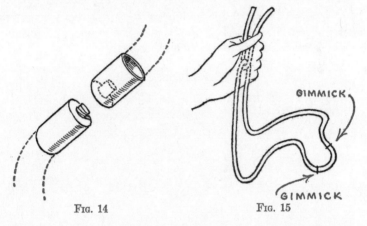

FIG. 14   FIG. 15

piece tie another short piece with a single knot, hold the rope
in the left hand, and present it as a single piece of rope.

Untie the knot in the short piece and hold the rope as in Fig.
15, the ends protruding above the hand. Show the rope thus;
then tie the short piece to the rope with a single knot.

Turn the rope round in the hands; cover the gimmicks at
each end of the short piece, one with each hand, and have a
spectator cut the rope in the middle of this short piece. Take the
scissors and cut the ends off close to each part of the gimmick,
detach these, and put them in your pocket with the scissors and
the small pieces. Show the rope apparently cut in the middle, one
end in each hand held far apart.

Bring the ends together in the left hand; under cover of this
action screw the second pair of gimmicks together and quickly

coil the rope round the left hand. Toss the rope into the air, catch it as it falls, and display it again in a circle.

Grasp the gimmick in the left hand, letting the knot hang down. Cut the rope on each side of the left hand and put the piece in your pocket with the scissors, thus getting rid of the second prepared section. Tie the ends and finish as explained in 2.

Finally, care must be taken not to overdo the trick. I have seen a performer begin with a rope about seven feet long and, after repeatedly cutting and restoring it with all sorts of twists and turns, finally toss out a rope about three feet long as proof of having restored the original rope—not a very convincing procedure. If you convince your audience that you really have cut the rope in the middle, the restoration is the climax and nothing more is required. Pass on to some other feat.

XIV

MAGIC WITH MONEY (BILLS)

"How goes the Money?
Wouldn't you like to know?
John Godfrey Saxe—Wouldn't You Like to Know.

TRICKS with folding money are popular with both audiences and magicians. The magician likes them because they provide for some amazing effects which require but little preparation and no cumbersome apparatus and, human nature being what it is, the spectators enjoy the discomfiture of the confiding individual who lends his money to the magician only to see it torn to pieces or burned. However, the confidence of the lender is justified, for in the end he gets his property back undamaged.

It is necessary to consider, first, the sleights peculiar to the manipulation of bills; then various subtleties in the preparation of duplicate bills, envelopes, lemons, oranges, etc.; and, finally a selection of the best bill tricks.

I. SLEIGHTS

1. PALMING

By rolling a bill tightly between the palms of the hands it can be squeezed into a small ball, which can then be manipulated in much the same way as the small balls for the cups and balls (see Chapter V). A bill thus rolled up can be shown between the tips of the right thumb and forefinger and, in the act of placing it in the left hand, it is rolled to the tips of the other three fingers—which carry it well down into the palm, where it will be held securely by a very slight contraction of the base of the thumb (Fig. 1). In the meantime the left fingers close on the tips of the thumb and forefinger—which are then withdrawn, leaving the bill apparently in the left hand.

Again, from the same position the bill can be rolled to the base of the little finger and held there by a slight contraction of that finger. The move can be made in a flash, and with a little practice the slight curve of the little finger becomes imperceptible.

When it is inadvisable to crumple the bill into a ball, another procedure is adopted. Fold the bill in half, the narrow ends coming together; then in half again and once more the opposite way, making a package about one and one-half inches by one inch; and press the creases firmly. Place one end in the fold at

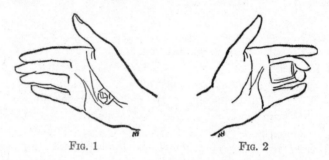

FIG. 1   FIG. 2

the base of the second and third fingers; bend these two fingers slightly, so that the other end of the packet is held in the fold of the top joints. In this position the bill is held in perfect concealment and the position of the hand is a natural one (Fig. 2).

2. SWITCHING A BILL

The methods of substituting a bill of your own for a borrowed one vary according to whether the bill is crumpled or folded. If crumpled into a ball, you secretly palm a crumpled bill in your left hand. Take the borrowed bill in the right hand, crumple it between the fingers, palm it in apparently placing it in the left hand, and show the substitute. This action must take place in turning to the left—to hand the bill to a spectator on that side, or to drop it into a glass on a table at your left. Either the regular palm or the finger palm can be used.

Or again the tourniquet (French drop) can be used. Have the substitute bill palmed in the right hand and take the borrowed bill in the left hand between the tips of the thumb and second finger, palm upwards. Pretend to take the bill with the right hand, really letting it drop into the left palm, and show the palmed bill in the right hand. In this case the action takes place in handing the bill to someone on your right (Fig. 3).

If, however, you have folded the bill, have the substitute, folded the same way, in the finger palm in the left hand. Show

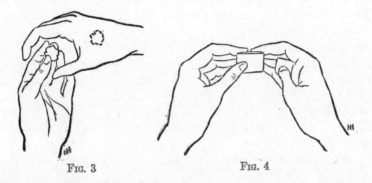

FIG. 3   FIG. 4

the borrowed bill at the tips of the right thumb and first and second fingers. Bring the hands together so that the tips of the fingers meet in front of you and, at that instant, push the substitute bill forward with the left thumb and pull the borrowed bill back into the finger palm with the right thumb (Fig. 4). Move

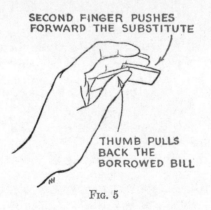

SECOND FINGER PUSHES
FORWARD THE SUBSTITUTE

THUMB PULLS
BACK THE
BORROWED BILL

FIG. 5

the left hand away, with the substitute bill in view, and drop the right hand naturally to the side. The move is made in handing the bill to someone on your left.

At times it is necessary to make the switch with one hand.

Hold the substitute bill in the finger palm and take the borrowed bill between the thumb and second and third fingers of the same hand. Pull the borrowed bill down over the substitute and push this upwards with the tip of the second finger; as soon as the edges of the bills clear, push the substitute with the tip of the thumb into the position previously occupied by the borrowed bill —that is to say, the two bills change places. Executed with the hand in motion, the substitution is imperceptible (Fig. 5).

A tuck made in either sleeve, in pulling the sleeve back a little, is very useful either for securing a substitute bill or for disposing of one after the substitution.

Another excellent method is to use a thumb tip. Fold the bill as described for the finger palm and put it at the bottom of a drugstore envelope; place this envelope fourth in a packet and a thumb tip in your vest pocket. Ask for the loan of a bill and instruct the owner how to fold it, giving him directions that will result in a package similar to the one in the envelope. While he does this, hand out the three top envelopes of the packet casually, as if merely to show they are quite ordinary, and get the thumb tip on your right thumb. Take the fourth envelope and hold it in your left hand by the sides with the address side towards the audience. Lift the flap, insert your thumb, as if to open out the envelope, and leave the thumb tip inside. Take the folded bill from the spectator, put it into the envelope, really into the thumb tip, and immediately withdraw this on your thumb, holding the envelope so that the substitute bill can be seen inside it.

Place your right hand into your coat pocket and bring out a book of matches, leaving the thumb tip behind; then stop and suggest that the number be recorded by the owner. He does this, replaces the bill in the envelope and retains it in his possession. Since you have memorized the number of your bill you can give a convincing exhibition of mindreading by revealing the number.

II. PRELIMINARY PREPARATIONS

One of the best methods of getting possession of a bill secretly is by means of a slit about an inch long in the address side of an envelope, parallel with the long side. The envelope is shown with the flap side toward the spectators, then the inside is shown with the fingers of the right hand covering the slit. Push the folded bill fairly inside the envelope (the flap side being toward the spectators) so that its end goes through the slit, where it is held with the left fingers. Fasten the flap and in due course pull the bill out of the slit with the left fingers and finger palm it. A small oblong piece of paper is generally pasted inside the envelope, so that when this is held before the flame of a candle the shadow is taken for proof that the bill is really in the envelope. An additional effect can be obtained by making this extra piece of flash paper. When the envelope is burned, the usual way of disposing of it, there is a sudden flare when the flame reaches the flash paper

A convincing touch is to paste a piece torn from the corner of a stage bill to the rear side of the envelope inside near the edge. This is hidden by the left fingers when the envelope is pulled open to show the inside, but when the bill is put in the envelope the right fingers pull it into view. Then the flap is moistened, but not stuck down until the flame has almost reached this piece. To the spectator this is proof positive that the bill has been burned and its subsequent restoration becomes real magic.

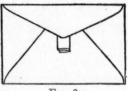

Fig. 6

By using a cheap, thin grade of envelope the slit need not be cut in it beforehand and the envelope can be handed out for examination. When it is returned and you hold it up (with the fingers of the right hand inside and the right thumb on the address side) to show that it is empty, it is an easy matter to make the required slit with the thumb nail.

There is still another method which allows for the examination of the envelope—the showing of the shadow of the bill itself after its insertion and the exhibition of both hands after the flap has been fastened down. In this case the bill is apparently inserted with the address side of the envelope to the audience, but it is really held on the outside by the left thumb. When the flap is moistened its tip is left dry, so that when it is pressed down it will hold the bill in place but can be pulled away later when required (Fig. 6). In the meantime the hands can be shown freely, also the actual shadow of the bill.

A favorite way of reproducing a bill is to find it inside a lemon or an orange. When duplicate bills are used, the fruit is prepared by removing the capsule left on the fruit when the stalk was broken. Insert an ice pick at this spot and make a hole large enough to take the bill, which you have folded and rolled very tightly. Push the bill in carefully so as not to break the rind, wipe off any juice which may have been squeezed out, and fasten the capsule in place again with a tiny drop of rubber cement. A lemon or an orange prepared in this way will stand the closest examination.

To insert a bill in a cigarette, another popular method of reproduction, roll the cigarette in a piece of note paper the same length and with the blunt end of a pencil push about two-thirds of the tobacco out, insert the bill, and fill the remaining space with the tobacco.

III.   TRICKS

1. The Lemon and Bill Trick

Effect. An unprepared lemon is handed out for examination; several bills are borrowed, wrapped in a handkerchief, and held by a spectator. The bills vanish and they are found inside the lemon.

Accessories. A lemon, a knife, a tumbler, and a handkerchief.

Preparation. In one corner of the handkerchief sew a wad of paper the same size and shape that the bills will assume when they are folded and rolled into a small packet. Place the handkerchief in your pocket in such a way that you can seize it by the prepared corner.

Method. Begin by handing out the lemon for examination, and while this is being done ask for the loan of a dollar bill. When one is handed to you ask for a five-dollar bill; if successful ask for a ten-dollar bill; and so on as long as the spectators respond. In any case, get three bills at least, even if they are all ones. While you are focusing all attention on the bills, casually take the lemon back and drop it in your right coat pocket —while you are still amongst the spectators.

Suppose you have obtained three bills. Stack them one on the other evenly; fold them in half lengthwise, then in half the opposite way, and hand the packet to a spectator to sign his name on the outside bill. While this is being done, stand with your left side to the spectators and place your hands in your coat pockets. With the right thumb nail cut the rind of the lemon at the stalk end; push the forefinger in, making a hole large enough to take the bills. Place the lemon with the hole upwards in the front corner of the pocket.

The signature having been written, take the bills, fold them in half once more, then roll them up tightly and bend the little roll in half. Hold this at the tips of your right thumb and forefinger in full view. Take out your handkerchief, seizing it by the wadded corner with the three free fingers of the right hand; take the opposite corner in the left hand, stretch it out, and show both sides. Bring the right hand, still holding the bills and the wadded corner, against the middle of the handkerchief and drape the rest of the fabric over that hand. With the left hand take hold of the wadded corner from above, finger palm the bills, bring the right hand from underneath, and twist the handkerchief tightly.

Hand the twisted handkerchief to a spectator, and have him tie a knot to come just below the wad. While this is being done, your hands go to your pockets again; with the right hand push the bills well into the hole in the lemon, bring it out casually and without remark, and put it in the tumbler in such a way that the hole does not show.

Return to the person holding the handkerchief, tell him to feel the bills to make sure they are still there, ask him if he will know his signature when he sees it again, and so on, merely to distract attention from the lemon. Have the knot in the handkerchief untied; then seize one corner, jerk the handkerchief away, spread it out (getting the prepared corner into one hand), show both sides, and replace it in your pocket.

Take the lemon, holding it with the hole to the rear; cut it round the middle and break it in half, showing the bills embedded in the sound half. Take them out with the very tips of the thumb and forefinger and drop the halves of the lemon into the tumbler. Open out the bills, carefully keeping them in full view the whole time. Have the spectator's signature identified, wipe the juice off the bills with your handkerchief, and hand them back to the owners.

There is no particular difficulty about the trick, but it must be worked smoothly and full advantage taken of the misdirection indicated in the explanation.

There are many variations of the trick. For example, by using one bill only you can switch it for one of your own, a duplicate of which you have placed in the lemon in the orthodox way. After the switch, have a spectator record the number, and in the meantime finger palm a piece of paper (on which you have written, "You are a fine custodian"), folded in the same manner as you will fold the bill.

Give the lemon out to be examined and let a spectator hold it in full view. Borrow a handkerchief and throw it over your right hand. Take the folded bill in the left hand and put it in the right hand, apparently; really drop it into the right sleeve, the right hand pushing up the palmed paper, the handkerchief covering the operations. Take hold of the slip with the left hand from above, through the fabric, and give both to a spectator to hold. Let it be seen that your hands are empty.

Order the bill to pass into the lemon; the spectator, however, maintains that he still has it, so you have him take the paper out and read the message aloud. Give a knife to the man holding the lemon; ask him to cut it carefully round the middle and break it apart. Let him remove the duplicate bill (which is then seen sticking out of one half), open it out, and call the numbers aloud. They correspond with the record, which to the layman is proof positive that the bill actually passed into the lemon. In the meantime you have had ample opportunity to allow the other bill to drop from your sleeve and to pocket it. Always have a crisp new bill to hand to the owner of the original bill in place of the lemon-soaked one.

The use of bills with the same numbers lends itself to many methods of reproduction. For example, you could pass the bill into a lemon first, have it identified; then pass it into a borrowed cigarette (as explained below), again have the number identified; then finally vanish it from your hands by sleight of hand, or a pull, and have the owner of the bill take it from his own pocket. In the course of the first two tricks you can easily find an opportunity to drop the triplicate bill into his coat pocket. Care must be taken not to carry the method to extremes.

2. THE BILL IN THE CIGARETTE

Effect. A cigarette is obtained from a spectator; the magician lights and smokes it. He borrows a bill, the number of which is recorded by the owner. The bill is placed in an envelope, which is burned. The cigarette is torn open and a bill is found in it. This is handed to the spectator and he identifies it by the serial number.

Preparation. Insert a folded and rolled dollar bill in a cigarette and put the cigarette in your left coat pocket under a new packet of cigarettes. Place matches in your right coat pocket. On the table have an ash tray and an envelope, prepared with a slit and corner of a bill as explained above.

Method. Begin by asking permission to smoke—the experiment you are about to show being hard on your nerves, so you say. Take out your own packet of cigarettes, with the prepared cigarette under it, in your left hand. Make a motion of opening the packet; then stop and, under pretense of not wanting to use anything of your own, borrow a cigarette. Receive it in your right hand, apparently transfer it to your left hand but really take the cigarette packet, retain the borrowed cigarette under it, and show the prepared cigarette in your left hand. Place this in your mouth, put the packet and the borrowed cigarette in your right coat pocket, and bring out the matches. Light the cigarette and replace the matches in the coat pocket.

Borrow a dollar bill, first having the owner record the number. Fold the bill in the usual way. Take the envelope; pull it open to show the inside, the right fingers hiding the slit and the left fingers the bill fragment. Place the folded bill in the envelope, one end going through the slit. Moisten the flap and pull the fragment into view. Pull the bill out with the right fingers and hold the envelope in the left hand, flap side toward the audience, the fragment of bill showing. Bring out the matches with the right hand and leave the borrowed bill in the pocket. Light the lower corner of the envelope and, when the flame is about to reach the bill fragment, close the flap and drop the burning envelope on the ash tray.

In the meantime you have allowed the cigarette to go out; lean over and relight it at the flame of the envelope. Explain to the owner that, having been folded into a tight wad, the bill will not be damaged and, when the envelope is reduced to ashes, pretend to search for the bill. You are taken aback at not finding any trace of it; the experiment has failed for the first time, you say. Apologize and say that you will make good. Thrust your right hand into your pocket; then suddenly recall the fact that you lighted the cigarette at the flame of the envelope, and note that the cigarette is not drawing well. In the meantime you have unfolded the borrowed bill in the pocket until it is only folded in half. Now tear the cigarette, extract the bill in it, unfold it, and show it. Say to the owner, "You gave me this bill, didn't you?" as if you were about to return it. He naturally replies, "Yes." Thank him, fold the bill in half, and thrust it into your pocket. A moment later, however, as if you had done this merely to get a laugh, bring out his bill, hand it to him, and have the number identified.

The method is an easy and effective one and, smoothly done, the switches will not be suspected. However, by using duplicate bills with prepared numbers, the pocket switch will not be necessary; but the borrowed bill must be switched for your own before the number is recorded. To do this, have your bill (the duplicate of the one in the cigarette) finger palmed in the right hand. Borrow a bill and fold it; then, as if as an afterthought, hand it back (making the switch) for the owner to take a note of the number.

The latest, best, and most direct method requires no switch of the bill or the cigarette.

Ask for a cigarette and have the obliging spectator place it between your lips and strike a match for you, as you call particular attention to the fact that you do not touch the cigarette yourself.

Borrow a bill (first having the owner record the serial number), fold it into a small packet, and roll it tightly. Insert it in the slit envelope in the usual way, getting it into the left hand via the slit and clipping it between the second and third fingers. Hold the envelope by the lower corner between the left thumb and fingers; strike a match and hold it behind the envelope so that the shadow of a little roll of flash paper, gummed in position beforehand, shows clearly.

While talking, accidentally bring the match to the envelope and set fire to it. Continue talking and do not look at the envelope until it is well alight; then suddenly realize your plight and drop the burning envelope on the ash tray. "Well, there goes the bill," you say as the flash paper flares up. Offer profuse apologies, and if you can make the spectators think you really have met with an accident so much the better. Take the cigarette from your mouth; hold it in the left hand between the thumb and second and third fingers, so that it covers the bill; and in your gestures let it be seen that your hands are otherwise empty. Seize the outer end of the cigarette between the right thumb and fingers, slide the bill against the back of the cigarette, and break the latter in half by bending the right hand end toward the body; nip the top of the bill with some of the tobacco from each half of the broken cigarette, and pull it out at the very tips of the right thumb and forefinger. Hold it up in full view; crumple the pieces of the cigarette in the left hand and toss them away. Open the bill slowly and carefully, so that everyone can see that there is no possibility of a substitution; then return it to the owner and have the number identified.

3. THE MULTIPLICATION OF BILLS

Effect. The effect of this excellent opening trick is that a single bill is suddenly multiplied into fifteen or twenty.

Preparation. To prepare, stack the required number of bills neatly one on the other, fold them lengthwise, then in half the opposite way and in half again. Tuck the packet in a fold of the left sleeve at the elbow, the opening of the fold toward the wrist.

Method. Show a single bill in the right hand; pull back the right sleeve with the left hand, casually showing all parts of the right hand. Transfer the bill to the left hand and with the right hand pull back the left sleeve, at the same time stealing the package of bills. Take the bill again with the right hand and hold the package behind it with the thumb.

Hold the bill vertically, between the fingers and thumbs of

both hands, at the ends (Fig. 7); bring the hands together and jerk them apart as if testing the bill, and under cover of this movement open out the packet lengthwise; then get the right thumb into the fold, remove the left hand, strike the bills on the back of the left hand, and fan them out quickly—displaying the sudden multiplication with surprising effect.

The trick may be used as an opener with a bill of your own, with a borrowed bill prior to using it for a trick, or as a means

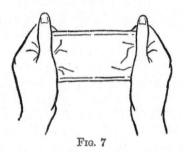

Fig. 7

of substituting a bill of your own for a borrowed bill—the duplicate of which is to be produced at the climax of a trick. In the last case put your duplicate bill at the bottom of the pile and, when the multiplication has been made, peel it off and hand it to the spectator from whom you borrowed a bill, as being his, with the request that he take a note of the number.

While this is being done, you may say, "Since this money has cost me nothing, I am always glad to distribute the bills as souvenirs"; you make a motion of doing so, then stop and add, "Perhaps I had better do my trick first"—and you pocket the bills.

XV

OUT OF THE HAT

"I never saw so many shocking bad hats in my life."
Arthur Wellesley, Duke of Wellington.
—upon seeing the first Reformed Parliament.

AN ANALYSIS of cartoons which use magic "to point a moral or adorn a tale," culled from metropolitan newspapers during the past few years, shows that more than fifty per cent depict the production of something from a hat. There is no doubt that the mention of magic suggests to the mind of the layman, in the majority of cases, a picture of a man pulling a rabbit out of a hat; yet one can visit a hundred magical performances at the present time and not once see a hat-production trick. The fashion just now is the manipulation of cigarettes and the making of fans with playing cards. This will pass, and the performer in search of a novelty can hardly do better than work up a modernized version of the hat trick. One of the greatest authorities on magic has said that if he wished to judge the caliber of a magician he would have him work a hat-production trick. To do that successfully but little sleight of hand, in the strict sense of the word, is necessary; but the performer must be deft and a master of misdirection, and for this reason a study of the technique of hat loading is an absolute necessity for anyone aspiring to be a finished, all-round magician.

The passing of the silk hat, possibly, has had something to do with the neglect of the trick; but we still have the derby hat and the felt hat, both of which can be used with even greater effect than the silk hat as savoring less of possible preparation. The necessary room for large articles can be obtained by keeping the sweatband turned up throughout. It would serve no good purpose to describe a series of hat productions; every performer has to work up his own methods of so misdirecting the attention of the spectators at a given moment that he can slip

273

his load into the hat imperceptibly. All that can be done is to give concrete examples of methods that have been found to be infallible; the student can then work out a series of "favorable moments" for himself.

1. The Street Magician

Here is one of the best possible examples of misdirection. Surrounded by curious spectators, the street magician produces a small rabbit or a guinea pig from a hat which everyone had seen to be empty a moment before. Obviously he must have put it in the hat. How? Simply by misdirection. He has the guinea pig in his right-hand coat pocket. After a trick in which he uses some small article—a lemon, for example—he puts the lemon on his little table, covers it with his hat, makes a feint of taking it away with his right hand and putting it in his pocket. When he asks the crowd, "Where is the lemon?" he is greeted with cries of "In your pocket." Turning sharply to someone on his left, he asks, "Did you see me take the lemon away? No? How could you when it is still here?" and he snatches up the hat with his left hand. All eyes go to the table; but in the meantime, he has seized the guinea pig in his right hand and with a backward swing of the body he brings his left hand back over the right hand and grips the hat by the brim with his right thumb, the fingers supporting the animal inside. Without pausing, he replaces the hat on the table and at the same time picks up the lemon with his left hand, thus keeping everyone's attention on the lemon.

He pretends to take the lemon in his right hand but palms it in the left and "passes" it toward the hat. Showing the right hand empty, he lifts the hat, revealing the guinea pig; and the astonishment caused by this apparition gives him another favorable moment for dropping the lemon from his left hand into his pocket.

2. Dropping an Object

In working the Miser's Dream (see page 42) with a soft hat it is necessary to have a saucer inside it to cause the sound of the fall of each coin to be heard distinctly by all. You can, of course, put the saucer in the hat openly, but it is much more magical to find it in the hat. The method is an easy one and useful for any hat load. You have the saucer in a loading pocket (a large pocket under the coat with a vertical opening) or simply under the coat on the left side, supported by pressure of the upper arm, and under the vest a silk handkerchief rolled into a ball.

Borrow a hat, take it with the right hand, and at the same time steal the silk with the left hand; step back a pace or two (do not turn your back), make some remark about the hat to the owner—you may ask if its crown is strong—and pass the hat to your left hand, holding it so that the crown is toward the audience. The introduction of the silk into the hat is thus quite covered and you let it drop inside. Look in the hat, shake it to make the silk expand, and tell the owner he has left something in it; grasp the brim on each side and turn the hat over toward yourself, letting the silk fall to the floor. At the same moment turn the mouth of the hat to your chest, seize the saucer, pull it into the hat, bend forward, and look at the silk over the hat. Lean down and pick up the silk with the right hand. A moment or two later discover the saucer in the hat, which in the meantime you have held in the left hand well away from the body.

3. USING THE PROFONDES

The idea of dropping something from a supposedly empty hat can be used to advantage in loading from the *profondes* (deep pockets in the coattails), if you work in evening dress. Suppose, for example, you have a load in the left coat pocket and that you have secretly introduced a lemon, obtained from your vest, into the hat. Look in the hat and remark, "Well, we have the hat empty at last"; with that turn the hat over with the right hand, dropping the left to the side. As the lemon hits the floor with a thud, seize the load with the left hand, turn your right side to the front, and bring the hat down with a sweep—covering the left hand, which inserts the load and takes hold of the hat. Without a pause stoop down and pick up the lemon, with the remark, "Now where in the world did that come from?" Put it aside, and then discover that there is something else in the hat and proceed to develop the load. Always allow a few moments to elapse between the actual loading and the discovery.

4. FROM A TABLE

The loading of articles from a table can be done perfectly—that is, imperceptibly—by the proper method; but the performer who passes the hat behind the table and sweeps off a load, hanging on a nail, is misdirecting himself only. The best way to learn the correct method is to practice with a wooden cannon ball. This has a hole bored out large enough for the insertion of the middle finger; it is set on a small shelf, or wire ring, behind the table in such a way that the hole points upwards

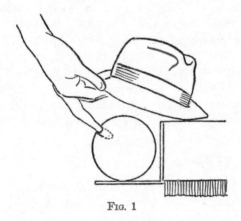

Fig. 1

obliquely at such an angle that when you hold the hat crown upwards, the thumb on the brim and the fingers inside, you can insert the middle finger in the hole, the other three fingers supporting the hat (Fig. 1).

With the ball thus set, holding the hat in the right hand with the middle finger free, go behind your table to pick up some article from it, bring the hat a little above the ball, lean forward to take the article with your left hand, let the right hand sink down until the front edge of the brim touches the table, insert the middle finger in the ball, lift it up into the hat; when the left hand, on which your whole attention has been fixed, has picked up the article, move away from the table, letting the right hand drop a little so that the crown of the hat is toward the spectators.

When you discover the ball in the hat, hold the hat with both hands, one on each side, the fingers inside; turn the hat mouth downwards and pretend to have great difficulty in getting the ball out, thus enhancing the surprise of its production. When you finally let the ball drop, you have another favorable moment for the introduction of another load from the coat pocket or from the *profonde*.

Any article that can be picked up by the first and second fingers can be loaded in this manner, for the hat can be held quite firmly by the thumb and the third and fourth fingers. The sleight requires practice for there must not be the slightest fumbling or even hesitation; so far as the spectators are concerned, nothing should be seen but the action of the left hand in picking up the object from the table.

5. The Wire Loop

When the load is of such a nature that it must be hung from a headless nail, a different plan is resorted to. Twist a piece of fine, flexible black wire into the shape in Fig. 2. The larger loop must be big enough to allow for the easy insertion of the middle finger, the smaller loop serves for hanging the bundle on a nail at the back of a table or chair, and the ends of the wire are twisted under the thread with which the load is tied together. The action is the same as that described for the cannon ball in 4. The right middle finger is inserted in the loop while the left hand takes some article from the table or the seat of the chair. The load is pulled off the headless nail and, as you move away, the right hand drops and the load is swung into the hat.

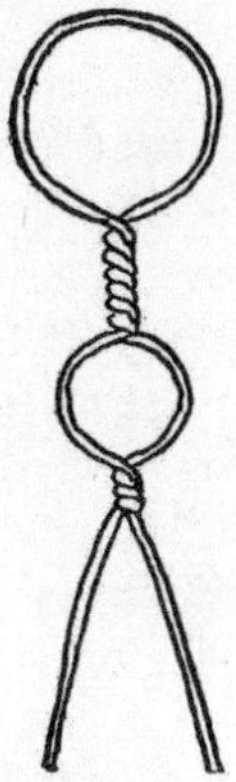

Fig. 2

So apparently unmanageable an object as a bowl of water can be loaded into the hat by this method. Fill a small bowl with water and place a rubber cover over it; tie a strong black thread round the bowl cover tightly crosswise, and suspend the bowl by the wire gimmick. Its subsequent production from a borrowed hat makes a startling climax to the rice bowl trick.

Simply vanish one of the bowls, by means of the faked tray and wire shape in a handkerchief, and then produce the bowl from the hat again, brimful of water.

6. RABBIT OR GUINEA PIG

A small rabbit or a guinea pig can be carried in the loading pocket of the coat on the left side and loaded into the hat under cover of the diversion caused by the dropping of an article to the stage. If you have a small waterproof mat on which to accidentally drop an egg, its smash will give you time to load an elephant.

The stuffed rabbits now obtainable at the magic stores can be made to look lifelike enough while being carried off stage immediately after the production, but whenever possible a live rabbit should be used. An easy method is to have the animal in a black bag, the mouth of which has four or five metal rings sewn to it. Put the rabbit in, and hang the bag by the rings on a headless nail at the back of a small threefold screen. In the course of the preceding productions throw a number of silks over the screen in such a way that in picking them up you can grasp the bag by the rings. When you have the hat empty, pretend that you will give the articles to the owner of the hat; pick up the silks and the bag and dump them into the hat, bag first. Discover then that there is something else in it, remove the silks, and bring out the rabbit. The bag must be lined with silk of different colors, parts of which are left unsewn so that when the bag is turned inside out it will pass for a bunch of silks.

7. FROM A TRAY

Drive a small, stout needle into the middle of the rear edge of a square Japanese tray; place the tray on your table with the needle end overlapping the table about an inch. Hang the load on the needle. In order to introduce the load into the hat, approach the table from the left with the hat in the left hand. With the right hand seize the tray toward the back and tilt it upwards without raising the front edge from the table, thus lifting the load behind the tray.

As soon as the tray conceals the load, place it over the hat, the load going inside and the left thumb holding the tray on the hat. With the right hand move the table a little forwards or to one side, take the tray with the right hand, and replace it on the table. The whole action must be carried through in such a way as to make it appear that the sole reason for moving the tray is to alter the position of the table.

8. A Double Production

For this very effective feat you will require two derby hats, one being a size larger than the other. Cut the brim from the larger hat and in the middle of the crown cut a semicircular slit, making a flap which can be pulled down (Fig. 3). Press the flap back into place, and inside the crown place a tambourine coil. Thus prepared, place this crown part, mouth upwards, on a small shelf at the back of your table. The smaller hat you entrust to a friend in front.

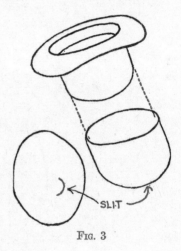

Fig. 3

In due course you ask for the loan of a hat and your friend hands you the derby. Proceed to make various productions from it, using the methods already described or others devised by yourself. In any case, at the end of the last production you must have a second tambourine coil in the hat. Some of the articles produced from the hat you have placed on your table; announce that you will replace them in the hat and return the lot to the owner. Hold the hat, crown downwards in your left hand, at the rear edge of the table immediately above the duplicate loaded crown on the shelf. Lower the hat into this and proceed to fill it with the articles on the table. No suspicion will be aroused by the action, for the hat is mouth upward and the brim does not go out of sight; however, when you lift the hat you bring away the loaded crown attached to it, the appearance of the hat not being altered in any way.

Finding it impossible to get all the articles back into the hat, take out those you have put in and declare that the hat is still full. In order to empty it more quickly ask permission to cut a hole in the crown. Without waiting for an answer, pick up an open penknife from the table, push the point into the cut already made, and pretend to cut the flap; pull the flap down, take hold of the end of the tambourine coil between the two crowns, and start it unwinding from the center. Take the wand and whirl out the coil from inside the hat in the usual way. The effect of the paper ribbon streaming out from the

Fig. 4

crown and the mouth of the hat is a sure-fire hit with any audience (Fig. 4).

When the coils are exhausted, dump the hat on top of the pile on the floor and try to push the other pile into it. It is then an easy matter to detach the false crown and conceal it in the paper ribbon. Failing to get the mass back into the hat, you say you will have the goods parceled and returned to the owner after the performance. Rub the crown of the hat, tap it with the magic wand, show that it is whole again, and return the hat.

With regard to the whirling out of the paper coil with the

wand—if you move the wand round always in the same direction, the paper will inevitably tangle on the wand instead of coming out in large, free circles. To avoid this tangling, every now and then reverse the motion of the wand (whirling first from right to left and then from left to right) and you will find you can keep the whole mass of paper whirling freely in the air with very pretty effect. It is surprising how few performers who use the coils know this. Instead of getting a continuous production they have to stop to disentangle the wand, and this spoils the effect entirely.

XVI

MENTAL MAGIC

"His eyes are in his mind."
Samuel Taylor Coleridge—To a Lady.

T RICKS which appear to be dependent entirely upon mental operations undoubtedly make the nearest possible approach to real magic. To the layman who does not know the secret, it appears to be impossible that an operator not only can tell him what he is thinking of but can even predict infallibly what he will think presently. Mental effects appeal strongly to the magician because of the absence of apparatus and tedious preparation too often associated with other magical effects.

Mental magic can be divided into two classes of tricks: those which can be done by an operator working entirely alone and those which require an assistant, generally a lady. There has been a great development in recent years in the mental effects which can be performed by one person and, while it is impossible to cover the whole field, examples will be given of the various methods used by performers who make a specialty of this work.

It is essential that no special apparatus of any kind be used. Naturally gimmicks of various kinds are employed, but of these the spectators should have no suspicion; all the visible articles should be of the most ordinary, everyday nature—such as envelopes, pencils, writing pads, slips of paper, slates, chalk, and so on. Any article which might be suspected of having been made specially to produce any certain effect must be ruled out. The performer's manner in presenting mental magic must be carefully studied. All the gestures so dear to the manipulator must be rigidly eliminated. There must be no ostentatious showing that the hands are empty, no suggestions of sleight of hand whatever. Many of the most subtle tricks of mind reading depend upon secret switches of billets, and these moves must be done under cover of perfectly natural moves. The audience must be led to believe that the performer is a mind reader and, therefore, to be successful he must act the part of a mind reader. All gags, jokes, and byplay must be carefully avoided. However, since the attention of the audience must be kept concentrated on every detail, great care must be taken not to make the demonstrations too long drawn out. From fifteen to twenty minutes should be regarded as the limit; but if the performer has made a specialty of the work and has devised a series of striking and well-diversified tests, the time might be lengthened to half an hour at the outside.

I. THE PERFORMER WORKING ALONE

1. IMPROMPTU MIND READING

A spectator writes a name, a telephone number, or a short question on a slip of paper. This is then torn to fragments and burned. The performer spells out the name, gets the telephone number figure by figure, or gives an appropriate answer to the question.

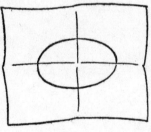

FIG. 1

Take a small slip of paper, not more than three and one-half by three inches, fold it in half and again in half the other way. Open it out and in the middle draw an oval with a pencil (Fig. 1). Invite someone to think of the name of a close friend, a telephone number with which he is familiar, or a short question. Under pretense of helping him to concentrate his thoughts, give him the paper and have him write the name, the number, or the question inside the oval, fold the paper, and return it.

Hold the folded part of the slip between the tips of the left thumb and first and second fingers so that they cover the part which has the oval and the writing inside (Fig. 2). Tear the paper in half downwards, as shown by the dotted line. Place the piece held in the right hand in front of that in the left hand; turn the pieces upward, keeping the folded part under the left thumb; and tear them in half, downwards again. Place the right-hand pieces in front, nearest to the spectators as before; with the left thumb pull the small folded piece, on the outside of the others, back and clip it between the first and second fingers. Tear the

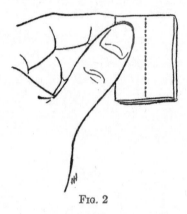

Fig. 2

other pieces again and again, drop them onto an ash tray, and either light a match and set fire to them yourself or ask a spectator to do so.

The result of these maneuvers is that the small folded part of the paper remains safely hidden in the left hand and you have merely to open it secretly, read the writing, and reveal it in the approved manner. If you are doing the trick seated at a table, it is easy to drop the left hand, open the slip with the thumb, and read the writing—covering the downward glance by putting your right hand to your forehead in pretended concentration. Or you may have a small note pad in your left outside coat pocket and, in the act of bringing it out with the left hand, open the slip against its face. Hold the pad upright, hiding the slip; read the writing; scribble something on the first page; then, as if dissatisfied, tear it off, crumple it with the slip inside, and drop it into your pocket. Then proceed to get the name or number, little by little, or write an intelligent answer to the question if such was written. Act as if you were getting the letters or figures through strained mental concentration, and in the case of a message or question never repeat it word for word. Make a mistake in a letter or figure occasionally—call an n for an m, a 1 for a 7, and so on—then correct yourself; in fact, use every artifice possible to induce the belief that you are getting the information through the channels of the mind only.

An excellent presentation is to have a person think of a playing card and write its name on the slip. You have a pack of cards in its case in your left coat pocket. After having torn the slip of paper and burned the pieces, bring out the card case, opening out the slip in the process; read the name of the card as you take the pack from its case; then put the case and the slip back in your pocket. Fan the deck and, after the usual pretended hesitation in getting the color, suit, and value, finally pull the card out, keeping its back to the spectator. Ask him to name the card he thought of, and slowly turn it to prove that you have read his mind.

After the pieces of the slip have been burned, never refer to the fact that any writing has been done; treat this as a mere incident, to enable the spectator to fix his thought more intently. Concentrate on the spectator. If he appears to be trying to help you, compliment him on his concentrative power; if he attempts to treat the matter lightly, upbraid him for inattention; and so on. The mechanical part of this trick is so easy that it makes an excellent experiment in the proper presentation of a mental effect.

2. THE BILLET SWITCH

This sleight is the key to many of the most subtle feats of pretended mind reading. The size of the slip of paper used is most important; when folded, it should be of such size that it can be held securely between the folds at the base and at the top joint of the middle finger by bending that finger slightly (Fig. 3). Take a piece of paper about two and one-half by three and one-half inches, fold it in half the long way, then in half the opposite way and again in half the same way. The resulting packet should be a little narrower than your middle finger and just the right length to fit into the required position. If this size is not just right, experiment with different-sized papers until the right one is found. Generally speaking, the little writing pads obtainable at the five and ten cent stores will be found just right; if not, have a printer cut your slips and clip them together.

The switch is made thus: Place a folded slip in the finger palm position and take a second slip between the tips of the thumb and second finger of the same hand. Pull this second slip back with the thumb until it overlaps the first (Fig. 4); then with the

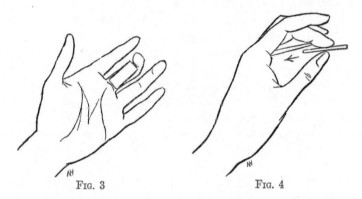

Fig. 3   Fig. 4

tip of the second finger push up the first slip and continue the action of the thumb and finger until the two slips have changed places, the first slip now being in view at the tips of the thumb and second finger and the second one finger palmed. The sleight is not a difficult one, but it must be done so smoothly that when the hand is in motion the change is imperceptible. It must be done with either hand with equal facility.

3. "The Quick and the Dead" Trick

1st Method. Slips of paper are handed to several spectators; one is asked to write the name of a deceased friend, the others to write the names of living persons. The papers are folded and mixed, yet the performer spells out the name of the dead person.

From a sheet of typewriting paper tear off a strip about two and a half inches wide, and rule it off into six equal parts. While you explain what is to be done, tear off the piece at one end of the strip. Show how it is to be folded—in half the long way, then twice the other way. Make a motion of dropping this into your pocket; in reality, finger palm it. Note that this piece has one machine-cut edge. Tear off the first piece from the other end of the strip of paper; this will also have a machine-cut edge on one side. Hand it to a spectator with the request that he write the name of a deceased friend and then fold it in the way you have just shown. As he does this, tear off another slip (both sides of which will have rough edges) and hand it to a second person to write the name of a living friend. Take the folded slip with the dead man's name and apparently drop it into a glass; in reality, switch it for the dummy slip—which goes into the glass, while you retain the written slip finger palmed.

Tear off the three remaining slips and hand them out for the names of living persons to be written on them. Have all four of these rough-sided slips folded the same way and dropped into the glass. Now you have to get an opportunity of opening the palmed slip and reading the name. For example, you may take a chair and sit down with your back to the spectators; instantly drop the slip into your lap and, grasping the seat of the chair with both hands, alter its position a little. Both hands are thus brought into full view quite naturally, and palpably hold nothing. Then open the paper, read the name, refold it, and finger palm it again—the work of a few seconds.

After a moment or two, say that you are not getting any impressions and decide that contact with the slips will help. Face the spectators; take from the glass one of the slips with two rough edges and hold it to your forehead, without any result. Drop it on the table and take a second rough-edged slip; again you get no impression, so you drop it with the first. The third time take the slip with the machine-cut edge (the dummy slip) and, in raising it to your forehead, switch it for the finger palmed duplicate. Now get the letters of the name one by one, hesitatingly, making mistakes and correcting yourself as the impression becomes clearer and so on, until you have the full name.

Give the folded slip to the man who wrote it, to be opened and verified. Take the remaining slips from the glass, adding the palmed dummy slip; add the three to the two slips on the table, tear them in half, crumple the pieces, and put them aside. Your hands are then empty and you are free to go on with the next experiment.

2d Method. This depends entirely upon a mental subtlety. Any piece of paper and any pencil can be used; close observation is all that is necessary. Having picked your subject, you ask him to think of some deceased friend—someone he is sure will be entirely unknown to you. Impress upon him to picture the name mentally very clearly. When he has fixed on a name, give him the paper and pencil and instruct him to write the names of four living friends, also unknown to you, and at any place in the list to write the name of the dead person. Rule five lines on the paper, making spaces for the names, and walk away.

While he is writing, you move about the room but you keep in such position that you can follow the motions of his hand. In fixing on the names of living friends, the subject will hesitate a little in writing them; but when he comes to put down the name of the dead person, on whom his thought is fixed, he will dash it off very quickly. Even if you were not watching him write, the very formation of the letters would reveal to you the name you want.

It is practically certain that no subject will write the name he has fixed upon in the first space and it is very unlikely that it will be written in the second space; the most likely position in which it will be found will be in the third or fourth place. These two spaces are the ones you will watch most closely, and the one which is written without hesitation is the one you pick. With very little practice you will find that the two clues will enable you to divine the name unerringly.

You may reveal the name by drawing a line under it, a rather bald conclusion. A better way is to take the paper and, in turning it over, read the name you have fixed upon as that of the dead person, and then reproduce it on the other side by automatic writing. Hold the subject's hand with your left hand, impress him to think intently of the name, make some meaningless scrawls at first, then write the name in very large letters.

4. A PREDICTION

1st Method. The performer writes something on a slip of paper, seals it in an envelope, and hands this to a spectator to hold. Several spectators then write single digits on a writing pad, one under the other; the pad is initialed and the column of figures added up. The total is found to correspond with the number previously written by the performer and sealed in the envelope.

Suppose you have written the number 38 on the slip which is in the envelope, held by a spectator. Take a pad and pencil and invite another spectator to write any digit he pleases. Go to a second person and have him write a figure under the first. Continue in the same way and mentally add the figures each time a digit is written. When the total passes 29, stop—for the addition of another figure might carry the total beyond 38. Inquire the initials of the last person, write them on the paper,

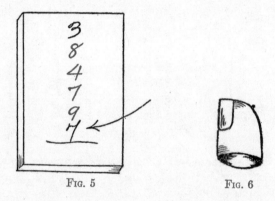

Fig. 5   Fig. 6

and at the same time write in a figure which will bring the total to 38. For example, if the genuine figures total 31, you would write a 7 under the other figures (Fig. 5), if 33 write in a 5, and so on. Draw a line under the column and hand the pad to another spectator to add up the figures. He calls the total and the spectator holding the envelope opens it, takes out your slip, and reads out the same number that you had written beforehand.

2d Method. A better plan is to use the gimmick known as a thumb writer (Fig. 6). This is a thumb tip with a tiny scrap of lead fixed to it as shown. Have this in your right-hand coat pocket. Take a pad and pencil and go from person to person, having each one write a digit, and as you take the pad each time keep track of the total. Again we will suppose you have written 38 on the slip which has been sealed in the envelope; when you note that the total of the column has reached within less than 9 of your number—31, for example—stop. You have already slipped the thumb writer onto your right thumb and you hold the pad with both hands, fingers in front, thumbs behind. While you say that you will have the figures added up by someone else, write in the required number—in this case 7— doing it without looking at the pad, but at the spectators as if choosing someone to make the addition. The rest follows as above.

5. Reading Names in Sealed Envelopes

A number of small white drug envelopes are given out, with white cards to match. The spectators write the names of famous

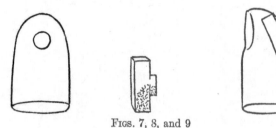

Figs. 7, 8, and 9

people on the cards and insert the cards, face down, in the envelopes, which they seal. The performer collects them and, holding the envelopes to his forehead, reads the names.

Another kind of thumb tip is required. This has a small round hole cut in it (Fig. 7) and a piece of fine sponge, cut as shown in Fig. 8, is inserted so that part of the sponge protrudes a little through the hole (Fig. 9). Saturate the sponge with rubbing alcohol, carbona, or tetrachloride, and place the thumb tip in your right outside coat pocket. After the envelopes have been collected, secretly get the tip onto your right thumb and take the envelopes one by one, the thumbs on the face toward yourself and the fingers on the back toward the spectators. Rub the sponge part of the right thumb tip across the face of the envelope as you lift it to your forehead. The paper instantly becomes transparent, enabling you to read the name written on the card. Reveal it in the usual way, hesitating and stumbling occasionally as if the information came to you by brain waves from the several spectators.

Tear off the end of each envelope with the left hand, extract the card, and show it. Proceed in the same way with three or four, which will be enough to read. Put the last card in your pocket, saying that you will keep it as a souvenir, and at the same time drop the gimmick into the pocket. Leave the other cards and the unopened envelopes on the table for inspection if anyone cares to make one. Crumple the opened envelopes and throw them aside.

6. BOOK TESTS

1st Method. A favorite stunt of mind readers is to read—by mental effort alone, apparently—a word selected at random from a book.

In its essence the trick rests upon the forcing of a certain page and word on that page, and any force that can be made to appear to be a genuine choice can be used. For example, the number of the page can be forced by the method given in the prediction trick (4) explained above. Suppose that by this method you have forced the number 38. Announce that this number is to designate the page in the book which is being used, and that the total of the two digits will designate the number of the word from the top of the page. Thus the person who holds the book is to look at the eleventh word on the thirty-eighth page. This word you have memorized so that you can either write the word on a slip of paper, seal it in an envelope, and give it out to be held before the number of the page is arrived at (presenting the trick as a prediction) or, after the spectator has found the word in the book, proceed to read his mind in the usual way.

2d Method. Again, you can arrange a pack of cards in such a way that any two cards, taken together, will have a total value of 14 or 15. Count Jacks 11, Queens 12, and Kings 13. For example, the cards may run: 4 J 3 Q 2 K A K 2 Q 3 J 4 10 5 and so on. When the arrangement is completed, there will be two Aces left over; these may be removed from the pack entirely or simply left in the card case when the pack is removed. The cards can then be cut any number of times with complete cuts, and any two cards removed from it together will total 14 or 15. Beforehand you memorize the fifth word on the fourteenth page and the sixth word on the fifteenth page of the book you will use.

Hand the book to a spectator; then introduce the arranged deck, make a false shuffle, and have the pack cut as often as is desired by another spectator. Invite him to remove any two cards together from any part of the pack, retire to a distance from you, add the values of the two cards, find the corresponding page in the book, add the two digits of the number, and find the corresponding word (counting from the first word at the top of the page). You have merely to note whether he is looking at the right or the left page, the right-hand page will always be the fifteenth and the left-hand page the fourteenth.

3d Method. In this procedure a chosen card is pushed by a spectator into a book at random. The first sentence at the top of the page thus selected is correctly visualized and written down by the performer.

Take a card—for instance, the Seven of Diamonds—open the book, which must be a rather thick one; memorize the first line on the top of the right-hand page; insert the card and, in closing the book, allow it to protrude about half an inch. Set the book on your table with the protruding card to the rear, and put a rubber band around it. Begin by forcing a duplicate of the Seven of Diamonds—the Hindu shuffle force described in Chapter XVII on playing cards is a good one to use—and invite the spectator to push the card into the book which you present to him with the duplicate card already in it protruding toward yourself. Push his card in to the same extent as the other card; replace the rubber band; and, as you return to your table, turn the book round and push the spectator's card right in, flush with the edges of the leaves.

Pretend to read through the closed book with great mental strain, and write on a slate the sentence you memorized. Place this on your table, with the writing away from the spectators. Invite the person who chose the card to come forwards. Under his close inspection move the rubber band and open the book at the place indicated by the protruding card, which he identifies as the card he himself pushed in. Ask him to read the first sentence on the right-hand page aloud; then turn the slate and also read aloud the words you have written. They correspond exactly, of course. It is not safe to let the spectator handle the book himself, for the duplicate card might drop out.

7. THE MIRROR PRINCIPLE

The use of a small mirror provides for some of the most striking of all mental effects. In the original form of this trick a small piece of thin mirror plate was fixed on the back of a pocketbook in such a way that it was concealed by a loose leather flap, which could be turned back at will (Fig. 10).

Facing a spectator, the performer gives him a sheet of paper, a pencil, and any flat object lying handy to serve as a writing support. He takes out his pocketbook, places a similar sheet of paper on it, and instructs the spectator to draw some simple object—holding the paper in such a way that the performer can-

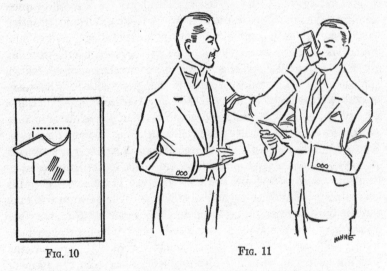

FIG. 10   FIG. 11

not possibly see it. As the spectator does this, the performer pretends to be drawing something on his paper; when the spectator has finished his design, he says, "Now I want you to concentrate on your drawing. Close one eye and continue to look at it with the other. . . . No, not that one"—and as he says this the performer holds his pocketbook in front of the spectator's open eye (whichever one it chances to be) and thereby catches the reflection of the drawing in the mirror (Fig. 11). Stepping back a pace or two, he draws a copy of the design. Both drawings are then shown to the audience.

If the necessary interposition of the pocketbook is made in a casual, offhand manner, no suspicion will be aroused and the subsequent effect is startling. A small convex mirror is now generally used in place of the pocketbook, and the reflection is obtained when grasping the subject's wrist to adjust the angle at which he holds a slate on which he has drawn a design. This action must be done casually and as if merely to make sure that there can be no suspicion of your being able to catch a direct glimpse of the drawing.

II. TWO PERSONS, OPERATOR AND MEDIUM

For many years the act generally known as the "Transmission of Thought" was presented by two people, using a talking code. One, a lady, seated blindfolded on the stage, named and described various articles handed to her partner, usually a man, by members of the audience. By a clever arrangement—in which all the articles generally found in the possession of the spectators were classified in groups of, say, ten articles—the framing of the questions indicated the class and the number in one of the lists. Thus a very slight alteration in the wording of a certain question could be made to indicate any particular article. Successful presentation of this system depended on long practice and devotion to this one trick only. If he lost his partner, the operator faced the necessity of training another assistant—a long and tedious process. In addition to this drawback, the many exposures of the principle in the public press, popular magazines, and books made the *modus operandi* so widely known that the talking code is now practically obsolete; that is, in the form of questions made by the operator directly to the medium.

A very clever modification of the act, in which the operator does not address the subject directly in any way, is now being used with success. For the details, however, I must refer the reader to the treatise entitled *The Calostro Mind Reading Act*, by Ralph W. Read, which can be obtained through the magic stores.

Another system has been developed, the silent system. For example, the blindfold used by the subject is so prepared that she can see the movements of the operator and the position in which he stands, the movements of his hands and arms, the direction of his gaze; and all these are used to transmit the required information. Here again long and arduous practice is necessary to acquire sufficient facility in the system before any public performance is possible. However, various artifices have been devised to overcome this difficulty, and some very effective presentations of pretended mind reading can be made with only a little practice and without the old question and answer code or elaborate signaling with the silent system. The following will serve as examples from which other tricks can be devised.

1. A Simple Thought Transference Feat

Effect. The subject, a lady, is genuinely blindfolded and seated in the center of the stage, platform, or part of the room set apart for the performance if it takes place in a parlor. Two red handkerchiefs are placed on her right shoulder, two white ones on her left shoulder, and two blue ones on her lap. Two members of the audience each whisper one of the colors of the handkerchiefs to the operator and a third whispers a small number. The lady then slowly takes the handkerchiefs of the colors chosen and ties them together in the desired number of knots, the operator maintaining complete silence.

Method. The operator makes a great point of the feat being carried through in absolute silence, but he manages to give certain signals to the subject before the experiment is supposed to begin. A code, after the style of the following, is used: 1. Thanks. 2. Thank you.   3. 'Sh.   4. Hush.   5. Excuse me.   6. Allow me.   7. Sorry to trouble you.   8. Many thanks. 9. Pardon?   10. Remember, please.

The first three can be used to signal the chosen colors first, and afterwards, if necessary, any one of them to signal the number of knots to be tied. The words should be spoken casually and quietly, just loud enough for the subject to hear, and directly to the spectator who has just whispered the request. After the signals have been given, the operator should stand facing the audience, motionless and affecting an air of deep concentration, while the lady should take her time in picking out the handkerchiefs, changing from one to another hesitatingly. Simple as it is, the experiment requires proper rehearsal and good acting on the part of both performers.

2. A Blackboard Feat

Effect. The medium is blindfolded and the spectators write numbers on a blackboard, which is placed in such a position that the medium could not see the figures even if a blindfold were not used. The medium then calls the correct total of the sum figure by figure, the performer remaining silent throughout. He then points to various figures and the subject calls them correctly; a spectator writes a figure on the board and the subject names it; finally the subject names correctly various cards taken from a shuffled deck.

Articles required. Fake blindfold, blackboard, chalk, and pack of cards. The prepared blindfold is best obtained from a magic shop and, in general, this applies to all trick apparatus; home-made articles are seldom satisfactory. For parlor work, to avoid the necessity of carrying a blackboard, several large sheets of white paper can be fastened with thumbtacks to the top of a small table overturned on a larger one. This, with a heavy black crayon, will serve the purpose admirably. A few cards, say six, are removed from the pack and placed in a certain order, which the subject memorizes. They are then laid on the table, face up, and covered by the blindfold.

Method. Introduce the medium and seat her so that she is back of the blackboard and to the left. Take the deck from its case and have the cards thoroughly shuffled by a spectator, whom you have invited to come forward. This done, take the deck and, as you lift the blindfold with one hand, with the other drop the pack, face up, on the six cards that were hidden by it. Hold the blindfold over the spectator's eyes and ask him if he can see through it. He announces that it is opaque and with it you blindfold the medium. Hand the chalk to the spectator and invite him to set down a sum consisting of four rows of four or five figures in each row. If you think it desirable, to avoid all suspicion of confederacy, you may have each of four spectators write a row of figures.

Announce that the medium will add the sum. Signal the figures to her thus: Stand with your left side to the board; right side toward the spectators; left hand resting on the board, the thumb in front and the fingers behind. The digits 1 to 5 are signaled with the hand near the top of the board—one finger extended for 1, two fingers for 2, three fingers for 3, four fingers for 4, and the hand clenched for 5. For 6, 7, 8, 9, and 0, hold the board near its lower side and repeat same signals.

As soon as the sum has been written down, add the first column mentally, draw a line below the figures, and signal the first digit of the total; at the same time add the second column mentally. When the medium calls the first figure, write it down and code the next. Proceed in exactly the same way until the total is completed. The subject must work in the approved style; that is, hesitatingly—occasionally making a mistake, such as calling a 1 for a 7 or a 0 for a 9, then claiming to see the figure more distinctly and correcting herself.

A series of figures is then touched in quick succession and the medium instantly calls them. This is managed very simply. Both must memorize the figures beforehand and the same series is always used. For example, the following couplet can be memorized:

> Eight kings threatened to save
> Ninety-five ladies for one sick knave,

coding 8, K, 3, 10, 2, 7, 9, 5, Q, 4, 1, 6, K. When the court cards are reached you tap on the blank part of the blackboard and the subject at once calls, "Nothing there." A second series —such as 13, 17, 14, 12—can also be memorized and called. After the last of the couplet figures has been named, place circles round two figures which total 13 and the subject calls that number, and so with the rest.

Next, hand the chalk to a spectator and invite him to write a figure on the board. Stand with your left side to the medium, the left hand on your hip, and signal with the fingers as before —holding the hand high for 1 to 5, low for 6 to 0.

Finish by taking the pack of cards; deal the first six, face up in a row, as you stand behind the table with your back to the medium. Take up the first card, look at it for a few moments, and the medium says, "I see a black card, a club, and it has . . . eight spots"—or as the case may be, and so on with the others.

3. ANOTHER BLACKBOARD TEST

This trick makes a most effective finish to any mind reading act. A blackboard, a very large slate, or a large sheet of white paper (set as for the second trick above) will be required. The test is worked in dead silence on the part of the operator and the audience. The medium is genuinely blindfolded and is seated toward the back in the middle of the stage or platform. The performer invites the spectators to indicate the figures they wish to be used by raising their hands, with the fingers extended or closed as may be necessary. These digits are written on the blackboard, forming, we will suppose, a sum of three rows of five figures. When completed, the performer draws a line under the sum and the medium instantly calls the total; for example, "Eighty-six thousand, two hundred and thirty-nine."

The effect is quite startling, but it is obtained by the simplest possible means. When the operator calls for figures, he writes them in columns (and not in lines) across the board, beginning with the last figure in each line. The first two figures, which he writes one under the other, are those really indicated by the spectators; but the third is whatever figure may be necessary to make the addition tally with the last figure of the total which has been memorized by the performer and the medium—86,239, as suggested above. Suppose the first two figures indicated are a 7 and a 4. The performer then pretends to see someone indicating an 8; he nods to the imaginary spectator and writes in the 8 below the 7 and the 4. He proceeds in precisely the same way until the sum is completed, always writing two figures genuinely indicated and the third an imaginary figure to make the total right. The signal to the medium to call the total is the drawing of a line under the sum by the performer. For effect she should call this as rapidly as it is possible for the performer to write the figures—thus, "Eighty-six thousand, two hundred and thirty-nine." Finally the operator checks the addition aloud, proving it to be correct.

The trick can be performed safely only before a fairly large audience, so that it is impossible for anyone to check up on every figure the operator writes on the board. To enable him to work without any hesitation, the performer can have the required total written in pencil in tiny figures on the frame of the slate or at the top of the blackboard; but the medium must have the figures of the total memorized perfectly.

4. THE KNIGHT'S TOUR

This is another favorite and very effective feat with which to conclude a mind reading test. Rule off one side of the blackboard or one of the sheets of paper into sixty-four squares, to represent a chess board. Show this and announce that your subject will call a knight's tour all over the board, visiting every square once only and beginning with any numbered square that the audience selects. For the benefit of those not knowing the game of chess, you demonstrate briefly the manner in which a knight can move. A number is then called and, as the medium calls the moves, the operator draws a line from the starting point to the square called and from that square to the next one she names, and so on until every square on the board is thus connected.

To be able to do this the lady must memorize the following list of numbers or, since this is a difficult task, she may have them written on a card fastened to the back of her fan or concealed by her handkerchief:

27, 17, 2, 12, 22, 32, 15, 5, 20, 26, 9, 3, 13, 7, 24, 30, 40, 55, 61, 46, 29, 14, 8, 3, 6, 16, 31, 21, 11, 1, 18, 28, 38, 48, 63, 53, 43, 33, 50, 60, 45, 39, 56, 62, 52, 58, 41, 35, 25, 10, 4, 19, 36, 51, 57, 42, 59, 49, 34, 44, 54, 64, 47, 37, and back to 27.

All she has to do then is to find the number called by the spectator, start with that number, and go straight ahead until every number has been called and she is back to the starting point.

5. MARVELOUS MEMORY

Effect. Spectators call the names of any persons or objects, and they are written down on a blackboard with the numbers from 1 on in consecutive order. The total number of such objects may range from twenty-five to fifty or more, yet the operator, with his back to the blackboard, names the whole list from start to finish (or the reverse way); and, on any number being called, he will name the object at that number or, the object being called, he will instantly call the number at which it stands in the list.

Method. Such a performance induces the popular belief that the operator is endowed with a marvelous memory. Such, however, is not the case. No special power of memory is required but simply the application of a mental trick, the association of ideas. In the first place, certain words are associated with particular numbers and the objects called are then associated by mental pictures with the word that represents the number attached to that particular object.

The first step, then, is to learn the numerical alphabet which follows:

1 is represented by	l		Clue,	one stroke
2 "	"	" n		"	two strokes
3 "	"	" m		"	three strokes
4 "	"	" r		"	last letter of "four"
5 "	"	" f-v		"	five
6 "	"	" b-p		"	similar shape
7 "	"	" t-d		"	" " "
8 "	"	" sh-ch		"	eight-aitch
9 "	"	" k-g (hard)		"	similar shape
0 "	"	" s-z		"	zero

The clues will enable anyone to memorize the list in a few minutes. By combining the letters, any required number can be indicated; for example, l-l represents 11, l-n 12, m-m 23, f-n 52, and so on.

The next step is to make up a list of words by adding vowels to consonants of the number alphabet, thus: 1. Ale.   2. Hen. 3. Emblem.   4. Arrow.   5. Ivy.   6. Bee.   7. Tea.   8. Shoe. 9. Key.   10. Lass. And so on.

These are given merely as examples. The student can choose words to suit himself; for instance, LioN might stand for 12, NuN for 22, MuMmy for 33. It must, however, be understood that the system is strictly phonetic, the sound of the consonants only being considered.

When the number words have been thoroughly memorized, all the operator has to do, when the objects are called and listed on the blackboard, is to associate each one with its appropriate number word by making a mental picture of the two in association—and the more absurd and grotesque the picture, the more easily it will be recalled. For example, suppose the first thing

called is Elephant. You have already pictured a huge glass of
Ale in your mind's eye, so you add to it an Elephant sitting on its
haunches about to pour the Ale down its mouth with its trunk.
Later, when you are asked to name the object at number 1, you
mentally picture the glass of Ale and at once you see the Elephant quaffing it.

Again, suppose number 2 is Clock. Picture a Hen sitting on a
nest opposite a Clock, timing herself laying an egg. When 2 is
called, you picture the Hen and at once you see the Clock;
whereas if Clock is called and you are asked its number, you
at once recall the picture of the Hen timing herself laying eggs.

A vivid imagination is of more assistance than a retentive memory in performing the feat and, of course, it is just as easily
applied to a hundred objects as to twenty or thirty. It is a good
plan not to use more than thirty objects, because of the time
taken up in writing a longer list. After all, the intention is to be
entertaining, and any tendency to become tedious or long drawn
out must be carefully avoided. A sure and rapid treatment of
thirty objects will be found to create more interest and wonder-
ment than the employment of twice that number, entailing the
taking of twice the length of time.

The act can be worked singlehanded by having a spectator
write the names on the board, but it is more effective to work it
with a lady assistant. As in the blackboard tests already explained, you blindfold genuinely, and seat your assistant back
of the blackboard and to the left. When you invite the spectators to call the objects, first call the number and then repeat
the object as you write it on the board, thus giving your assistant
time to form the necessary mental picture.

When the list is completed, you may have her call off the
objects rapidly in order from 1 to 30, then backwards from
30 to 1. Next invite the spectators to call any numbers and she
names the objects, or vice versa. Strike out each object, as
called, until the whole list has been gone over. By using the
couplet already given in this chapter ("Eight kings threatened
to save . . .") the medium is enabled to call the objects that
you apparently pick out at random. Of course, when you arrive
at a court card you point to a blank space.

Finally, by using a trick blindfold you can invite a spectator to point to any number, and the medium will call it and the object. This is a mere matter of signaling with the left fingers, as has been explained already (see page 296).

Mastery of the system will repay the student handsomely. There is no apparatus to carry, you are ready to perform the feat at all times, and it is always received with enthusiasm by the largest and the smallest audiences.

XVII

PLAYING CARDS

"Patience, and shuffle the cards."
Miguel de Cervantes—Don Quixote.

FROM the time the first engraved playing cards were produced, about the middle of the fifteenth century, they have been the favorite implements of the workers of magic tricks. Before that time cards were painted by hand and only the nobility and the very rich could afford to buy them. The discovery of a payment to one Gringonier, a court painter, for painting a pack of cards for the mad king Charles of France gave rise to the foolish legend, still current, that cards were invented for the amusement of a madman. The art of engraving brought cards into the hands of the common people, and so rapidly did the magicians—jongleurs, as they were then called—adapt them to their purposes that the curious reader will find in Reginald Scot's *The Discoverie of Witchcraft* (1586) a clear description of some of the sleights used by skilled card performers of today, who little know to whom they are indebted for them.

Of recent years there has been a great advance in the art of manipulating cards, mainly in the direction of simplicity and subtlety as against the use of difficult sleights. For example, the textbooks place great stress on the absolute necessity for making the pass, a sleight whereby the halves of the pack are righted after a cut has been made. This is an extremely difficult sleight and, being faced with it at the outset, many would-be card tricksters give up the struggle and turn to some other branch of the art which appears to be less difficult. The fact is, however, that the basic sleights with cards are easy and anyone who can make the regular overhand and riffle shuffles can with very little trouble master a large number of the best card tricks. The simplified methods of today are in great part a reversion to those in use in Scot's time as the following quotation from his book proves:

303

"But in showing feats and juggling with cards the principall point consisteth in shuffling them nimblie and alwaies keeping one certain card in the bottome or in some knowne place in the stock foure or five cards from it. Hereby you shall seeme to worke wonders . . . in reserving the bottome card you must alwaies (whilest you shuffle) keepe him a little before or a little behind all the other cards lieing beneath him."

This last is nothing more nor less than the so-called modern "jog," one of the best weapons in the armory of the up-to-date card man.

The essential sleights in card conjuring are few in number and if the student will follow the descriptions with the cards in hand and apply a little intelligent practice to them he will have no difficulty in mastering the tricks dependent on them.

I. SHUFFLES

1. THE OVERHAND SHUFFLE

A neat overhand shuffle is still "the principall point," as laid down by Scot. The proper position of the pack is important.

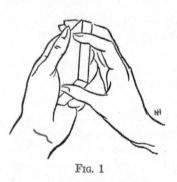

Hold it in the left hand, at an angle of about forty-five degrees, the thumb on the back near the outer end and about the middle, the forefinger from the second joint resting against the outer end, the little finger curled against the inner end, and the second and third fingers resting on the bottom card (Fig. 1).

FIG. 1

To shuffle the cards, raise the lower portion of the pack between the right thumb at the inner end and the tips of the second and third fingers on the outer end, the forefinger resting on the middle of the upper side and the little finger resting free.

Bring the right-hand portion down on the remainder in the left hand (Fig. 1), pull off a few cards with the left thumb, and raise the right hand again. Repeat the same movements until the cards in the right hand are exhausted and the whole shuffled pack is again in the left hand. The positions of the left first and fourth fingers are important, for they serve to keep the cards together neatly.

This shuffle is applied to secret purposes as follows:

(1) *To retain the bottom card.* In drawing out the lower part of the pack press the tips of the left second and third fingers against the bottom card, holding it back so that the upper part, which remains in the left hand, falls on it. This action can be repeated as often as desired.

(2) *To retain the top card.* Press the left thumb on the top card; lift off all the other cards with the right hand and shuffle them onto that card, which then becomes the bottom card of the deck. Lift the lower portion of the pack and shuffle off into the left hand until the bottom card only remains in the right hand, then throw it on top. Practice this sleight by turning the top card face upwards so that you can follow it easily.

(3) *To bring the top card second from the bottom and again to the top.* Press the left thumb firmly on the back of the deck and the tips of the second and third fingers on the bottom card; with the right hand lift out all the intervening cards so that the top card falls on the bottom card, both being retained in the left hand by the pressure; then shuffle off on top of them as usual. You can now turn the pack over to show the bottom card (the card you are controlling being next to it and hidden by it) and then show the top card, yet by repeating exactly the same movements as before you shuffle the card back to the top. Here again it is well to reverse the top card when learning the sleight.

(4) *Running the cards.* This is the technical term for pulling off cards singly with the left thumb in the shuffle. By this you can place any required number of cards on top of the card you are controlling. Very little practice will enable you to do this with ease and certainty if the cards are in good condition. Never practice with cards that are sticky and dirty from use.

(5) *The jog.* This term means simply a protruding card. Turn the top card face up so that it can be followed easily. Begin the shuffle as usual by lifting the lower portion with the right hand, but at once draw that hand inwards a little toward the body so

that when the first card is drawn off by the thumb it will protrude slightly over the left little finger (Fig. 2). Move the right hand back to its original position and shuffle off the remaining cards. With the right thumb and second finger seize all the cards under the protruding card and throw them on the top of the pack, the action passing for a casual cut. The faced card will again be on the top. Naturally, several cards can be retained on the top in the same way.

(6) *The break*. This is the technical term for a separation between two portions of the deck secretly held at the inner end.

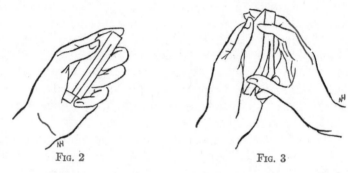

FIG. 2   FIG. 3

Jog one card, as in the preceding paragraph, then, instead of making a final cut, seize about three-quarters of the deck with the right hand for another shuffle and press the right thumb slightly upwards against the protruding end of the jogged card. Squeeze the ends of the cards rather tightly and it will be found that a break will be formed below the jogged card. Shuffle off all the cards until the break is reached and throw the rest on top (Fig. 3).

The jog and the break are two of the strongest weapons of the card magician. They are not difficult and rapid execution is not at all necessary, rather smoothness and regularity in the action.

(7) *Partial shuffle, controlling several cards*. We will suppose that you have several cards on the top of the pack which are to be kept under control secretly and returned to the top while making an apparently fair shuffle. Call this packet A. Turn the top card so that you can follow the action. Seize the lower por-

tion of the pack between the right thumb and second finger only, leaving the third finger free, and lift about three-quarters of the deck. Call this part B. Bring B down in front of A; drop a packet (C) from the top of B; at the same moment press the tip of the right third finger against the outer end of A, pushing its inner end against the inside of the right thumb. A is thus held firmly between the third finger and the thumb, with a break between it and B (Fig. 4).

Shuffle off the remaining cards of B on top of C, and when the break is reached throw A on top of the pack as the last move in the shuffle. Note that this sleight accomplishes the same result

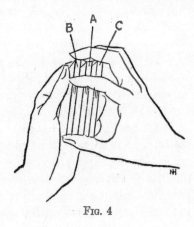

Fig. 4

as the jog and the break in the preceding paragraphs but with one shuffle only.

(8) *To retain control of a card which has been drawn from the pack by a spectator, noted by him, and replaced in the pack.* Invite a spectator to draw a card from the deck and note what it is. Begin an overhand shuffle by drawing off three or four small packets into the left hand; have the chosen card placed on top of them and shuffle off the remaining cards in the right hand on top of it—at least that is what you appear to do. In reality, when you bring the right-hand packet down on the chosen card, merely slide the left thumb down over it but do not draw off any cards. Then tilt the left-hand packet onto the left thumb,

drop a packet from the right hand on it, tilt the left-hand packet back onto the fingers, repeat the sliding of the left thumb without drawing off any cards, then tilt the packet onto the fingers and drop a packet from the right hand. Repeat the same movements until the cards in the right hand are exhausted. The chosen card is then on the top of the deck to be dealt with as may be necessary for the trick in hand.

Smoothly done, the action of the left thumb creates a perfect illusion.

An alternative method is to have the drawn card returned on top of the first packets shuffled into the left hand, run two cards on top of it, jog the next card, and shuffle off the remaining cards freely. Make a break at the jogged card, shuffle to the break, and throw the rest on top.

(9) *To retain the whole deck in a set order.* Begin the shuffle by lifting the lower half of the deck with the right hand, run five cards from the right-hand portion onto the left-hand packet; then throw the remainder of the right-hand packet a little forwards so that it overlaps the lower portion by about half an inch, the protruding part resting on the top joint of the left forefinger. Seize the lower portion between the right thumb and second finger, run five cards, and throw the rest on top. The action is very simple: the first shuffle reverses the order of five cards; the second shuffle brings them back to their original order; the remaining cards are not disturbed, but the illusion of a real shuffle is perfect.

2. THE RIFFLE SHUFFLE

To retain a card or cards on the top with a riffle shuffle is the simplest thing in the world. You have only to see that it, or they, drop from the right-hand portion last of all.

To retain cards on the bottom, after cutting the pack and putting the two portions together for the riffle shuffle, with the left thumb lift the cards above those to be retained on the bottom and riffle the cards from the right-hand portion into these cards only, so that the bottom cards of the pack remain intact. In both cases cover the operation with the hands as much as possible (Fig. 5).

I would urge the reader to practice the foregoing sleights thoroughly before going any further. I have found by experience in teaching that anyone used to handling cards—a bridge player, for example—can learn them inside of an hour. To execute them rapidly, without looking at the hands and while talking, is merely a matter of further practice.

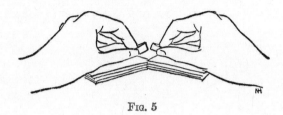

FIG. 5

3. THE HINDU SHUFFLE

I first saw this shuffle done by one Hassan, a Hindu magician, in Australia some thirty-odd years ago. Since then, as I found it was the only shuffle used by the Hindu magicians, I dubbed it the Hindu shuffle and the name has been adopted by the profession. The shuffle itself is a genuine one, but it lends itself admirably to the wiles of the conjurer.

To execute the genuine shuffle hold the pack in the left hand between the top joints of the thumb near the outer end of one side and the top joints of the second and third fingers on the other side, the forefinger at the middle of the outer end, the little finger free, and

FIG. 6

the pack sloping slightly toward the front (Fig. 6).

Take hold of the inner end of the deck by its sides between the top joints of the right thumb and second finger, the forefinger resting on the top of the pack, the third and fourth fingers resting free. Move the left hand outwards, taking with it several cards from the top of the deck gripped by the left thumb and the second finger. As soon as these cards clear the outer end of the deck, release the pressure of the left thumb and the second finger and let the cards fall into the left hand, the left first finger preventing them from leaving the hand (Fig. 7).

Bring the left hand back to its original position, seize another small packet from the top of the deck between the left thumb and second finger as before, move the left hand outwards (Fig. 8), and let the packet fall on top of the first cards that were drawn off. Repeat the same movements until the cards in the right hand are exhausted. Note particularly that the left hand does the work; the right hand barely moves at all. A little practice is required to enable you to draw the cards off in small

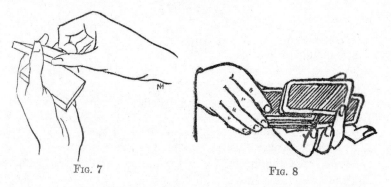

Fig. 7   Fig. 8

packets smoothly; the slanting position of the pack and the stop formed by the left forefinger cause the pack to be assembled neatly in the left hand. Great rapidity is not necessary.

The shuffle is adapted to trick purposes as follows:

(1) *To control a chosen card.* A card having been drawn by a spectator, while he notes it, prepare for the Hindu shuffle. Draw off several small packets of cards and hold out your left hand for him to place his card on top of them. This done, bring the left hand back to the right hand to resume the shuffle, but a moment before the next packet is drawn off by the left hand press the right third finger on the side of the left-hand packet and lift several cards from the top by holding them between the tip of that finger and the right thumb. Continue the shuffle in the regular way until the packet held by the third finger is reached, then drop that packet on top as the last movement of the shuffle. The chosen card is then at the top of the pack.

(2) *To control several cards at the same time.* We will suppose that three spectators have each drawn a card. As the last one

notes his card, prepare for the Hindu shuffle. Draw off several small packets into the left hand and have him replace his card on top of them. Lift several cards with the right third finger as explained in the preceding paragraph and go to the second man. Draw off a couple of packets into the left hand; however, in making the third movement, draw no cards off, but let the stolen packet drop onto the cards in the left hand. Hold out the left hand to the spectator and have his card placed on top of them; that is, on top of the first card replaced.

Repeat the pickup with the third finger; draw off several more packets from the top of the cards in the right hand as you go to the third man, calling particular attention to the fact that the cards are replaced in different parts of the pack. Again drop the stolen packet on the cards in the left hand and have the last card replaced on top. Repeat the pickup with the right third finger and complete the shuffle, dropping the stolen packet on the top in the last movement. All three of the chosen cards are now on the top and in their proper order. The process not only is convincingly deceptive but it saves time by controlling all three cards with one shuffle.

(3) *To force a card.* "Forcing" a card means that you compel a spectator to draw a certain card that you want him to take, at the same time leaving him convinced that he has had a free choice. Have the desired card on the top of the pack and begin the Hindu shuffle by drawing off about a dozen cards in one packet; then, in drawing off a second, small packet, steal several cards from the top of the first packet in the usual way with the right third finger. As you continue the shuffle by drawing off small packets, invite the spectator to call "Stop" at any time he pleases. At the word "Stop" you simply drop the stolen cards on the cards in the left hand without drawing any cards from the right-hand packet, hold the left hand out to the spectator, turn your head away, and tell him to look at the card on which he stopped you.

Then proceed in whatever manner the particular trick calls for. You may bring the card to the top by continuing the Hindu shuffle, or you may drop the rest of the cards on it and hand the pack out to be shuffled. Knowing the card, you can find it when you please.

(4) *Sighting a card.* It is often necessary to obtain knowledge of a certain card secretly. This method is a useful one.

Invite a spectator to shuffle the deck, retain one card, and hand the rest back to you. Begin the Hindu shuffle, drawing off several packets, letting them drop rather unevenly, and tapping them with the cards in the right hand to even them up. To do this turn the right hand, bringing its cards to a vertical position, and tap the outer end of the packet against the inner ends of the left-hand cards, thus bringing the bottom card of the right-hand packet into your view (Fig. 9). Note the card and immediately renew the shuffle.

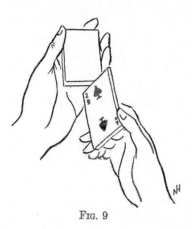

FIG. 9

Invite the spectator to replace his card whenever he pleases, and when he does so drop all the cards in the right hand on it. The card you sighted is thus brought on top of the selected card. This key card serves as a marker whereby you can at any time discover the chosen card immediately below it.

If you care to take a small risk to get a great effect, hand the deck to the spectator to shuffle, at the same time indicating an overhand shuffle with your hands. When he has made a couple of movements of a shuffle, thank him and take the pack back. Not once in a hundred times will the cards be separated.

It should be noted here that if when you control a single card by the Hindu shuffle you manage to pick it up alone with the third finger you can sight it by this tapping and squaring process. At the beginning it is better not to attempt to pick up one card only, for any hesitation at this point is likely to arouse suspicion.

II. SLEIGHTS

1. A SIMPLE PASS

It is the custom nowadays, when you wish to have a chosen card returned to the deck, to place the pack on the left hand, cut off about half the cards with the right hand, hold out the left-hand packet for the chosen card to be placed on top, then put the right-hand packet on top of all. At the same time you slip the tip of the left little finger between the two packets—a process which must cause the old masters to turn in their graves. Far more artistic is it to spread the pack fanwise for the return of the chosen card and then slip the tip of the little finger above it in closing the fan.

Again you may hold the pack in the right hand over the left and drop several packets from the bottom onto the left hand, one after the other, as you invite the spectator to replace his card somewhere in the deck. When about half the cards have

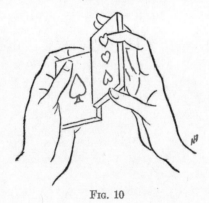

Fig. 10

been dropped, stretch out the left hand to him, have the card replaced, and then put the right-hand packet on top of all— slipping the tip of the little finger between the packets.

Now, to control the card and bring it to the top, first press the outer ends of the cards tightly together so that there is no sign of any break, then bend the outer end of the pack upwards and let the cards escape from the end of the second finger singly but rapidly; this is known as ruffling the cards. Take hold of the top packet between the right thumb at the inner end and all four fingers, close together, at the outer end; make a quick, sharp remark to the spectator—such as, "You are sure you will know your card again?"—to draw his eyes to yours; and immediately, without looking at your hands, lift the top packet with the right hand, drop the left thumb under the lower packet, turn it face up against the curved left fingers (Fig. 10), and instantly begin shuffling the right-hand packet onto the other cards. At the end of the shuffle turn the pack face down in the left hand. The chosen card is on the top.

Do not be deceived by the simplicity of the action. The sleight is used by many of the best card magicians just as described.

2. THE PALM

Here is the *pons asinorum* of most card conjurers, yet to palm a card is one of the easiest of the sleights to be learned. The trouble lies partly in lack of confidence and partly in ignorance of the correct method. The first thing to be learned is the correct position in which to hold the card in the hand. Place your right hand palm upwards and lay a card on it, face up, so that the outer index corner is at the fold of the top joint of the left little finger and the inner corner is against the fleshy part of the base of the thumb (Fig. 11). Bend the four fingers slightly, keeping them pressed together, and turn the hand over. You will find that you can hold the card securely and that the hand has a perfectly natural appearance, for, when in repose, the hand is always partially closed.

FIG. 11

Retain the card in your hand and practice picking up articles, handling them, taking matches from your pocket, striking one, making the overhand and Hindu shuffles and so on. Do this until that inevitable paralysis of the wrist and the forearm, always present when palming is first tried, and which some performers never overcome, disappears entirely. Keep the wrist and arm flexible but always remember that the back of the hand must be kept toward the spectators. When you feel quite at ease with one card palmed, practice with several; and gradually increase the number until you can handle objects quite naturally with half the pack in the palm of your hand.

The next step is to learn how to get the card or cards into the palm secretly. To palm the top card of the deck, hold the cards

in the usual position for dealing them; bring the right hand over
the pack to square the cards, the four fingers being together at
the outer end and the thumb at the inner end of the pack. Move
the fingers and thumb along the ends several times in the usual
way, squaring them; at the moment when the fingers cover the
deck completely, push the lower end of the top card toward the
right with the left thumb (Fig. 12). Bend the right little finger
slightly on the top right corner, thus pressing the opposite
diagonal corner against the base of the right thumb; move the
right hand along the top and bottom of the pack to the right-
hand side, press the palmed card firmly into the palm with the

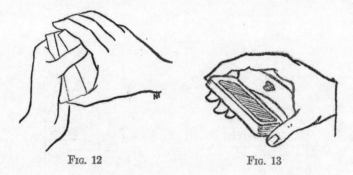

Fig. 12   Fig. 13

tip of the left middle finger, and grip the pack between the first
two fingers of the right hand and the thumb (Fig. 13).

To palm several cards at once, first slip the tip of the left
little finger under them, then treat them in just the same way
as one card. On no account must the right hand be moved away
after palming a card; always complete the action of squaring the
ends and then hold the deck if only for a few moments. Later,
when the left hand takes the pack or you place it on the table,
no suspicion of palming can be aroused, for your actions are
perfectly open and natural.

Audacity and easy, natural gestures with the hand that has
the card, or cards, palmed are the secret of success in palming;
on the other hand, furtive glances at the hand, keeping the hand
and arm stiffly at the side of the body, and using the left hand
to perform actions (such as taking the pack from a spectator)

which should be done with the right hand spell failure. Many of the most effective tricks with cards depend upon perfect palming, and the neophyte should not be satisfied until he can palm a number of cards and use the hand which conceals them with perfect freedom.

3. Replacing Palmed Cards on the Pack

A problem that recurs constantly in the working of card tricks is this—you have a card, or cards, palmed in the right hand, a spectator has shuffled the pack and is ready to return it to you, how are you to take it naturally and without exposing the palmed cards?

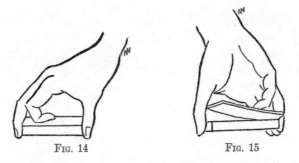

Fig. 14   Fig. 15

The usual solution is to take the pack from the spectator with the left hand and put the palmed cards on top with the right hand. One might just as well tell the spectator right out, for the inference from such action is plain. Yet the solution is an easy one—simply hold out your left hand palm upwards and, making a natural gesture with the right hand, invite the spectator to place the pack on it, face down, and make a free cut. As soon as he takes the top portion, pick up the lower part with your right hand, adding the palmed cards, and put the packet on top of the cut, thus reassembling the pack without any suspicious move. Point out to the spectators that not only has the pack been freely shuffled but a final cut has also been made.

In adding the palmed cards to the packet you pick up, the moment the right hand covers the packet bend the forefinger and press its tip on the middle of the back of the palmed cards

(Fig. 14). This not only disguises the operation but the bend caused by palming is taken out.

The difficulty in replacing palmed cards on the pack is this—if the pack is taken naturally it will be grasped between the thumb and fingers, the rest of the hand being arched well above the pack, and to bring the hand down flat is not natural. To overcome this, take the pack between the thumb and fingers, keeping the hand arched; bend the little finger in on top of the palmed cards and with it press them down on the top of the pack (Fig. 15). The movement requires practice, but if done with the hand in motion the sleight is imperceptible to the closest watcher.

4. THE GLIDE

This is a very easy and useful sleight. The effect is that the bottom card of the pack is shown and dealt on the table; in reality

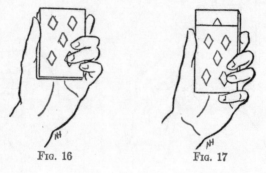

FIG. 16   FIG. 17

the second card is taken, the bottom card remaining in position. To do this, hold the pack face down in the left hand, the thumb at the middle of one side, the other side resting against the first joints of the fingers which are curled under the pack, the tips of the second and third fingers resting on the middle of the bottom card, the little finger free. Hold the pack upright to show the bottom card to the spectators (Fig. 16); then turn the hand, bringing the pack face down; pull the bottom card inwards with the tips of the second and third fingers; with the tip of the right second finger draw the next card forwards, seize it between that finger and the thumb, draw it away, and place it face down on the table. Bend the little finger behind the bottom card and press it back level with the others (Fig. 17).

Sometimes it is necessary to draw several cards off the bottom after the glide has been made, in which case the action of the little finger does not come into play until the last card has been drawn out.

5. THE DOUBLE LIFT

As its name implies, this sleight is the lifting of two cards at once, holding them together so that they appear to be one card only.

1st Method. Hold the pack in the left hand in position for dealing. Bring the right hand over the cards, the fingers at the outer end, the thumb at the inner end; square the pack perfectly; then wedge the ends slightly, by pushing back with the

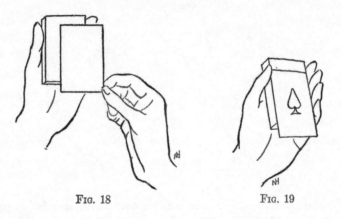

FIG. 18   FIG. 19

fingers and pushing the thumb forwards. With the right thumb lift the inner ends of the two top cards, the tiny steps between the cards making this easy, and slip the tip of the left little finger under them. This is the preliminary preparation before attention is called to the cards. Turn the right hand palm upwards and seize the inner right-hand corners of the two cards (Fig. 18); turn them face up on the top of the deck so that the inner ends protrude about half an inch toward the body (Fig. 19). Call attention to the visible card, naming it; then take hold of the lower right-hand corners as before and turn the card face down level with the pack.

2d Method. Hold the pack in the left hand as for dealing and with the left thumb push a few of the top cards to the right, spreading them a little. The edge of the right-hand side of the second card will strike against the tip of the second finger; with a slight upward pressure draw this finger back, squaring the cards under the two top ones. Insert the tip of the left little finger under the two cards thus separated from the rest. Extend the second and third fingers and with them draw the two cards back square with the deck. Run the right thumb and fingers lightly along the edges of the two cards to insure perfect alignment; then turn the two cards as one, in exactly the same manner as in the first method.

The sleight is used to show, apparently, that a chosen card is not on the top of the deck, or to change one card for another. The action must be done naturally and without hesitation. Neatly done, it is one of the most useful of the modern card sleights.

6. THE FORCE

We have already seen that a card can be forced by means of the Hindu shuffle (see page 311). The following method, the indicator card force, can be used as an alternative. Bring the desired card to the top of the pack and, as you approach a spectator, draw out about one-third of the bottom portion of the pack and shuffle overhand, jogging the first card. Insert the tip of the left little finger under the jogged card. It rests, therefore, on the back of the card you are about to force. Take off the top card of the deck, hand it to the spectator face up, and invite him to insert the card at any point as you ruffle the cards. Keeping the little finger in position, place the right thumb at the inner end of the deck and with the right second finger bend up the outer ends of all the cards; then let them escape in succession from the tip of the finger, illustrating what he is to do.

Bend the ends of the cards upwards again, and this time allow about one-third of the cards to escape rapidly; then slow the movement a little, thus making sure that the indicator will not be inserted too near the bottom of the pack but at a point a little below the card to be forced (Fig. 20). The moment the indicator card is pushed into the deck, drop all the rest of the

cards on top of it (Fig. 21); turn the left hand, bringing the pack
to a vertical position; with the right thumb push up the packet
of cards above the little-finger level with the top of the indicator

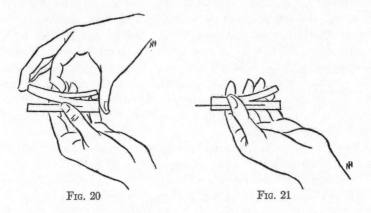

FIG. 20   FIG. 21

card; seize this card and the packet thus brought behind it and
draw them away clear of the pack (Fig. 22). Turn the left hand to

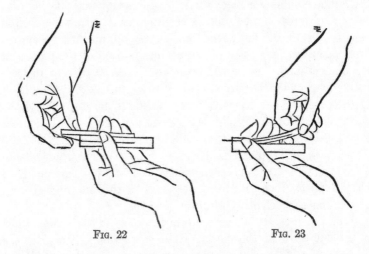

FIG. 22   FIG. 23

a horizontal position and hold the remaining packet out to the
spectator to take the top card; that is, the force card.

It may happen that the indicator card will be inserted above
the break held by the little finger. In that case keep the pack in

a horizontal position, seize the inner end of the packet above the break with the right hand, hold the indicator card in place with the left thumb, and draw the packet away toward the body (Fig. 23). The indicator card will then lie face up on the force card; lift it off and have the spectator take the next, which he will believe he has chosen freely.

7. THE FALSE COUNT

1st Method. To make it appear that you have more cards than you really hold. For example, you have seven cards and it is necessary to count them as eight cards. Hold the seven cards in the left hand vertically, face outwards, the thumb on the middle

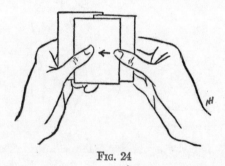

FIG. 24

of the back pressing the packet against the inside of the first three fingers, the left little finger curled against the bottom. Push off the top card and take it in the right hand between the tips of the thumb and the first and second fingers. Count "One." Push off a second card with the left thumb and take it in the right hand in front of the first card. Count "Two." Push off a third card and, at the moment the hands meet, with the right thumb push the first card to the left (Fig. 24); with the left thumb pull it flush with the packet, while the right hand carries away the third card. Count "Three." Then finish the count, one card at a time; one card having been counted twice, the final count will be "Eight."

Two or three cards can be pushed back in the same way, increasing the count accordingly. It is essential that the cards be taken off by the right hand in perfect rhythm.

2d Method. To make the count less than it should be. Hold the cards face down in the left hand, in position for the glide, and draw back the bottom card. We will suppose you have nine cards and it is necessary to count them as six. With the right thumb draw off the top card against the right fingers (Fig. 25). Count "One." Pull off the next card on top of the first one.

Fig. 25

Count "Two." Do the same for "Three" and "Four"; but at "Five" take all the cards above the drawn back card as one card, snap the remaining card in the left hand with the left thumb and finger, and count "Six."

Here again the count must be made in the same tempo throughout, and the outer end of the left-hand packet should point downwards so that the spectators cannot form any estimate of how many cards it contains.

III. FLOURISHES

This branch of the art of card manipulation has expanded so much during recent years that some specialists present complete acts using flourishes only. The acquisition of such skill requires too much time spent in patient practice to be worth while for the average performer, who will get far more satisfactory results by devoting himself to the actual presentation of tricks. There

are, however, a few flourishes with which every performer should
be familiar.

1. THE FAN

Take the deck by the ends between the right thumb at the
lower end and the second and third fingers at the upper end;
place it in the fork of the left thumb, the tip of the thumb resting at the middle of the back at the lower end. Press the right
middle and third fingers downwards, bending the cards (Fig. 26),

FIG. 26

and move them to the right and downwards so that they describe
a semicircle with the right thumb as a pivot; at the same time
allow the cards to slip away from the tips of the fingers in succession. There is only one secret in making the flourish and that is—
practice. First results will seem discouraging, but little by little
the cards will spread further until the spreading of a perfect
semicircle of cards is accomplished by a rapid sweep of the hand.

2. SPRINGING THE CARDS

The effect of this flourish is that the cards are apparently
drawn out in the air, between the hands, concertina fashion. Take
the pack in the right hand between the thumb at the lower end
and the second and third fingers at the upper end, holding it a
few inches away from the left hand. Squeeze the pack between
the thumb and fingers, making the face concave; then allow the
cards to slip away in succession into the left hand (Fig. 27).
When this action becomes familiar, practice moving the right

hand slowly away as the cards escape from it and, as the last card leaves the right hand, bring the left hand up to the right, rapidly gathering all the cards between the hands with a loud slap. Finally, practice doing the same thing swinging the body and the hands from right to left and upwards. This action creates an optical illusion, the cards appearing to cover an arc of some eighteen inches or more.

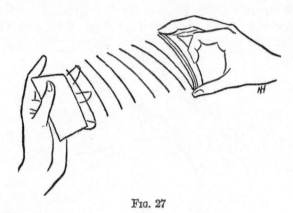

FIG. 27

3. SPREADING THE CARDS

It is sometimes necessary to spread the cards on the table, and this same springing action is utilized. Hold the pack in the right hand on the table top, bend the cards as described above, and

FIG. 28

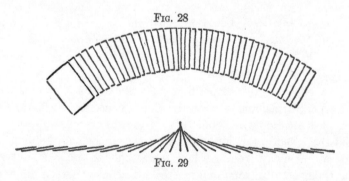

FIG. 29

allow them to escape in succession as you sweep the hand around in a semicircle from right to left (Fig. 28). If the table has a cloth on it, a pretty effect is obtained by lifting the first card and turning it over—when the whole line of cards follows suit (Fig. 29). If the spread has been made evenly by turning the card at the other end of the line, all the cards will be turned over again. When spreading the cards face down, remark, "You see there is no preparation on this side"—turn the cards over—"or on this"—turn them again, and gather the whole deck with one sweep.

This same spread can be done on the forearm, and also the turn over. The effect is very striking, but considerable practice is necessary.

IV. TRICKS WITH CARDS

Before attempting to follow the explanations of the tricks to be explained, the reader must understand fully that the effect of a card trick is just what the performer makes it. To have a card drawn from a pack noted, replaced, and the pack shuffled, then to discover it and hand it back with the words "That's your card," may be very intriguing to a fellow magician who does not happen to know the particular sleight you have employed; but to a layman it is a mere curiosity. That sort of thing is not magic. Every trick should have a plot, no matter how far-fetched or how ridiculous in cold blood; it should be clothed with sprightly talk, garnished with amusing incidents in the development of the plot, and, above all, have a definite climax. Worked up on these lines, the simplest trick can be made to appear as a brilliant feat of magic. It is impossible to devote the space which would be necessary to develop in this manner every trick that follows, but one example will be given which will serve as a pattern.

1. THE MAGIC BREATH

Invite a spectator to shuffle the deck and remove any card he pleases. Take the pack back and, after he has noted his card, begin a Hindu shuffle (see page 309); have the card replaced and control it in the usual way, bringing it to the top of the deck. Execute an overhand shuffle, sending the chosen card to the bottom of the deck and bringing it back to the top.

Address the spectator, "With your permission I propose to try a little scientific experiment with you. Some people have what is called a magic breath, and, with the help of the cards, I am going to find out if you are one of them. I'm afraid you are not one of the chosen. However, I may be mistaken; we'll soon see. Now I want you to think of a number—say up to fifteen, as we don't want to take up too much time. You have thought of one? Very good. Now fix your thoughts intently on that number; concentrate on it firmly. Ready? Now just breathe on the cards. Thank you. If you have a magic breath, it will have sent your card to that very number you thought of from the top of the deck. What was your number? Thirteen? Let us see if your breath is magical. I am a little doubtful about it myself."

Deal twelve cards face down on the table in a pile and take the thirteenth card in your right hand face down. "Now the result." Turn the card face up. "Is that your card? No? Well, you know I told you I was afraid that you are not endowed with a magic breath." Push the card in amongst the twelve cards dealt off the pack, lift the whole packet, and replace the cards on top of the rest of the deck. Do this very openly, so that there can be no suspicion of any secret maneuvers.

Continue, "Remember, you chose a card freely, returned it to the pack, and the cards have been thoroughly shuffled. I have not even touched your card, and I don't know what card it is or where it is in the deck. However, that creates no difficulty for me, because I have a magic breath. See, I merely breathe gently on the cards—just a zephyr so to speak. Will you take the cards in your own hands and test the result for yourself? What number did you say? Thirteen? Very well; deal twelve cards on the table face down."

This done, you continue, "What was your card? The . . . of . . . Turn up the next card—the thirteenth—and there it is, you see. I think that, perhaps, instead of thinking while blowing you blew while thinking, a very different thing. Try it again at home some time."

The elements of the trick are very simple. The chosen card, being at the top of the pack for the first count, naturally becomes the thirteenth, or whatever other number may be chosen, when the counted cards are replaced on the others. Disguised by the plot and the patter, it becomes quite a striking experiment.

2. THE CARDS TO THE POCKET

No better trick than this could be proposed as a test of a performer's ability in the presentation of a trick with cards. It is a perfect experiment for the learner to study. The only preparation required is to have a half dollar in the right-hand trousers pocket.

Effect. Ten cards, freely taken from any pack, pass one by one from the performer's left hand, up his sleeve, and down into his right-hand trousers pocket.

Method. Begin by inviting two spectators to come forwards and seat themselves, one on each side of you. Invite one to shuffle a pack of cards, cut it into three heaps, and choose one of the heaps. Take the chosen pile, count off ten cards, and have all the other cards placed aside. Turn to the man on your left and say, "It is necessary for you to memorize these ten cards, so that you can satisfy yourself that I use these cards only in my experiment." Run the cards very rapidly from hand to hand before his eyes and say, "Now you will remember the cards, won't you?" Turn to the other assistant and repeat the rapid spreading of the cards and say, "Will you do the same? Now that you both know all the cards we will proceed." Of course, they haven't been able to distinguish even one card clearly and the audience is amused at their discomfiture.

"I was too quick for you? Perhaps, after all, it will be better if I call the names of all the cards for everyone to follow." Spread five cards in the left hand and call their names; then do the same with the other five cards in the right hand. Place the two packets together in the left hand and slip the tip of the left little finger between them.

Continue, "To understand my experiment you will have to exercise a little imagination. I want you to think that these ten cards"—bring the right hand over the packet and square the cards lightly—"are certain packages of goods"; palm the top five cards in the right hand and take the remaining five cards in the same hand by the outer corners between the thumb and the first and second fingers, keeping as much of the packet in view as possible (Fig. 30). "And this hand"—tap the left palm with the cards in the right hand—"is a dispatching station"—replace the five visible cards in the left hand—"from which they will pass up my sleeve, across my chest, down into my pocket (the receiving station)"—gesture accordingly with the right hand, passing it up over the sleeve and across the chest into your right trousers pocket—"which, by the way, is quite empty. No, I quite forgot I still have a half dollar." Seize the coin with the tips of the thumb and fingers and pull the pocket out. Show the coin, thus covering the half-closed condition of the hand; then push the pocket in and leave the coin and the five cards inside it.

"Now let us try the experiment"; snap the right fingers on the back of the cards in the left hand, incidentally showing that the

Fig. 30

right hand is empty. "Ten cards here. First card . . . pass." Bring out one card from the pocket, being careful to straighten the card by bending it the opposite way; do the same with the others in turn. "Here is the first card, the . . . of . . . Only nine cards left." Take the five cards from the left hand, spread them very slightly, and replace them in the left hand. "Number two . . . pass." Snap the packet, showing the right hand empty as before, and bring a second card from the pocket. "Eight cards here now." Take the packet and spread it slightly as before. Repeat these maneuvers, exactly, for the third card.

"There should be seven cards left. I'll count them." False-count the five cards as seven, order one card to pass, and bring another card from the pocket. "Four cards have passed. How many should I have now?" you ask, turning to the man on your left. "Six? Perfect. Right, first guess." False-count the five cards as six. Continue, to the same man, "Will you hold the ends of the six cards tightly? Fifth card . . . pass. Count them onto my hand." Hold out your left hand, palm upwards, and the cards are dealt one by one onto it. "Five cards only; one has gone." Turn to the man on your right, "Will you put your hand into my pocket and take the card out?" He does so, and you take advantage of this surprise to palm three cards in the right hand.

"Wait a moment. I forgot I had a half dollar in that pocket." Thrust your hand into the pocket, leave the three palmed cards, bring out the coin, and show it. "It's nice to meet an honest man." Make a gesture of replacing the coin in the trousers pocket; then, with a sly look at the audience, put it in a vest pocket.

Hold up the two cards in the left hand, squared together. "Five cards are left. I'll send two at once to save time. Pass. Pass." Let your right hand be seen empty, casually not ostentatiously, and bring two cards out. "That makes eight and you can see there are just two cards left."

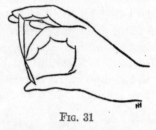

Fig. 31

Take one card in each hand and show them; then take them by the ends, face outwards, in the right hand, the thumb on the lower ends, the second finger on the upper end, and the forefinger pressing on the middle of the back (Fig. 31). Turn to the left; snap the cards into the left hand and immediately turn that hand over, half closed.

Look rather slyly at the audience; then, with a shake of the head, continue, "Oh, no, they haven't gone yet." Take them in the right hand—thumb on the bottom, fingers on the top edges—and repeat the gesture of putting them in the left hand; but,

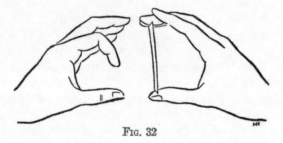

Fig. 32

this time, press the tip of the left first finger against the middle of the face and snap the two cards back into the right hand (Fig. 32), at once turning the left hand over—half closed, just as before. Raise the left hand diagonally to the left, following it intently with your eyes and pointing to it with the right forefinger. A moment later snap the left thumb and fingers, turn the hand and show it empty, thrust the right hand into the pocket, and bring the cards out one at a time.

The last operation is the only difficult part of the trick. The action in the feint and the actual palm must appear to be exactly the same and to have the same sound as the cards snap against the left palm the first time and the right palm the second time. A little practice before a mirror will soon enable you to get the right result. The trick appears to be a bold one, and most performers are afraid of it; but if proper attention is given to the misdirective moves detailed in the explanation, the reader should have no difficulty in adding this brilliant trick to his repertoire.

3. FIVE CARD DISCOVERIES

The great majority of card tricks are based on the discovery— in more or less startling ways—of a card which has been freely chosen by a spectator, returned to the pack, and buried ("drowned," as the French say) therein. Instead of completing a trick with one card, then proceeding to have another card drawn and doing a trick with that one, and so on, it is much more effective to have several cards chosen and returned to the pack before going on with the discovery processes. Not only does this procedure save time, always valuable, and so help to keep the attention of the audience, but it adds greatly to the effect— for it appears impossible to the layman that a number of cards can be controlled and produced separately when the pack is being constantly mixed up in the production of each card. Two sequences providing for the discoveries of five cards follow. These will serve as models from which the reader can arrange combinations of his own.

Combination of four tricks. Hand the deck to a spectator, A, with the request that he shuffle it, take out one card, and give the pack back to you. Do the same with four other persons, B, C, D, and E. Ask all five to note and remember their cards. Beginning with the last man, E, have the chosen cards returned to the deck in the course of a Hindu shuffle (see page 309), controlling them and finishing the shuffle with the five cards on the top of the deck in the order in which they were drawn. You can now execute a false shuffle or palm off the five cards and have the pack shuffled by a spectator.

In either case, with the five chosen cards on the top, place the pack in your breast pocket and proceed to give an exhibition of the development of your sense of touch. Explain that in handling the card the personal vibrations of the drawer were transmitted to it, and that by means of them you will find the card in the shuffled pack. To make the task harder ask A to name a small number at which he would like you to find his card. Suppose that seven is called. Six times in succession you take cards from the bottom of the deck; then, for the seventh, touch his fingers to get the right vibrations, dive your hand into the pocket, and bring out the top card. Hold it face down and ask A to name his card, which you slowly turn face up. Take the rest of the cards from the pocket, put the seven cards on the bottom, and go to the second spectator, B.

Ask for the loan of his handkerchief; as he takes it from his pocket, palm the top card and take the pack in the same hand. Receive the handkerchief with the left hand, taking it by a corner. Transfer

Fig. 33

the pack to the left hand, take the opposite corner in the right hand, and stretch the handkerchief out; then cross your arms to show the other side. Let the fabric fall over the right hand and with the left hand lay the deck on the middle, immediately over the palmed card; grip it through the handkerchief with the right hand, holding the pack vertically, the bottom card facing the audience. With the left hand draw the upper part of the handkerchief over the pack, so that it hangs down in front; push the folds at the top of the deck on each side to the back, so that they partly cover and hold B's card in place; and grasp the whole at the top with the left hand. Run the right hand down the folds of the handkerchief below the pack, twist them together, and hold them; turn the pack down sideways with the left hand, release it, and hold the handkerchief with the right hand (Fig. 33).

Invite B to name his card. Order it to penetrate the handkerchief and show itself. A slight up-and-down shake with the right hand will cause the card to free itself from the folds and appear gradually, as if working its way through the handkerchief. Let it flutter to the floor, seize the lower end of the pack through the fabric with the left hand, turn the hand over, and show that the deck was fairly wrapped up. Return the handkerchief and proceed to C.

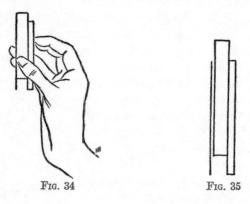

FIG. 34   FIG. 35

Execute another false shuffle, leaving the three top cards intact. Place the cards in the right hand in the position shown in Figure 34, at the same time pulling about one-third of the pack down at the back (making a step) and spreading the face cards down a little to hide it. Fig. 35 shows a side view of the arrangement. Ask C to name his card and order it to rise from the middle of the deck. With the tips of the right first and second fingers push the rear card—C's card—slowly upwards with a regular movement. When its lower edge has arrived at the top of the step, seize the card and the top of the deck with the left hand, press the bottom edge of the card against the step, square the pack by pressing it down on the right palm, remove the pack with the left hand, and show the card protruding from the middle of the deck.

Push the card into the pack, remarking, "Well, that completes my trick. I have found the cards each in a different way." Turn to your table, run the top card to the bottom, and put the pack down. Naturally, D and E remind you that they also drew cards. Pretend to be embarrassed by the oversight. Point out that the pack has left your hands, that you have lost contact with the vibrations, and so on. "I don't like to try it," you continue, "but there is only one course left—that is to rely upon chance. I will throw the whole pack into the air and try to catch the two chosen cards from amongst the whole fifty-two cards."

Take the pack in the right hand, the thumb on the face of the bottom card, fingers on the back of the top card. Squeeze the pack rather tightly; lower the right hand, then jerk it upwards

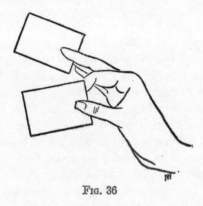

Fig. 36

sharply, retaining the top and bottom cards and letting all the intervening cards slip upwards; grip the two cards tightly and with the same hand strike the pack, scattering the cards in all directions. At once slide the two cards apart by pushing the face card upwards with the thumb; slip the first and second fingers between them and grip one between the thumb and forefinger, the other between the second and third fingers (Fig. 36). Hold the cards with their backs to the spectators and ask D and E to name their cards. Turn the faces of the two cards and show that you have succeeded.

This last catch is easier, cleaner, and more effective than the old method of wetting the thumb and fingers to make the cards stick to them.

Annemann's five card findo. I am indebted to Mr. Theodore

Annemann for permission to describe this series of five discoveries which appeared in his famous monthly *The Jinx*. The arrangement is an excellent one and the various subtleties introduced should be carefully studied.

Five cards are freely chosen by five spectators, whom we will again call A, B, C, D, and E; Mr. Annemann prefers that the first person shall be a lady. Control the cards and bring them to the top of the pack in the order of choice by means of the Hindu shuffle (see page 309). Then execute an overhand shuffle, running seven cards onto the top of the pack; jog the next card and shuffle off. Make a break at the jog; shuffle to the break and throw the rest of the cards on top, thus making A's card the eighth card from the top, the other four remaining in order below it.

Invite A to step forwards beside you and name a number between one and ten. In the meantime you have slipped the tip of the left little finger below the two top cards, which prepares you for the numbers five, six, seven, and eight. If four, or a smaller number, is named, merely remark, "It *should* be a more difficult one," and a higher number is then certain to be named. If five is chosen, deal the first two cards as one onto A's hand, then single cards at two, three, four, and five; point to the top card and have the card named. Make a double lift and the eighth card, A's card, shows. If the number chosen is six, deal two cards as one to start with and, after dealing five more cards one at a time, let the lady name her card and turn it over herself on top of the deck. If seven, deal fairly throughout and have her turn the top card; if eight, deal seven cards and have the eighth turned. In any case, place the eight cards on the bottom of the pack so that B's card becomes the top card.

B now steps forwards and stands at your left. Hand the deck to him, instruct him to deal the cards onto your left hand, and, when he has dealt the fourth card, say, "And you may stop dealing at any time you like. It's entirely up to you." When he stops, push off the last card he dealt with your left thumb, take it with the right hand, and shake it a little without showing its face—as if merely to draw attention to it—as you continue, "This is as far as you want to go?" and drop the card carelessly on top of the packet again. Look directly at B; with the left second finger push out the bottom card (his card) a trifle and press the tip of the left thumb against the tip of this second finger. As he replies and while you are still looking at him, bring the right hand over, take the bottom card, and move the left hand away as you say, "Then tell everybody what card you looked at." Stretch your right hand out to the right at full length and, as he names his card, slowly turn its face to the audience with the fingers only, moving neither the hand nor the arm.

Put B's card on the cards in the left hand, take the rest of the pack from him, and place them on top of the packet in the left hand. The three remaining selected cards are now on the bottom of the pack in order, from the face card up. B retires and C steps forwards. Hand him the top card of the pack, saying, "Is this the card you took, sir? No? I'm glad it isn't, for my finding it might lead you to suspect that I am merely deceiving you with card tricks. You appear to be a rather difficult subject, so we'll leave everything to chance this time. Use the card as an indicator and push it face up into the pack, anywhere you please." In the meantime you have undercut—that is to say, drawn out from the bottom—about fifteen cards, placed them on the top of the pack, and slipped the tip of the left little finger below them.

Riffle the ends of the cards for the insertion of the indicator card and let the rest fall on top of it. Raise the pack to a vertical position, push up the packet above the little finger, grasp it and the indicator card together with the right hand, and draw the hands apart. The indicator card then lies directly against the face of C's card; remove the indicator as C names his card.

As C returns to his seat and D comes forwards, put the packet in the right hand below the cards in the left hand and move C's card and the indicator card to the top. The fourth and fifth chosen cards are now on the bottom and again you cut the pack, holding a break with the tip of the left little finger. Hold the deck in the left hand at arm's length to the left. Tell the spectator he is to think of his card, watch you riffle slowly through the pack, and, when he feels an uncontrollable impulse, he is to call "Stop." Bend the left forefinger under the pack and with the thumb riffle the left outer corners of the cards in such a way that the audience can see the action.

When D calls "Stop," don't move either the hand or the arm;

turn your head to him and say, "Are you sure that was a real impulse? You may try again if you like. It's up to you." When he is satisfied, bring the left arm down in front of you with a swing, tipping the pack down with the backs of the cards toward the spectators. With the right hand, the thumb at the back, the fingers in front, lift off the packet above the break. D names his card and you turn the packet over slowly to reveal it.

D retires and, as E comes up, place the packet in the right hand underneath that in the left and move D's card to the top. Sight the bottom card, E's card; make an overhand shuffle, bringing it to the top; and slip the tip of the left little finger under the second card. If E's card is a red one, you say to him, "Was your card a black one?" If it was a black one, ask him, "Was your card a red card?" thus insuring that the answer will be "No." Explain that that leaves you up against a stone wall and that the card will have to be left to find itself. Continue, "Will you see that your card is amongst the others as I fan them through?" Keep the first two cards together, thus concealing his card; and, as you fan the cards, spell out its name, remembering to take two letters for the first two cards taken off as one card. When you reach the card on the last letter, put the right forefinger on it in front and keep on fanning the cards against that finger. With the right thumb push the top card toward the left at the back of the fan, then with the left thumb pull it further along; push back the right forefinger to make an opening in the fan, into which the card slips as you gather the cards together.

Ask E if he has seen his card. You know the answer will be "No" and you hand the deck to him, telling him to look through it and see that his card is really there. He does this and you tell him to keep the deck and name his card aloud. Instruct him to deal the cards face down onto your hand and as he does so you spell the name of his card. Stop him on the last letter and have him turn the card himself. Climax.

4. TWO CARDS CHANGE PLACES

Invite a spectator to assist you and place him on your left. Let him shuffle a pack of cards to his own satisfaction and hand it back to you. Then remark that any card will do for the peculiar experiment you are about to try and that you will use the top card, whatever it may happen to be. In the meantime you have prepared for the double lift and, in apparently turning the top card, you turn two cards as one. Suppose the card that shows is the Seven of Clubs; call attention to it, name it aloud, and turn the two cards face down on the pack. Deal off the top card—an indifferent card—face down to your right, as you say, "Please remember this card, the Seven of Clubs."

Continue, "Now, we will take the next card"; and again you make a double lift, showing this time, let us say, the Four of Diamonds. Turn the two cards down on the pack; deal off the top card, calling it the Four of Diamonds (really it is the Seven of Clubs), to the left and have the spectator place his hand on it.

Slip the tip of your left little finger under the top card of the pack, the Four of Diamonds. Pick up the indifferent card on your right, keeping its face toward you; look at it and say, "Now I have this Seven of Clubs, while you hold the Four of Diamonds. Please keep your hand firmly on your card." Place the indifferent card on the top of the deck, square the two cards at the top lightly, and—thanks to the break held by the tip of the left little finger—you are prepared for another double lift.

Continue, "You know it was an Irishman who said that, not being a bird, he couldn't be in two places at the same time. All scientists are agreed that even for a bird that is impossible, but I maintain that an object not only can be in two places at the same time but even that it may be nowhere at all. I'll use these cards as an example. Watch. I merely say 'Pass,' and here is your Four of Diamonds"—make a double lift and show that card—"and you will find that you have the Seven of Clubs." The spectator turns his card and finds it is the Seven of Clubs.

Casually turn your two cards face down on top of the pack, make an overhand shuffle, and lay the pack on the table. Any search the spectator may make for a duplicate card will be futile and only heighten the effect of the transposition. Although the method is so simple to work, the trick is a bewildering one to the onlookers. It affords excellent practice in the execution of the double lift.

5. THE AMBITIOUS CARD

The plot of this very popular and most intriguing trick hinges upon the fact, so you state, that a card, having been chosen from amongst its fellows, becomes ambitious and always assumes the place of honor in the pack, the top.

To illustrate this peculiar fact, hand a pack of cards to a spectator to be shuffled thoroughly. Take the pack back and spread the cards, allowing him perfect freedom of choice. When he has noted the card he has chosen, have it replaced, control it by one of the methods already explained, and bring it to the top of the pack. While you are outlining the plot and asserting that the chosen card will eventually rise to the top of its own accord, square the pack lightly and slip the tip of the left little finger under the second card from the top. Make a double lift, showing the face of the second card—an indifferent one—and then turn the two cards face down.

Invite the spectator to name his card, give the cards a little shake—to help the chosen card along, as you say—turn the top card face up, and show that the chosen card has arrived.

Turn the card face down and take it in the right hand. Push the next card halfway over the right side of the deck and slide the chosen card under it. Square the two cards with the rest of the deck and, in so doing, insert the left little fingertip underneath them. Hold the pack slanting upwards, so that the absence of the little finger is not noticeable. "In such a short journey," you say, "the card comes through instantly." Make the double lift and show it.

Turn the two cards face down and take them as one card between the right thumb and the first and second fingers; with the left thumb push off the next card halfway off the right-hand side of the pack and slide the two cards underneath it. Square the three cards with the deck, at the same time securing a break below them with the tip of the left little finger. "Again it comes to the top immediately," you say, and, making a triple lift, you show the chosen card.

Turn the three cards face down. Take off the top card with the right hand and, keeping it face down so that no one can get a glimpse of its face, push it into the middle of the deck. "This time it will take a moment or two longer to arrive," you continue; then, as if you noticed some skepticism as to whether the card was really placed in the deck and was already on the top, say, "Oh, no, the card really has gone, you see"—and you turn the top card, showing an indifferent card. In replacing it on the top of the deck, secure a break, as usual, under the next card—the chosen one—and again hold the deck so that this cannot be noticed. Shake the cards a little, make the double lift, and again show the selected card.

Turn the two cards face down on the deck; take off the top card and insert it in the middle, pushing it home and squaring the pack. Hold out your left hand flat, palm upward with the pack lying on it; shake the cards a little, then slowly turn the top card. It is the chosen card again. "It really is a curious thing," you remark. "Try it for yourself when you go home."

The trick is subject to almost infinite variety as to the sequence of the moves bringing the card to the top, every performer having his own methods. It is advisable to learn the sequence given above before attempting any variations.

All of the tricks I have explained can be done with any deck, at any time and without preparation, and it is such tricks that are the most useful to anyone taking up magic as a hobby. The space allotted to playing cards in this work precludes the treatment of tricks with special packs, prepared cards, and prearranged decks. The reader who wishes to follow up the subject cannot do better than consult *The Encyclopedia of Card Tricks* (published by Max Holden, New York City) and *Greater Magic* (published by Carl W. Jones, Minneapolis, Minnesota). Both books are obtainable from any magic dealer.

INDEX

341